IMAGES
of America

BIRMINGHAM
AND JEFFERSON COUNTY
ALABAMA

IMAGES *of America*

BIRMINGHAM AND JEFFERSON COUNTY ALABAMA

The Jefferson County Historical Commission
The Birmingham Public Library
The Bessemer Hall of History

ARCADIA PUBLISHING

ISBN 978-0-7385-8730-1

Published by Arcadia Publishing
Charleston, South Carolina

Printed in the United States of America

Library of Congress Catalog Card Number: 98-87867

For all general information contact Arcadia Publishing at:
Telephone 843-853-2070
Fax 843-853-0044
E-Mail sales@arcadiapublishing.com
For customer service and orders:
Toll-Free 1-888-313-2665

Visit us on the Internet at www.arcadiapublishing.com

Contents

ACKNOWLEDGMENTS

Three organizations, the Jefferson County Historical Commission, the Birmingham Public Library, and the Bessemer Hall of History, sponsored this book. Profits from the sale of the book go to support these organizations in their work.

The Jefferson County Historical Commission administers a marker program that designates and marks historic structures and sites, and the commission presents its Thomas Jefferson Award annually to individuals and organizations that have made significant contributions to historic preservation or the study of history. Other publications that the commission has sponsored include Carolyn Green Satterfield's *Historic Sites of Jefferson County* and, most recently, *Birmingham: The Magic City*, an audio tape history and tour guide.

The Birmingham Public Library's system is made up of a downtown Central Library, the Linn-Henley Research Library, and 19 branches. Through the Jefferson County Library Cooperative, Birmingham Public shares resources with more than a dozen other libraries in the county. Besides working to provide the finest library service possible, Birmingham Public aids and encourages the study and appreciation of local history through its research collections, exhibits, lectures and workshops, and the publications of the library press.

The Bessemer Hall of History Museum, housed in the old Southern Railway terminal, exhibits material chronicling the history of the Bessemer area. Items of particular interest include Native-American artifacts excavated from a local mound site, Civil War material relating to the 28th Alabama Regiment, and photos and artifacts highlighting Bessemer's industrial heritage. The museum also houses a research collection on Bessemer history.

A number of individuals and organizations made significant contributions to this project. Of special note are Steven Gilmer (who also shared his considerable expertise), William J. Skelton, Mr. and Mrs. Jim Ed Mulkin, and the Leeds Chamber of Commerce.

The members of the Jefferson County Historical Commission contributed their time and expertise, especially Virginia Pounds Brown, who logged many miles and worked many hours gathering information. Louise Ayer Tommie provided much needed research assistance and advice, as did Linda Nelson, Alice Bowsher, Sam Rumore, and Gillian Goodrich. Barbara King held down the fort.

The staff of the Birmingham Public Library did their usual fine job, especially Don Veasey, who shared his considerable knowledge of Birmingham architecture, Caryl Johnston, Yvonne Crumpler, Becky Scarborough, and Danny Dorroh.

We express our gratitude to the staff of the Bessemer Hall of History, the Special Collections Department at Samford University, and the Methodist Archives at Birmingham-Southern College. Thanks also to those who shared information, Catherine Allen, Russell Cunningham Jr., Dr. LeRoy Holt, Tom McEniry, Margaret Hallmark, Margaret Miller, Eleanor S. Haslip, Claradel Holcombe, Lucile Hamrick, Alex Woodall, Penelope P. Cunningham, Becky Strickland, and the folks at the Bright Star restaurant.

Introduction

The Austrian Postal authority issued the first postcard, made of buff paperboard with no illustration, in 1869. During the following year the North German Confederation, Britain, and France issued their own government-printed cards, and the United States followed in 1873. Coming at a time when many countries had developed reliable postal systems and when more people than ever had achieved some level of literacy, postcards were a phenomenal success. The cards were inexpensive, and allowed the sender to dash off quick messages without the trouble of paper, envelopes, and additional postage. Business people recognized the postcard as a cheap means of advertisement, and government agencies used them for sending brief communications. During the first month of availability in Austria, 1.5 million cards were sold. First year sales in Britain exceeded 75 million.

Picture postcards, introduced in Germany and first appearing in the United States at the Chicago Industrial Exposition of 1873, proved even more popular than their plain cousins. Illustrated postcards became collectibles, and the illustrations captured a multitude of subjects from flowers, animals, and pastoral scenes to historic sites, cityscapes, and naked women. By 1903 Japan was printing 500 million postcards per year; Germany was printing more than a billion. In the United States the golden age of postcard collecting began around the turn of the century and lasted until 1914. Picture postcards were often used for ordinary communication, and people would select and send cards to collecting friends or relatives. Tens of millions of cards were sold each year. Collectors could purchase postcard albums, and might keep these albums in their foyer or parlor for guests to peruse.

During the height of the collecting craze in Birmingham, a former cigar salesman named William H. Faulkner opened the Post Card Exchange on Second Avenue, North. Faulkner offered customers a large inventory of cards and published his own images of local scenes. Some of the cards included in this book are Post Card Exchange imprints. The Exchange operated from 1909 until 1917, and Faulkner remained in the card and novelty business in Birmingham until the 1940s.

Prior to the First World War, Germany was the largest producer of postcards. Germans were masters of chromolithography, the coloring process used on the best cards. Many manufacturers in the United States would send their cards to Germany for coloring, but with the outbreak of war many Americans stopped buying German products. American postcard images were noticeably inferior, and postcard collecting never regained its pre-war popularity.

The quality of postcard images declined again after 1930 with the introduction of "linen cards" printed on a cheaper paper stock, and around 1945 the modern chrome era began. These are the type cards, with slick photographic images, still produced today.

The most attractive subjects for postcard producers have always been large cities and busy tourist spots; however, postcards have been popular for so long, and so many have been produced in such a wide variety, that images of places like Birmingham, Bessemer, and smaller towns like

Wylam, Leeds, and Brookside were produced and can still be found in some collections. These cards are valuable as collectibles and as historical documentation. The postcard image of a main street, park, home, or business may be the only surviving record to show how that place looked in the late 19th or early 20th century.

With that said, the reader of this book will still notice that postcards are like any other form of historical documentation. The record is incomplete. In some cases cards have not survived, and in many cases cards showing certain places or people simply were not produced. Postcard makers were business people, and they published cards that they believed would sell. This explains why Birmingham and Bessemer are better represented than smaller towns and outlying areas, and why some schools or churches are shown but others are not. This caveat aside, postcards are still a fine source for visual information about Jefferson County's history, architecture, and an earlier lifestyle.

James L. Baggett
Birmingham, 1998

One

Main Streets and Downtown

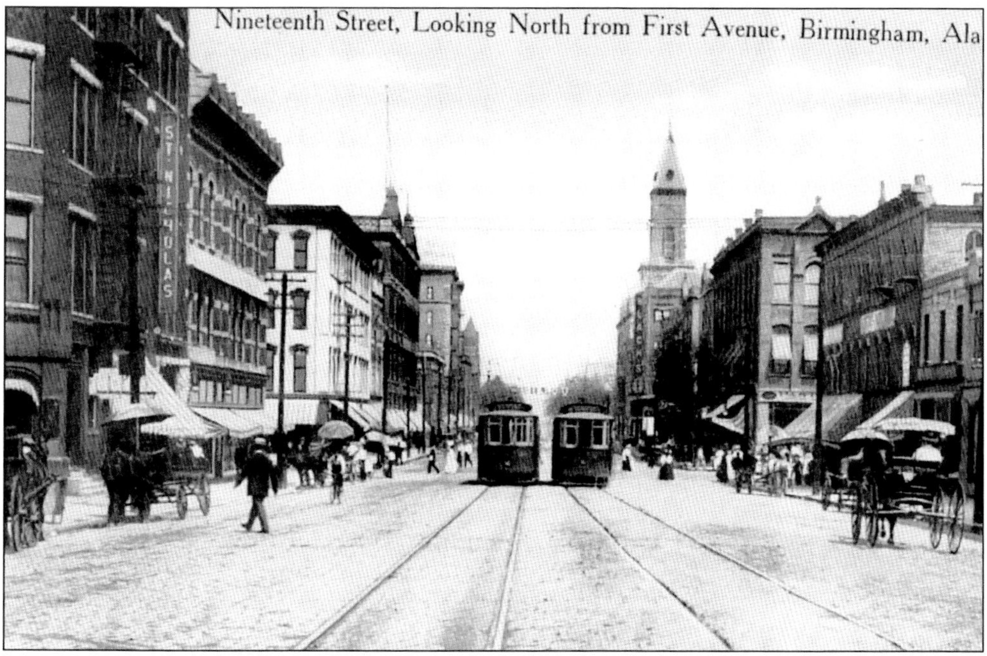

The 20th century dawned on a prospering Birmingham recovering from an 1890s economic depression. Nineteenth Street, North, pictured here, teems with shoppers. A horse-drawn buggy and mule-drawn wagons have moved to either side of the street, making way for the streetcars in the center. Before automobiles, streetcars were a popular and inexpensive mode of transportation. Commuters could ride for 5¢ in town, or go to outlying areas like Ensley and Pratt City for 10¢. The tower visible on the right side of the street tops the Birmingham City Hall, built in 1901. In the far distant on the left is the tower of First Methodist Church. (BPLA.)

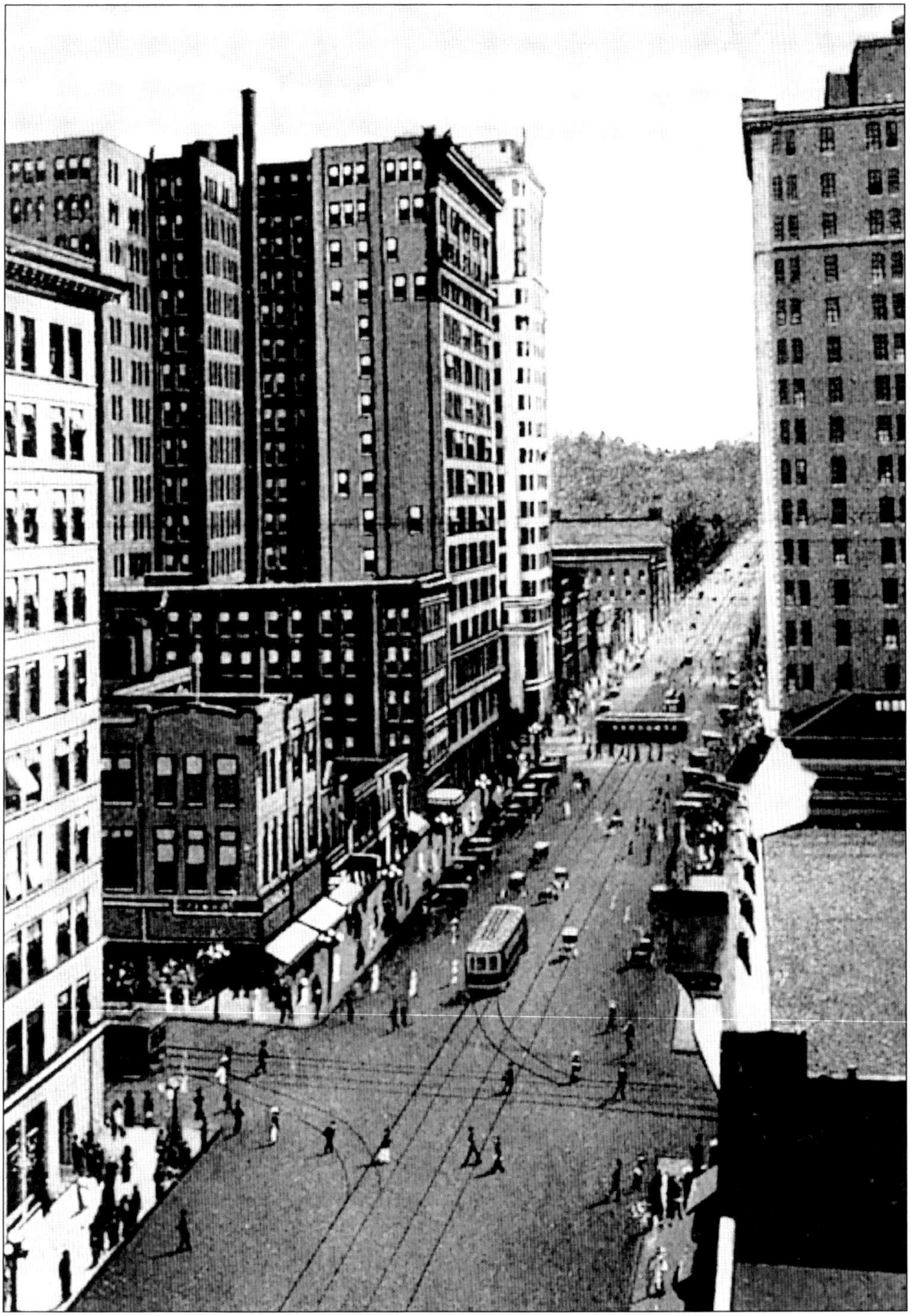

In the original survey for the city of Birmingham commissioned by the Elyton Land Company, Twentieth Street was intended to be a main business thoroughfare. It remains so today. Birmingham Green now occupies the area down the center of the street formerly used for streetcar tracks. (BPLA.)

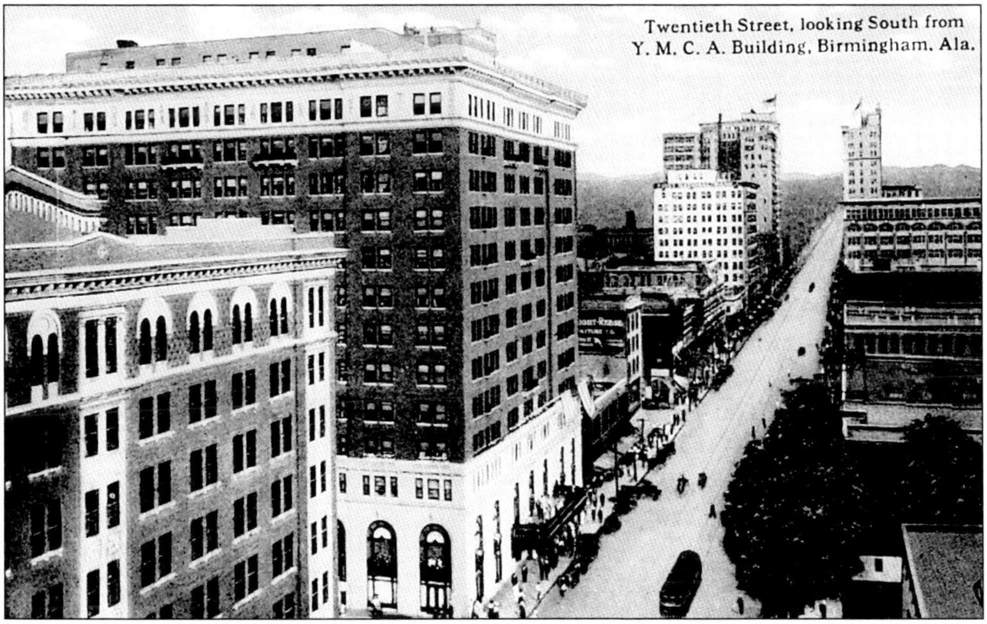

In this image of Twentieth Street, the Molton Hotel is visible in the left foreground, and the next building as one goes down the street is the original Tutwiler Hotel. (BPLA.)

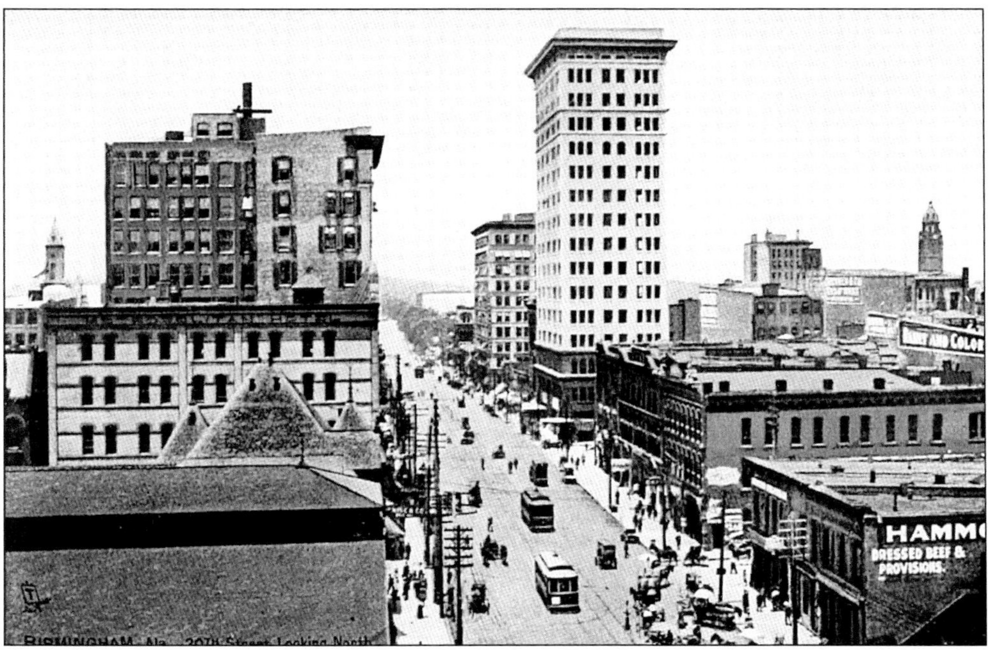

This northward view of Twentieth Street was "photochromed," or colored in Saxony, Germany. Prior to World War I, German manufacturers colored many cards sold in the United States. (BPLA.)

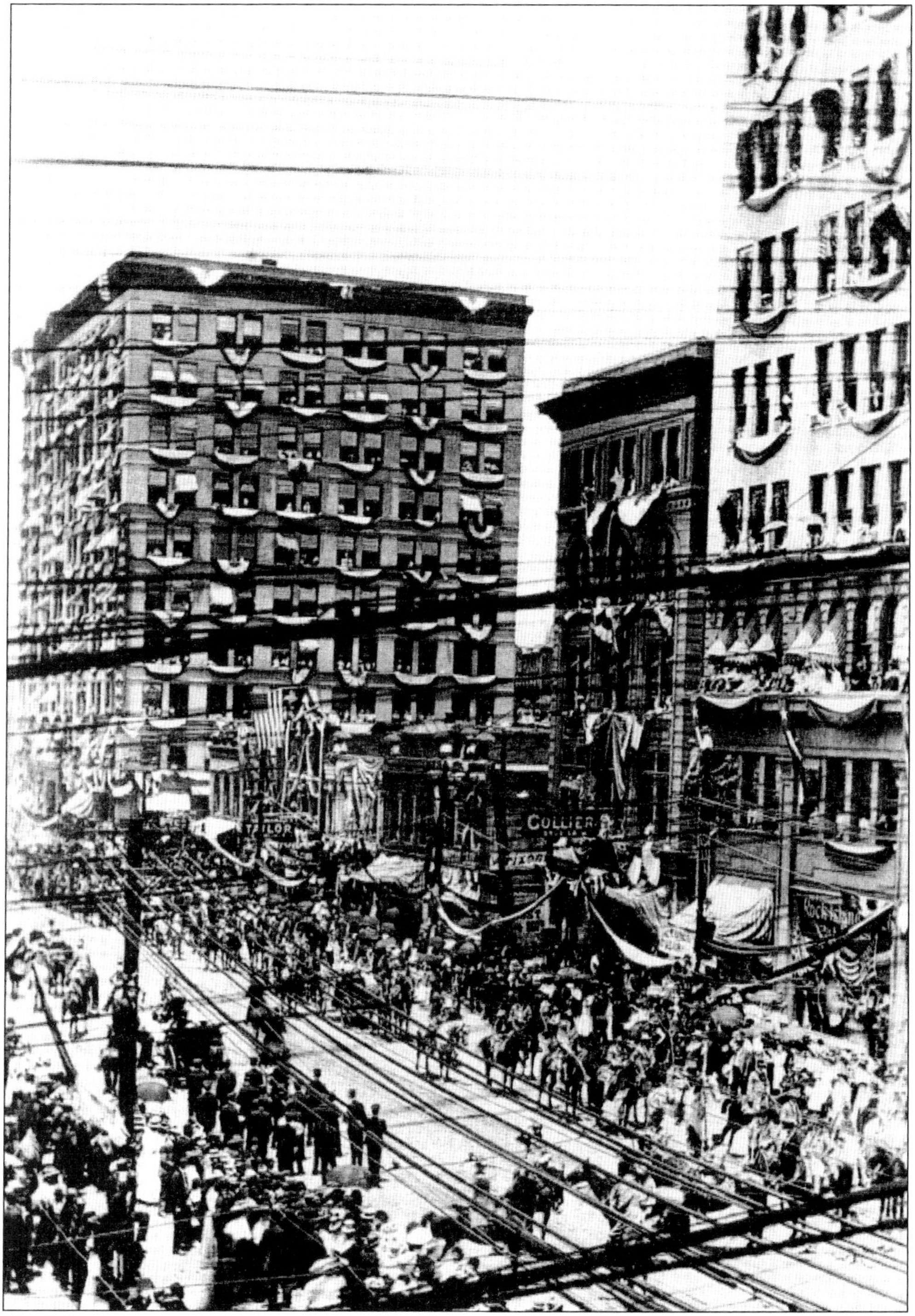

Confederate veteran reunions were held in Birmingham in 1894, 1908, 1916, and 1926. This card shows one of the veteran parades down Twentieth Street. A handwritten note on the verso reads, "Taken by Clarine during Confederate Reunion. Birmingham, Ala., June 9–10 1908." (SG.)

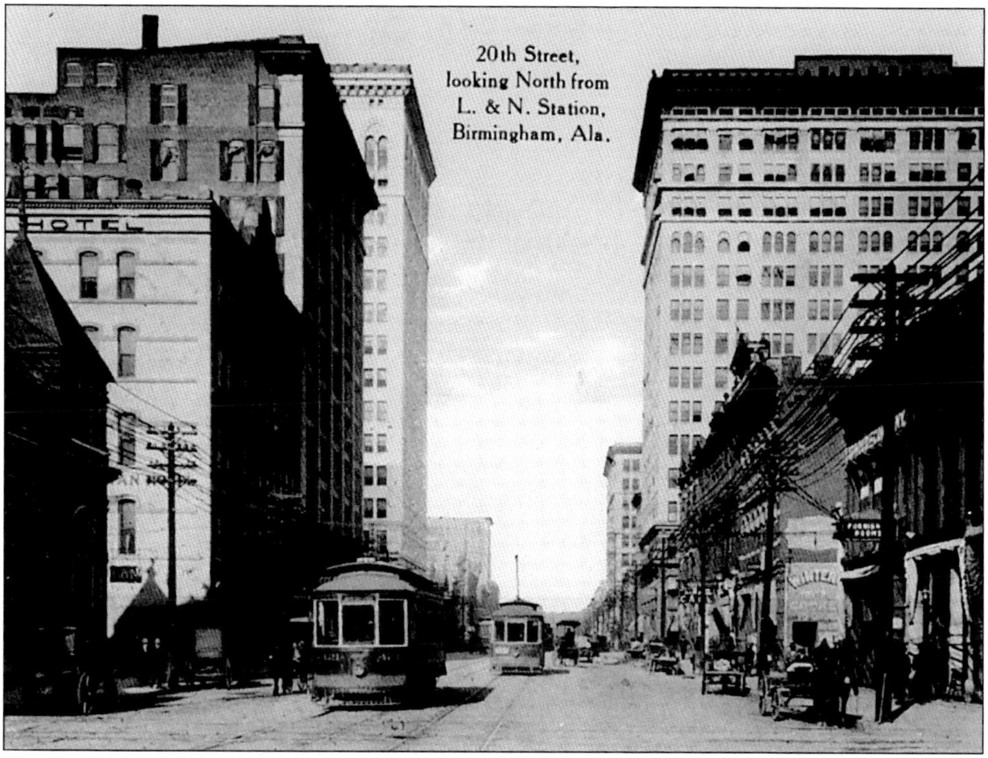

Above and below are two views of Twentieth Street, one looking north from the railroad tracks in the center of town, and the other looking north from Five Points South. (BPLA.)

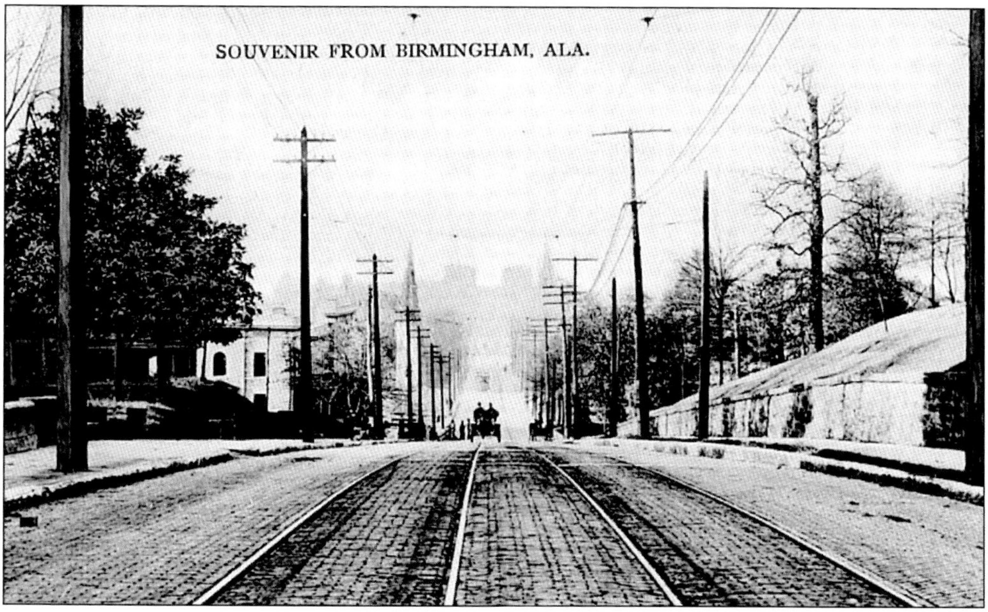

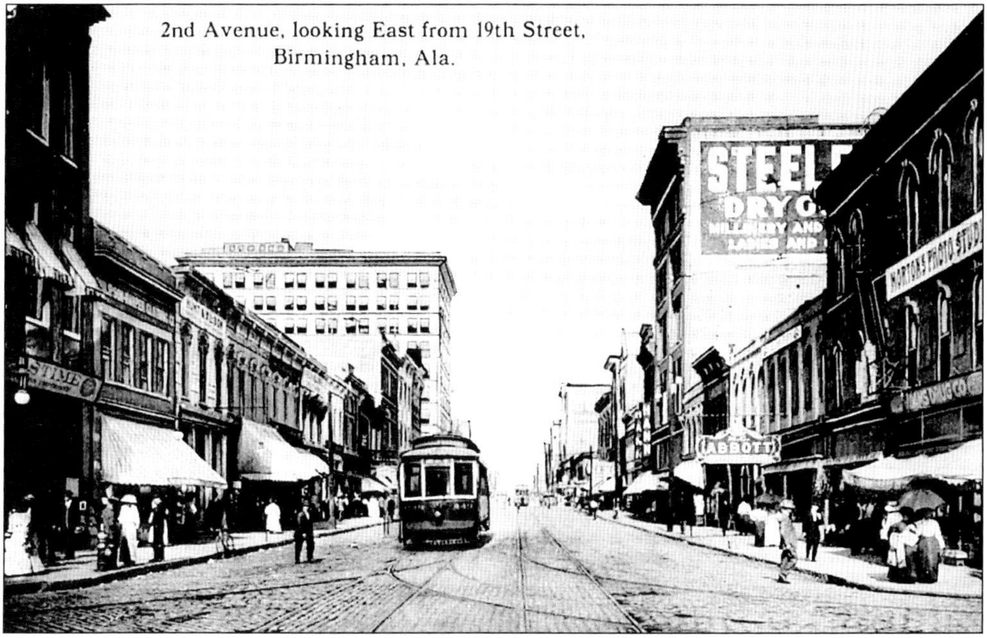

Pictured above is an image of Second Avenue about 1902. Visible on the far right of this image, in the red brick building, is Morton Photo Studio. Hugh T. Morton operated a studio in at least two locations downtown at different times, and manufactured and sold "photo oil paints," probably used to color black-and-white photographs. (BPLA.)

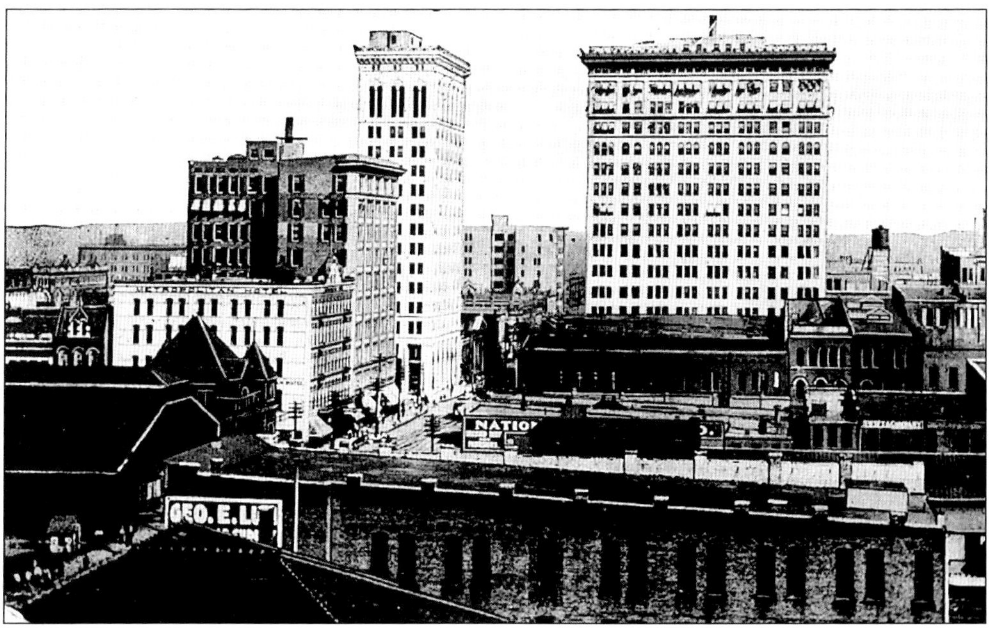

This "Bird's Eye View" shows three Birmingham skyscrapers, the Brown-Marx (large building on right), the Empire (tall building left of center), and the Woodward (foreground next to Empire). Detail views of these buildings appear on the following three pages. (BPLA.)

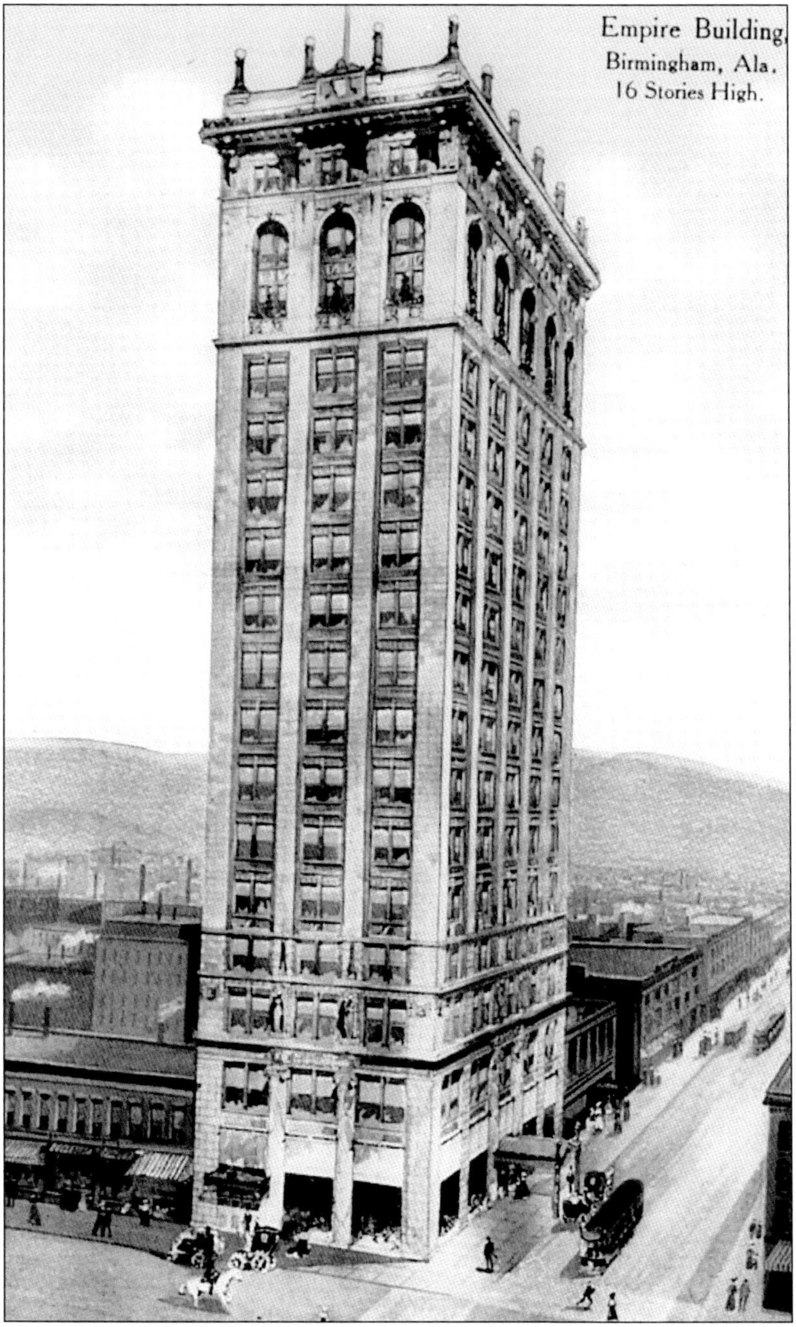

The Empire Building, located at the corner of First Avenue, North and Twentieth Street, was designed by architects William T. Warren and William Leslie Welton and constructed in 1909, replacing the Bank Saloon. Above the paired arches are Roman busts depicting the architect Welton as Emperor William, and Frederick Larkin, the contractor's representative, as Frederick the Great. City National Bank renovated the structure in 1965, and Colonial Bank now occupies the building. (BPLA.)

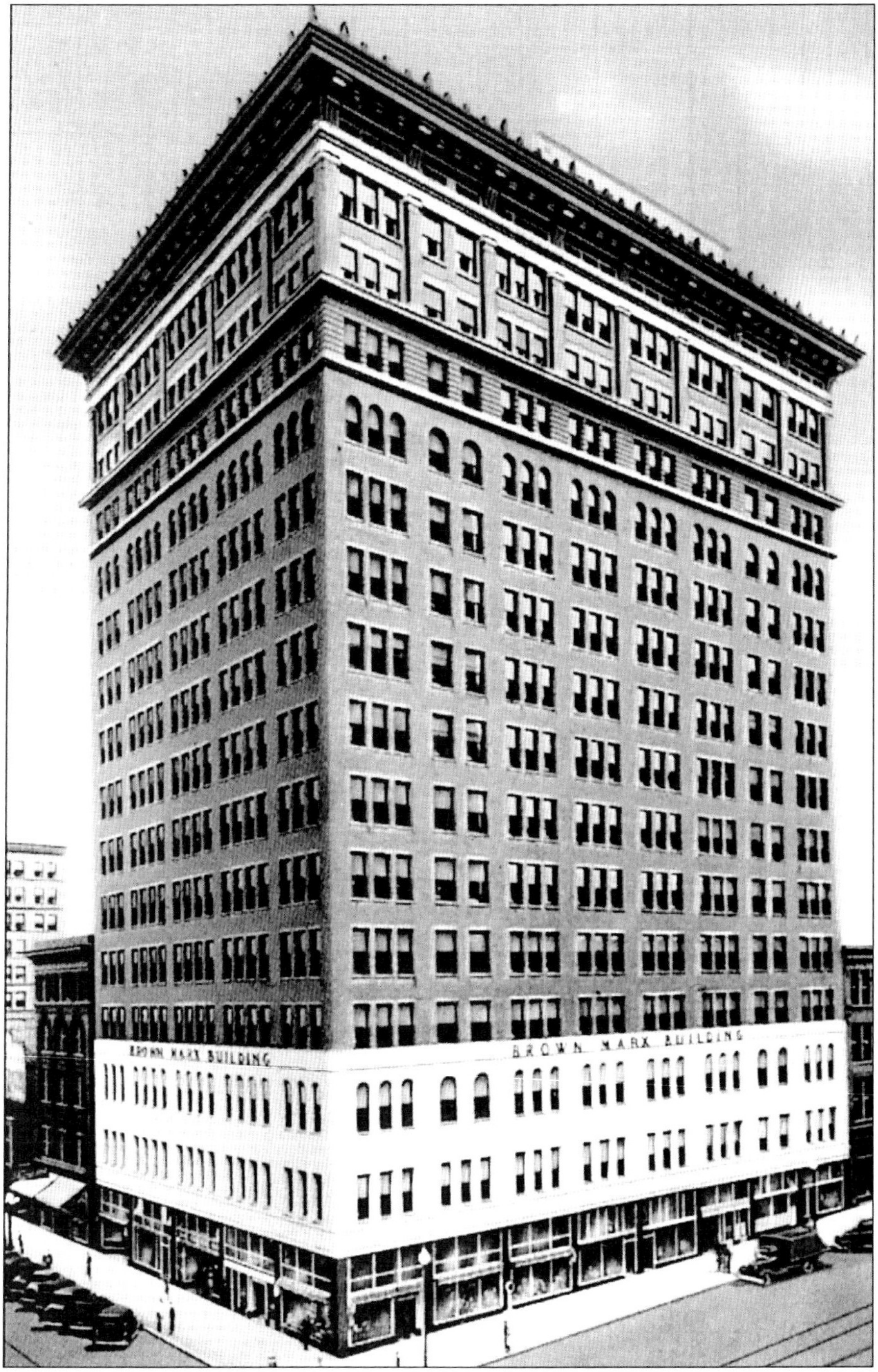

Standing on the corner across from the Empire Building, the Brown-Marx was constructed in two stages and completed around 1906. On the verso of this postcard the caption reads, "Located in Birmingham's thriving business district, the Brown-Marx Building is one of the finest. Shoppers from a hundred mile radius come to Birmingham to do their retail shopping." (BPLA.)

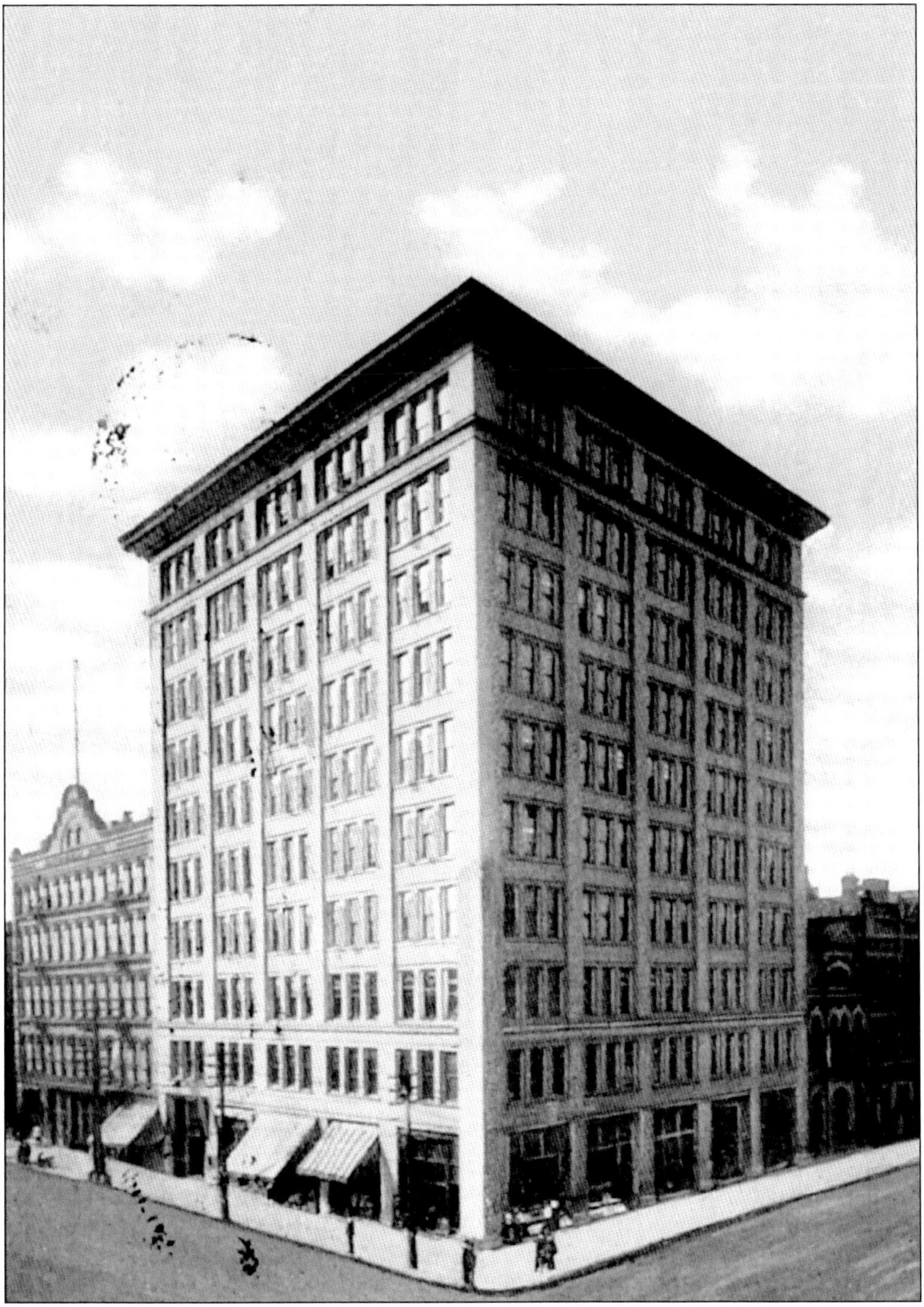

The Woodward Building, financed by William Henry Woodward and designed by architect William C. Weston, was completed 1902. It was Birmingham's first steel frame commercial office building. Ten stories high, the structure raised doubts among local real estate experts, who said all that space could not be rented. Upon opening, the building quickly filled with tenants. (BPLA.)

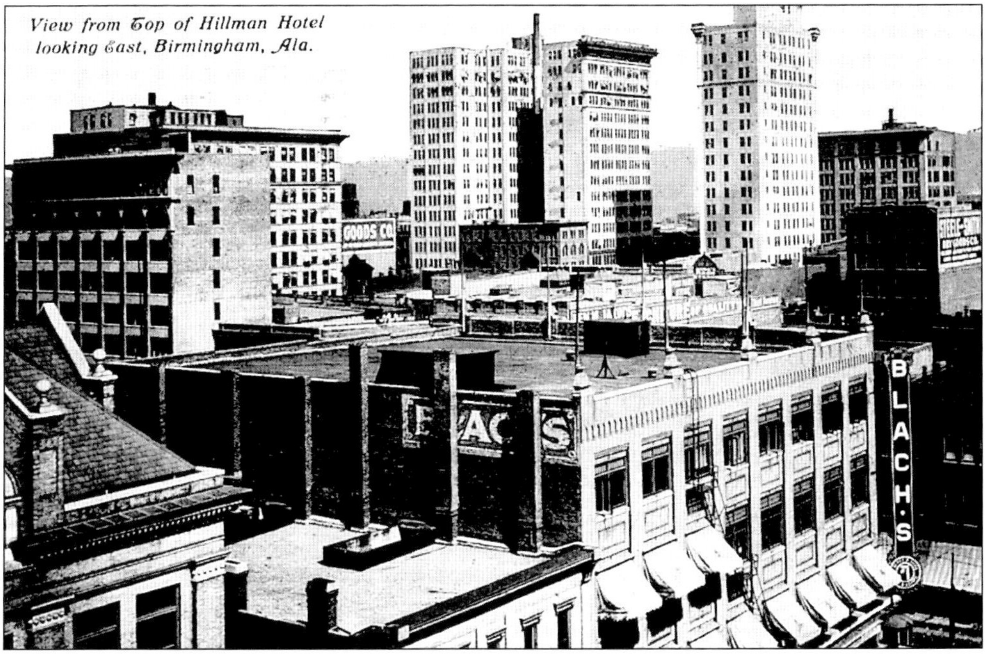

The image above shows Nineteenth Street, North looking southeast. Blach's department store, visible in the foreground, occupied the site of a future Kress store. (BPLA.)

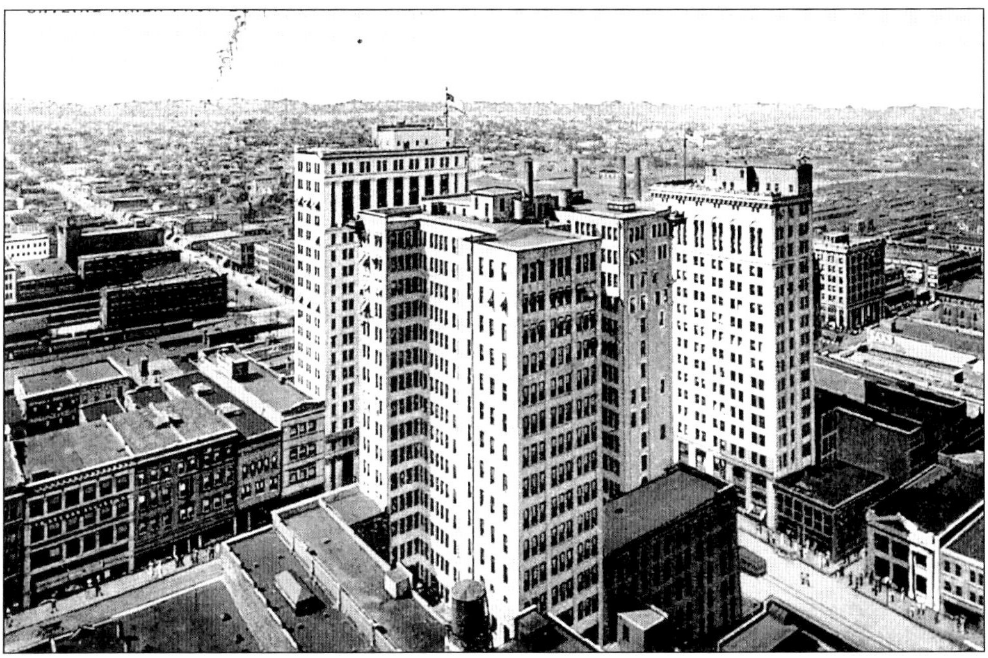

This skyline view includes the American Trust and Savings Bank Building. The tallest building on the left with an American flag on the roof, American Trust, is pictured in detail on the next page. (BPLA.)

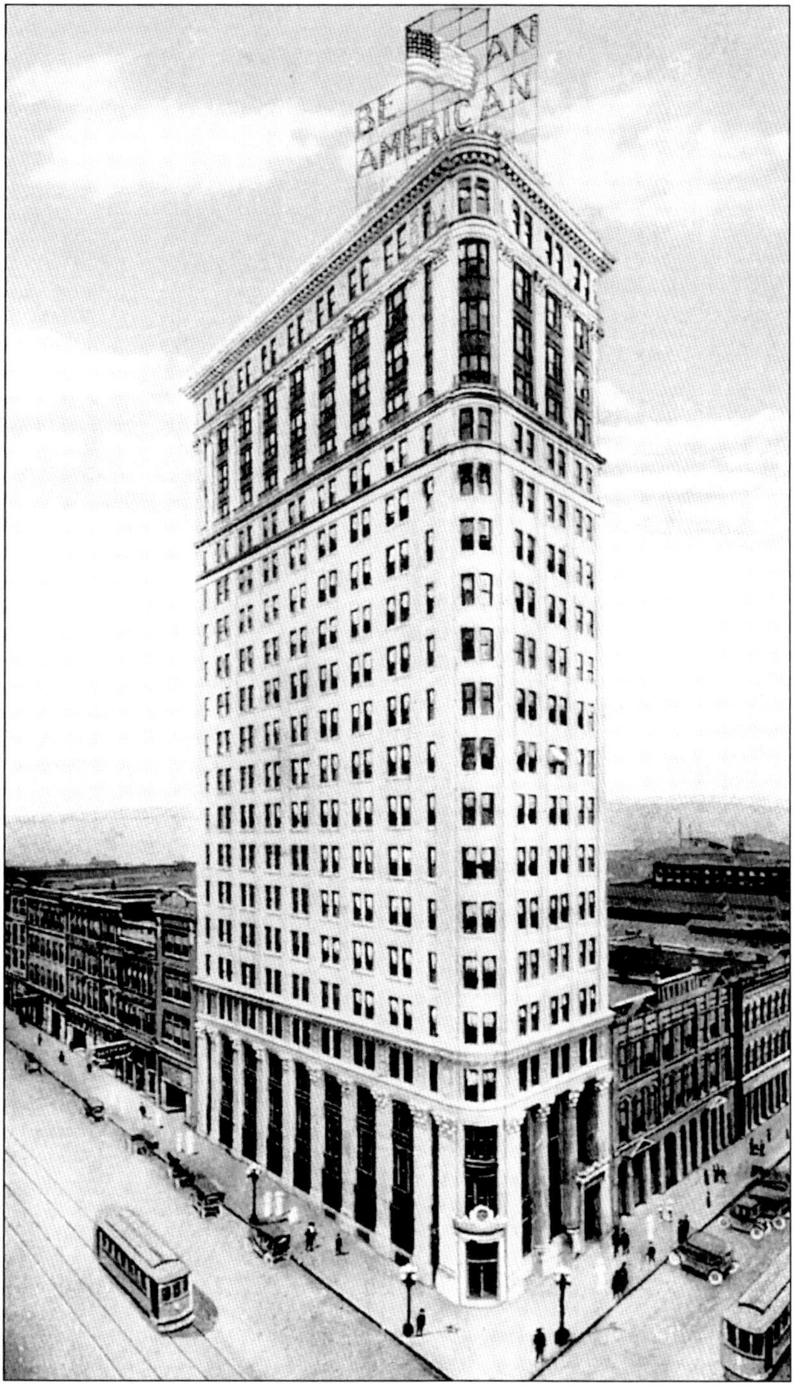

Completed in 1912, the American Trust and Savings Bank Building is located on the southeast corner of First Avenue and Twentieth Street, North. In 1930 American Trust merged with First National Bank, and in 1970 this building was renamed the John A. Hand Building, to honor a former president and chairman of the board of First National. Designed by William Welton, the building is currently undergoing renovation. (BPLA.)

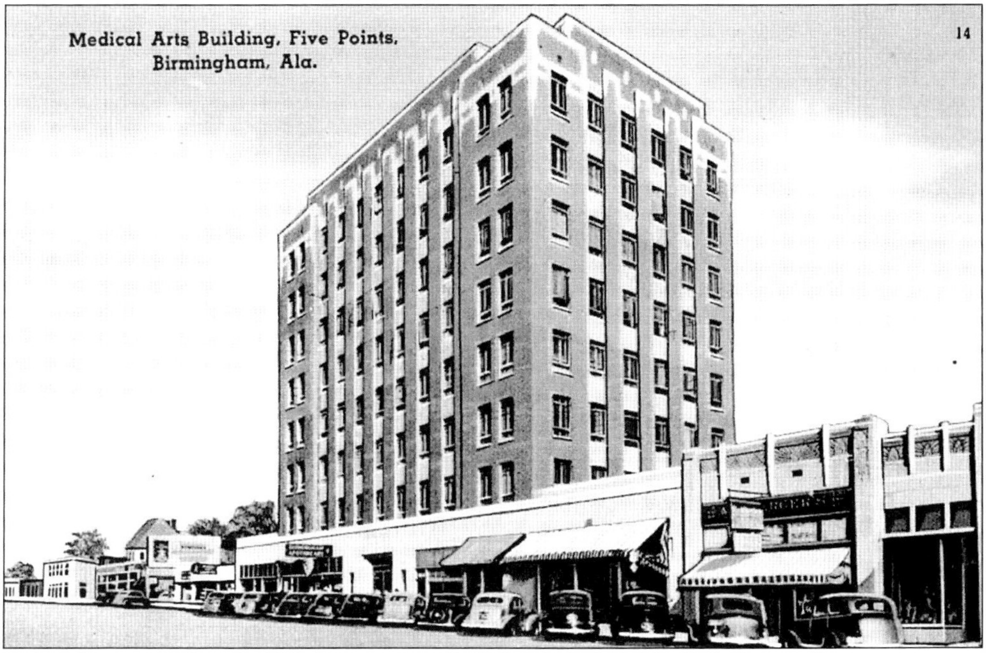

The caption on the verso of this card reads, "Birmingham's Medical Arts Building was designed especially for physicians, surgeons and dentists. It is located in the semi-business district of Five Points—a fashionable residential section. The Basement includes parking facilities for residents and their patients." Designed by architect Charles H. McCauley, the building was completed in 1930 and is now occupied by the Pickwick Hotel. (BPLA.)

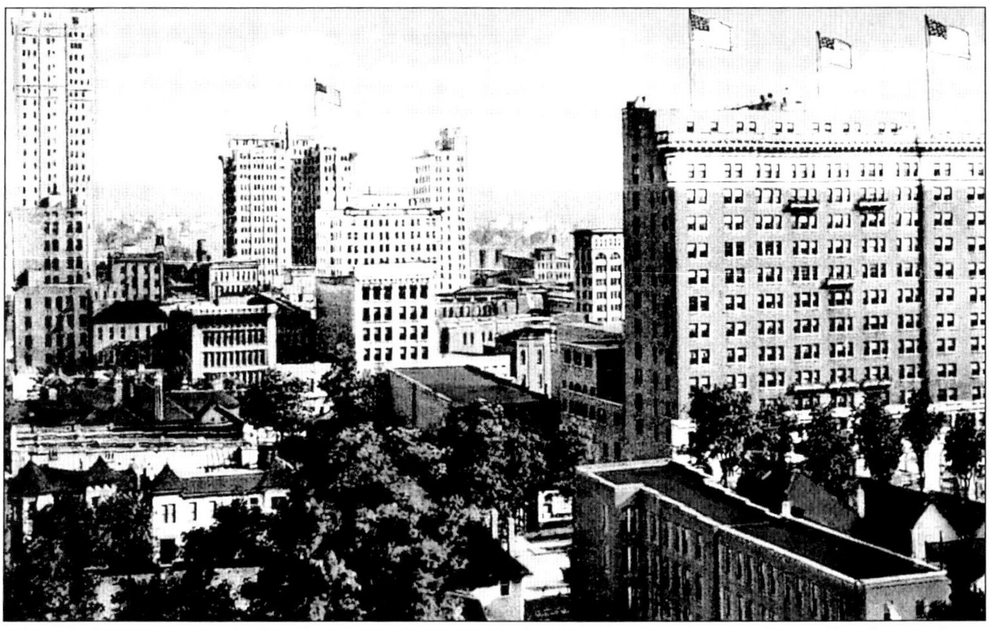

This skyline view includes the Tutwiler Hotel, the large structure on the right flying three American flags. Just peeking out from behind the Tutwiler is the Farley Building, shown in detail on the next page. (BPLA.)

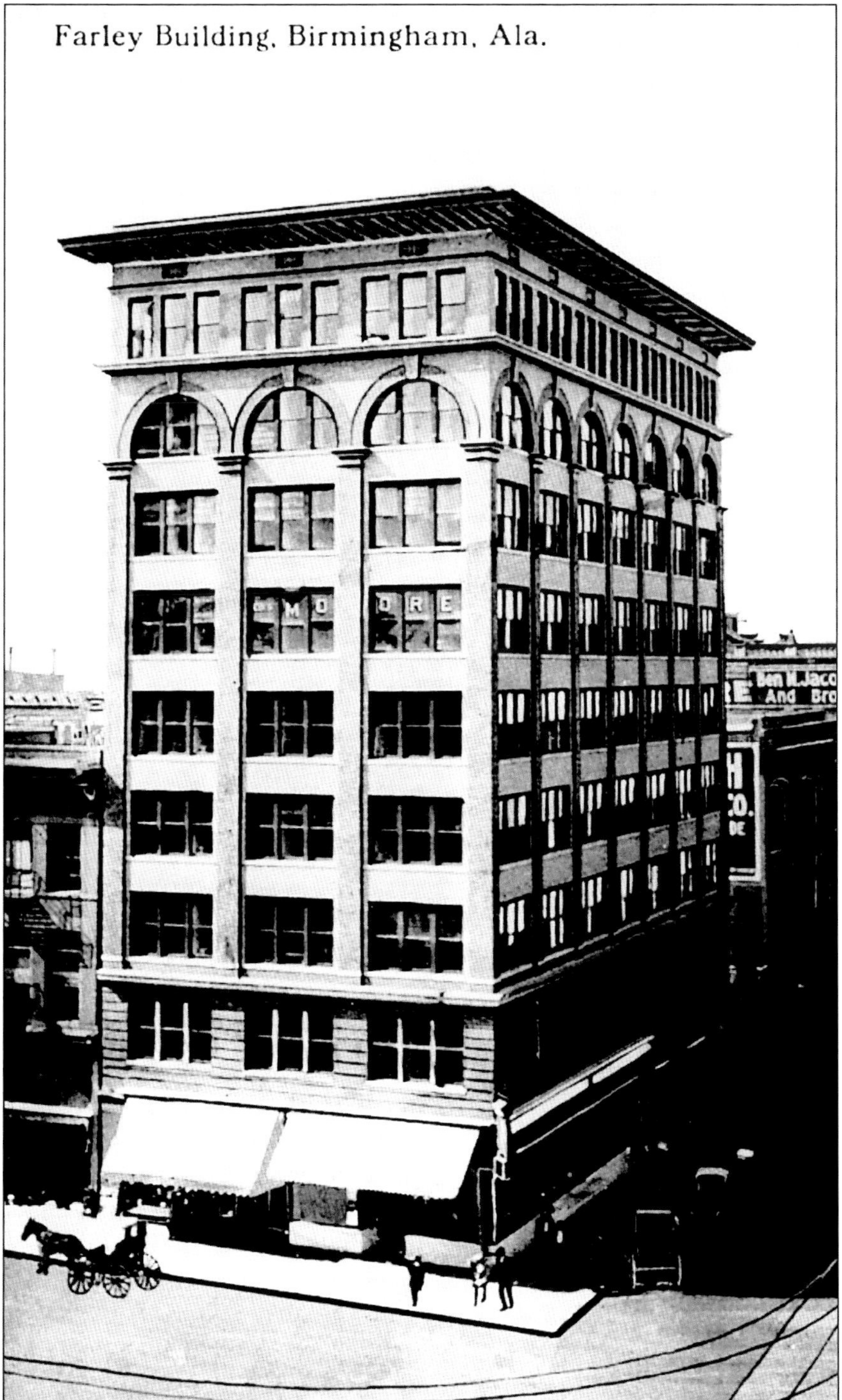

Located on Third Avenue, North and completed in 1909, the Farley Building was named for John G. Farley, a Civil War veteran who never lived in Birmingham but did invest in various Birmingham business ventures, including the building bearing his name. (BPLA.)

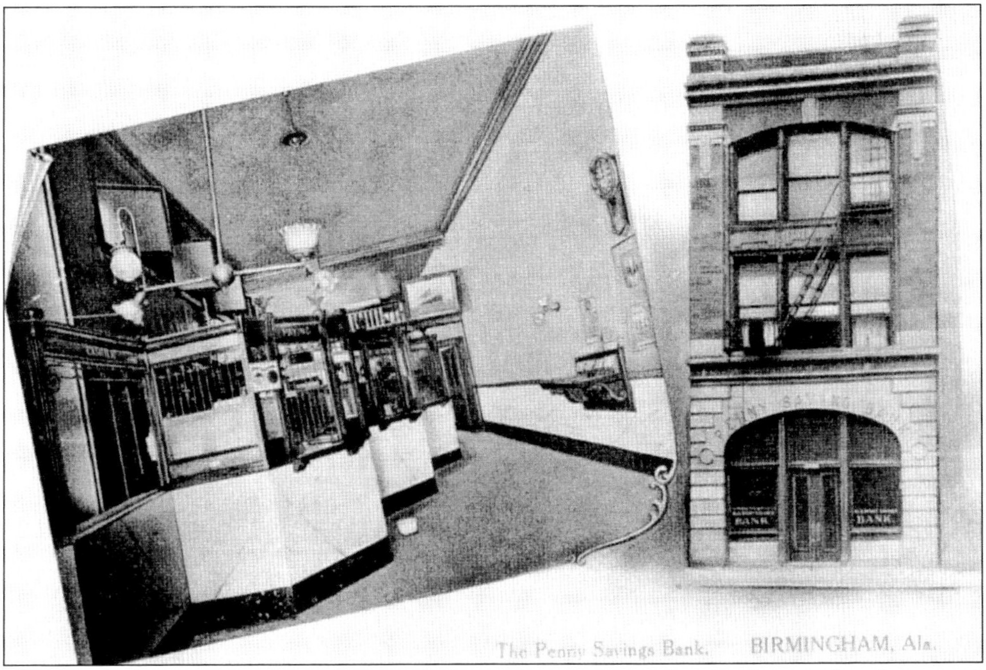

The Penny Savings Bank, founded in 1890, was Birmingham's first bank owned and operated by African Americans. One of the financial institution's organizers was William R. Pettiford, minister at Sixteenth Street Baptist Church from 1883 to 1893. The building pictured above was located at 217 Eighteenth Street, North. In 1913 the bank opened a new, six-story building at 310 Eighteenth Street. The bank survived for 25 years, and in 1915 the Grand Lodge Knights of Pythias purchased the second bank building. (SG.)

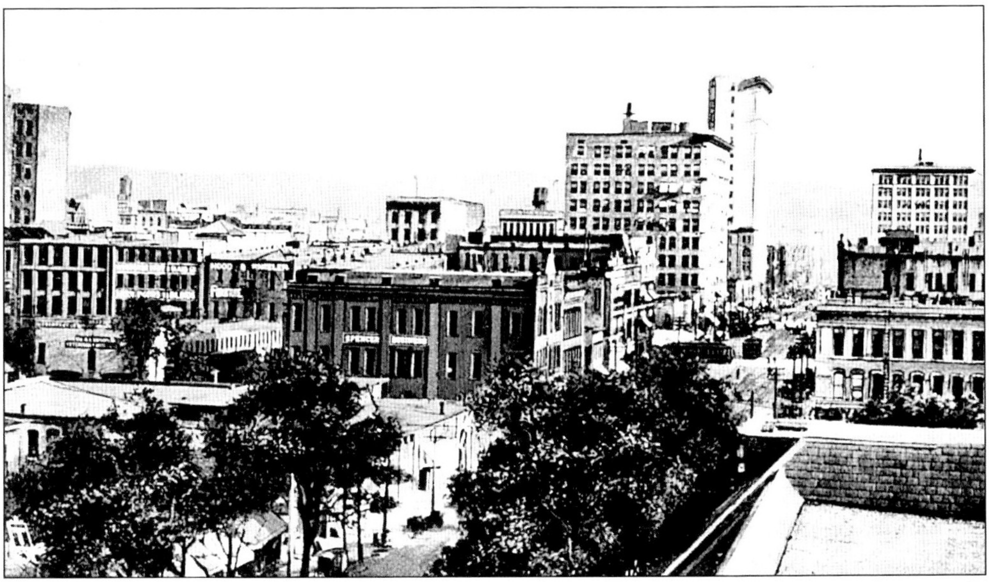

Judging by the stamp on the back, this card was probably given out by A.C. Oxford, an early Birmingham photographer, as a souvenir at a Confederate veteran's reunion. Just visible, the tallest building on the far left is the Title Guarantee Loan and Trust Company Building, which is shown in detail on the next page. (BPLA.)

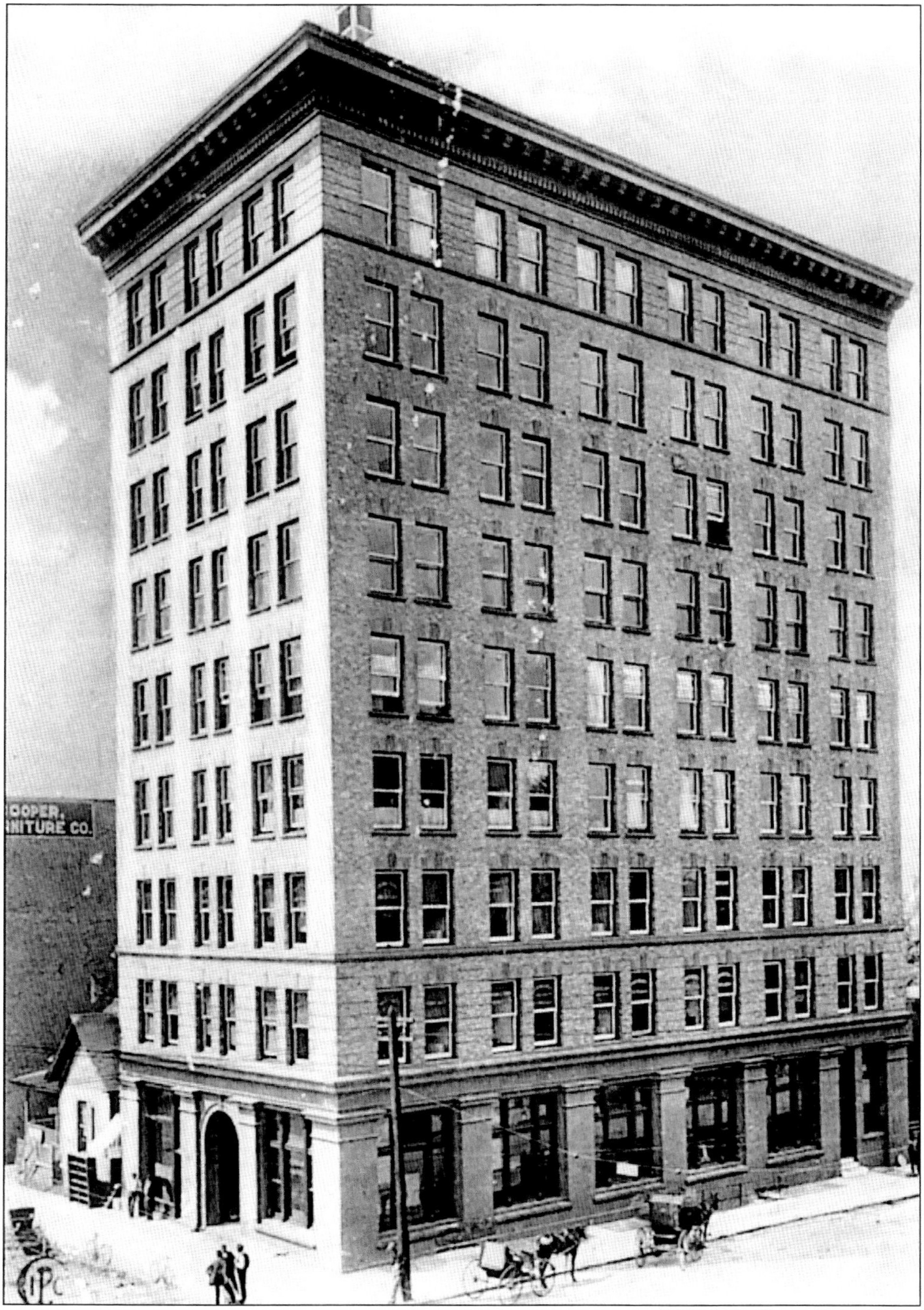

The Title Guarantee Building, completed in 1903 and designed by architect William C. Weston, was the only Birmingham building with its own power plant. Building tenants were provided free electricity. Located at 2030 Third Avenue, North, Title Guarantee was constructed in an area of Birmingham that had been primarily residential. On the image above houses are visible beside and behind the new office building. (BPLA.)

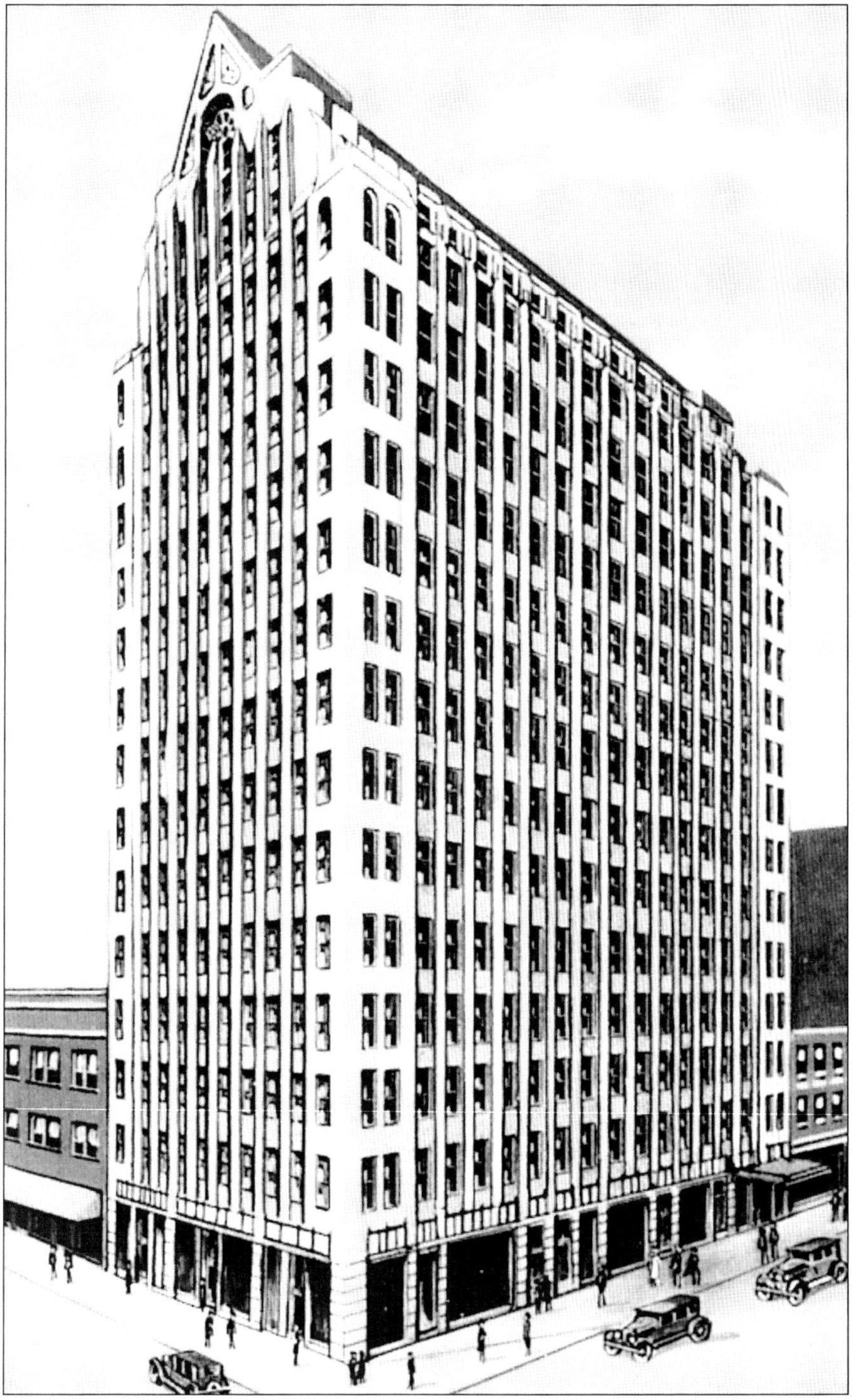

The caption on the verso of this card reads, "The Watts Building, one of Birmingham's newest office buildings, consists of more than 300 offices, and stores on grade floor and basement. Estimated cost one million dollars." This building, located at 2004 Third Avenue, North and completed in 1928, replaced an earlier four-story structure built in 1881 also called the Watts Building. (BPLA.)

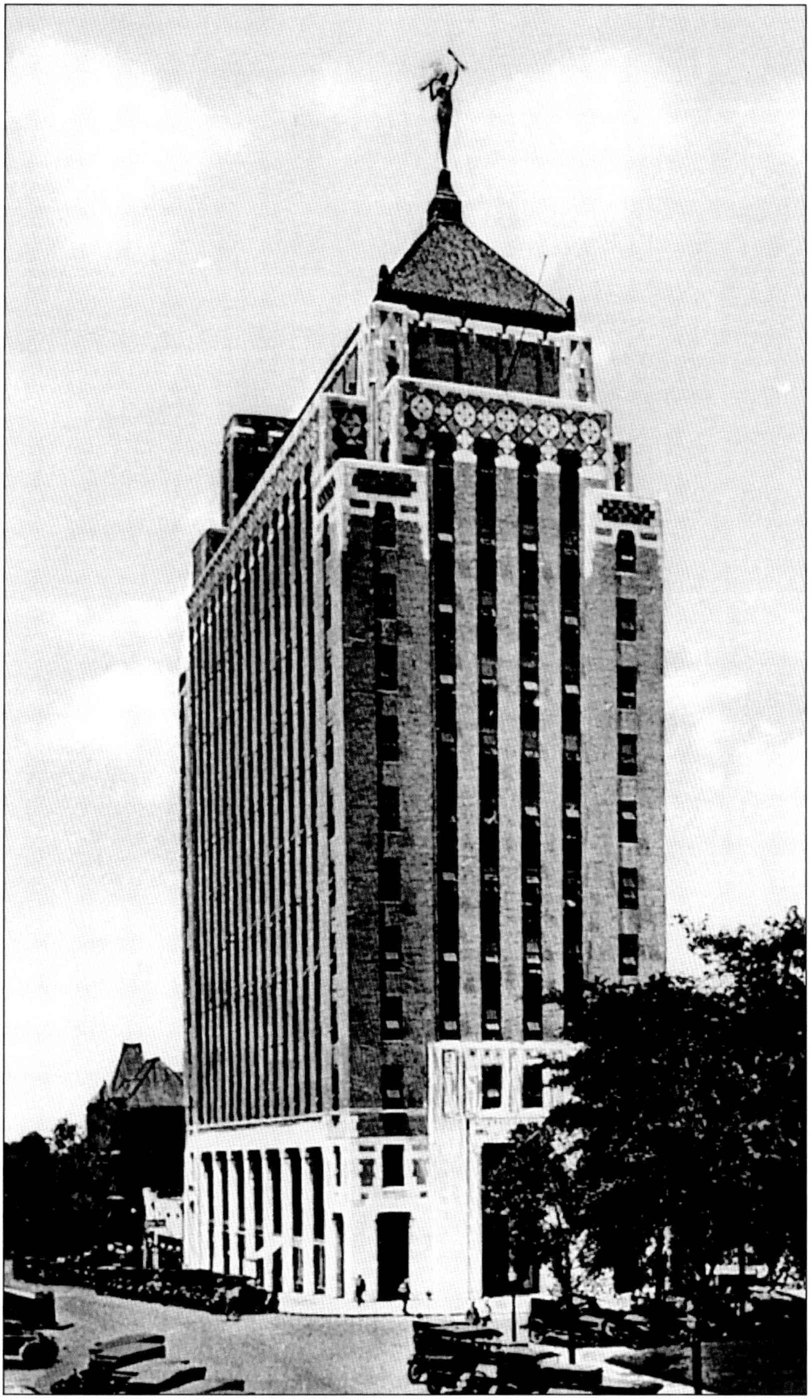

Located on the corner of Sixth Avenue and Eighteenth Street, North, the Alabama Power Company Building is primarily attributed to the architectural firm of Warren, Knight, and Davis and was completed in 1925. The caption on the verso of the card reads, "The Office Building of Alabama Power Co. has been pronounced by the London Daily Express as one of the three most beautiful public utility buildings in the world." (BPLA.)

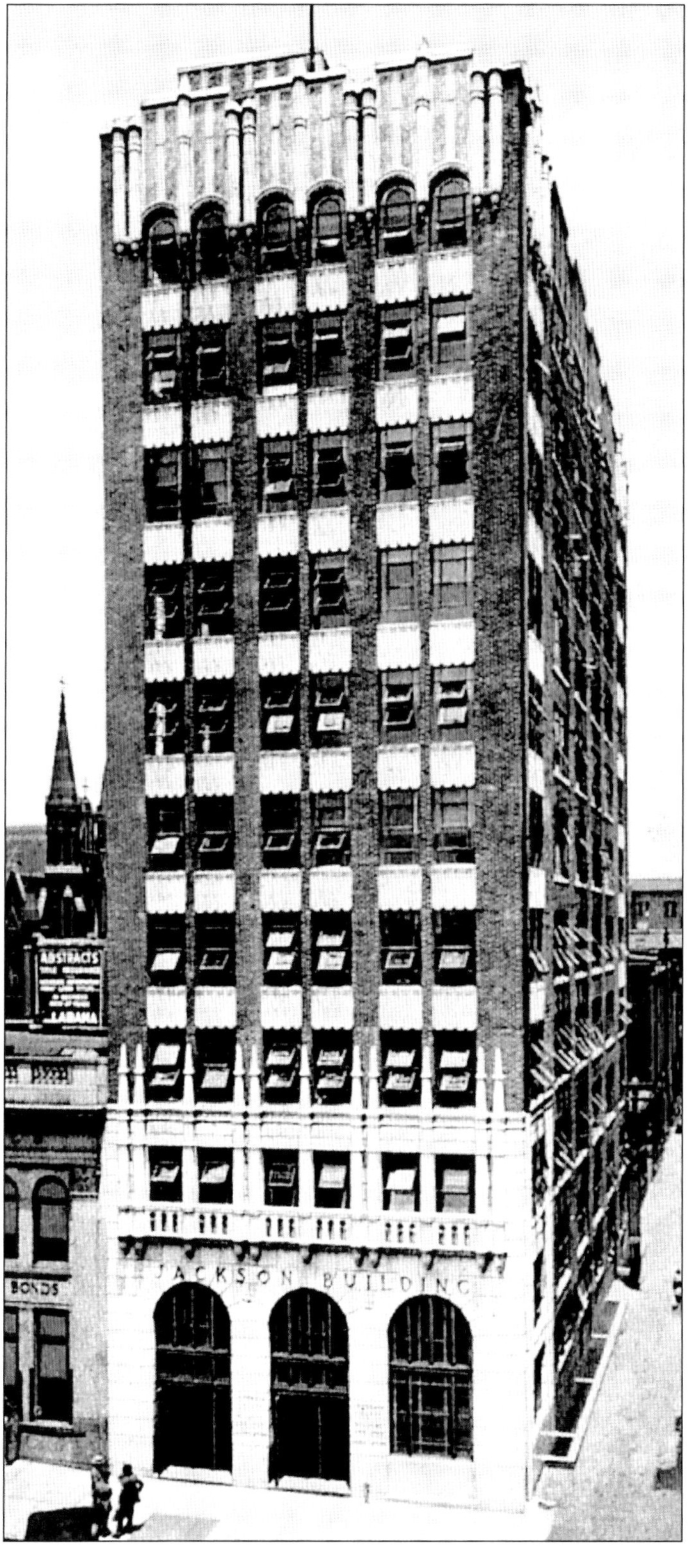

The caption on the verso of this card reads, "The Jackson Building, Birmingham, Alabama. Located on Twenty-first Street between Second and Third Avenues, 10 stories, of fireproof construction, with 120 ideal offices. This is the new home of the Jefferson County Building & Loan Association, which has been in successful operation for the past thirty-three years and is closely associated with the growth of this city as being a prominent factor in making many thousands home owners." (BPLA.)

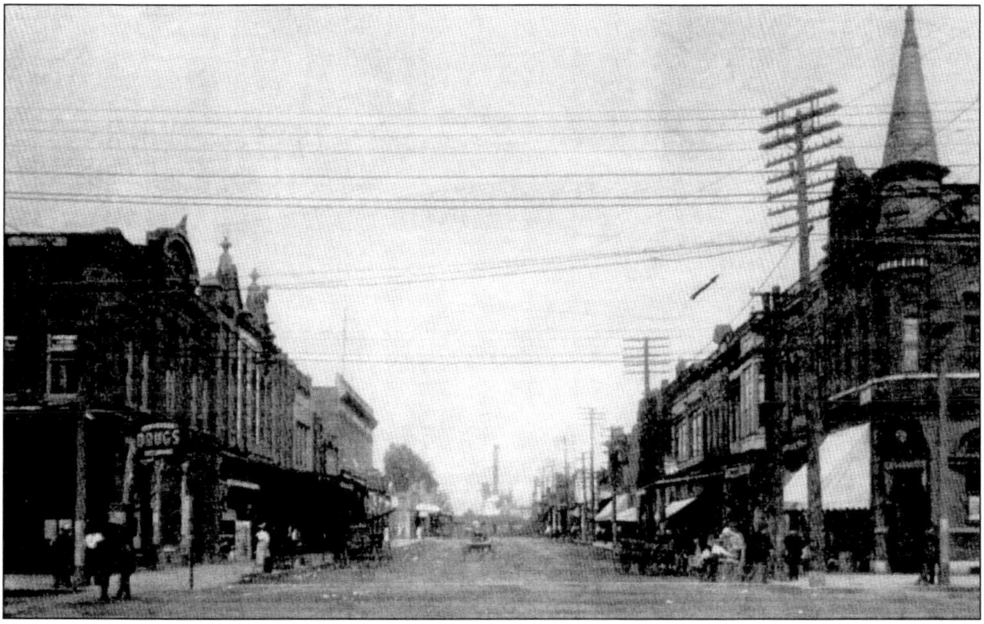

Above, below, and on the following page are three views of Bessemer's business district from three different time periods. On the right side of the street is the Berney Bank, opened in 1888 as the first bank in Bessemer. The card above is an earlier image than the card below, even though the bottom card does not show power lines. Postcard makers would sometimes "remove" objects like power lines and poles to make the area pictured more attractive. (BHH.)

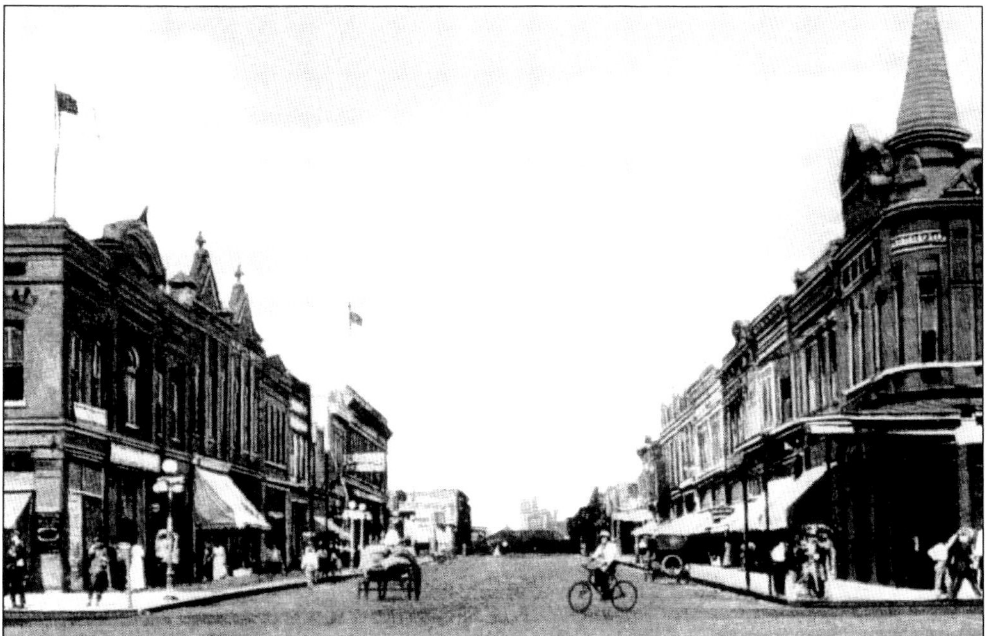

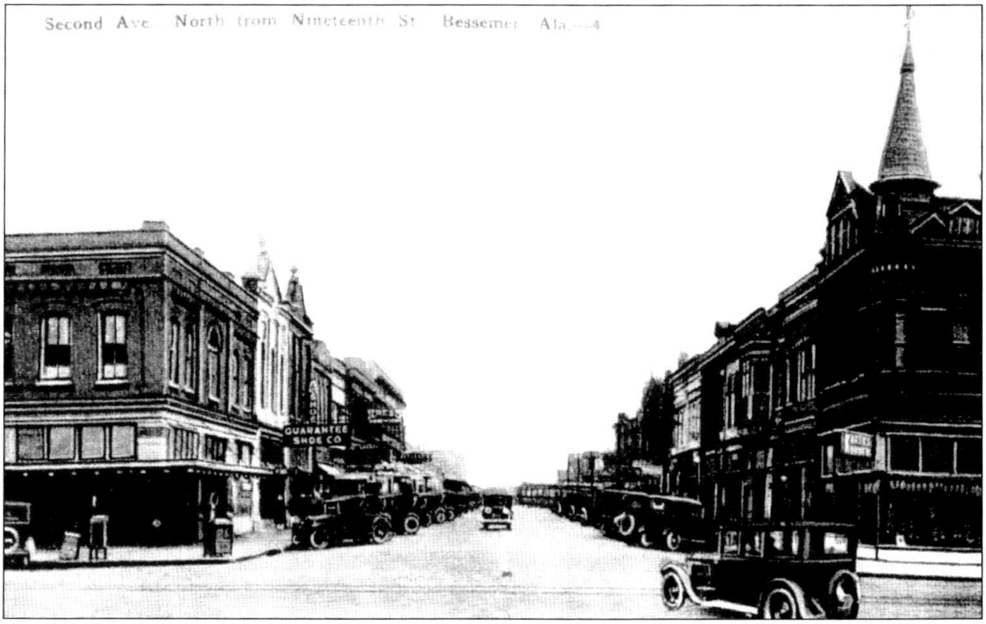

In this view, automobiles have now replaced horse-drawn wagons and bicycles in downtown Bessemer. (BHH.)

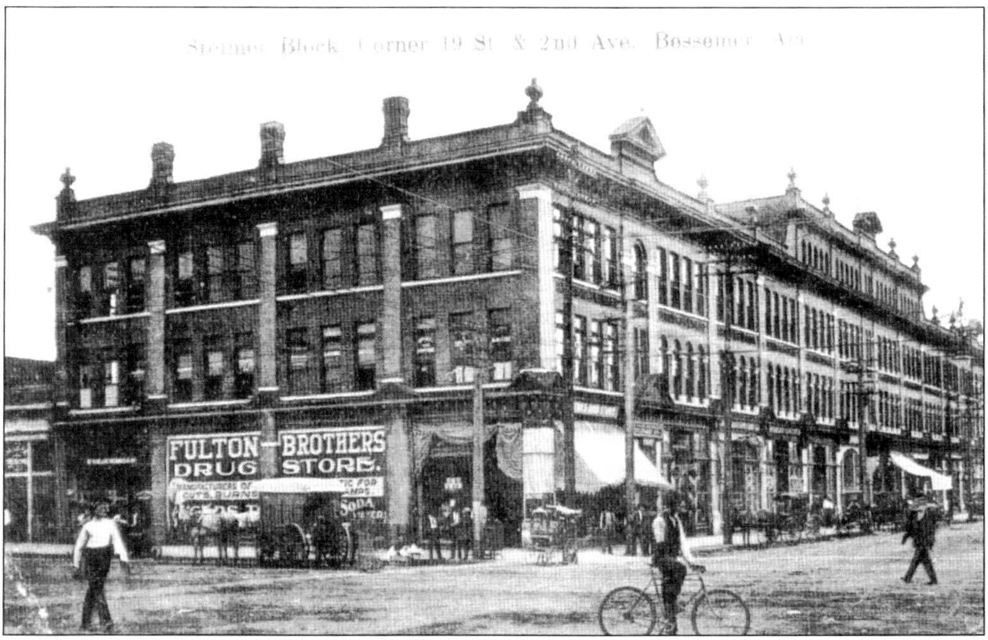

This card showing Bessemer's Steiner Block is another example of German printing. The verso indicates that the card was published by "Ownes Bros. Co., Boston, Berlin, and Leipzig." (BHH.)

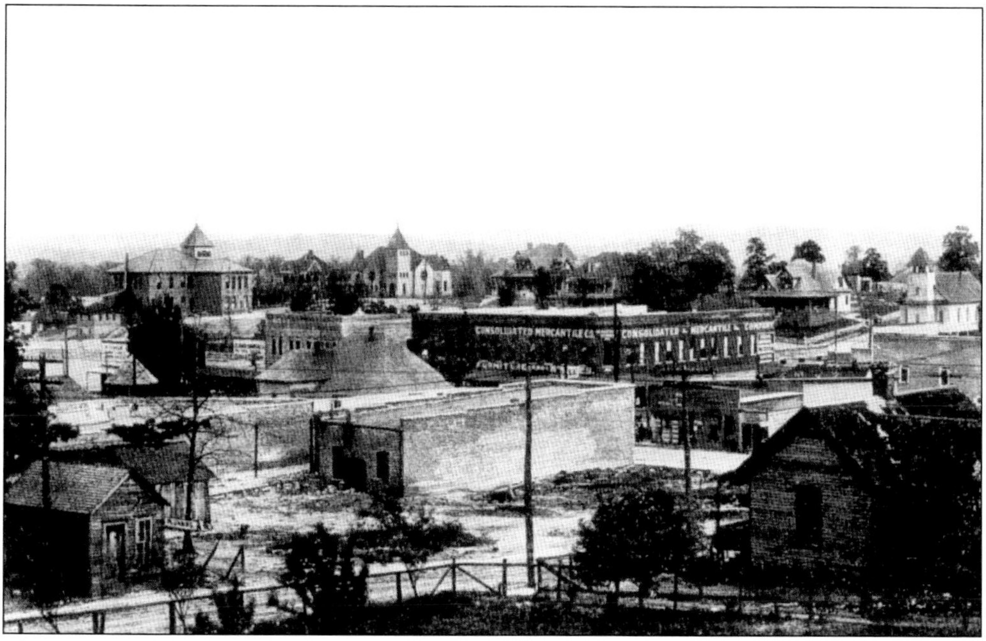

The area that became Wylam was settled after the Tennessee Coal, Iron and Railroad Company opened two mines there in 1886. Lacking sufficient manpower to operate the mines, the company advertised for workers, and immigrants came to Wylam from as far away as England, Scotland, Wales, France, Italy, Germany, Poland, Russia, and Yugoslavia. The town incorporated in 1900 and by the 1920s boasted 5,000 residents. (SG.)

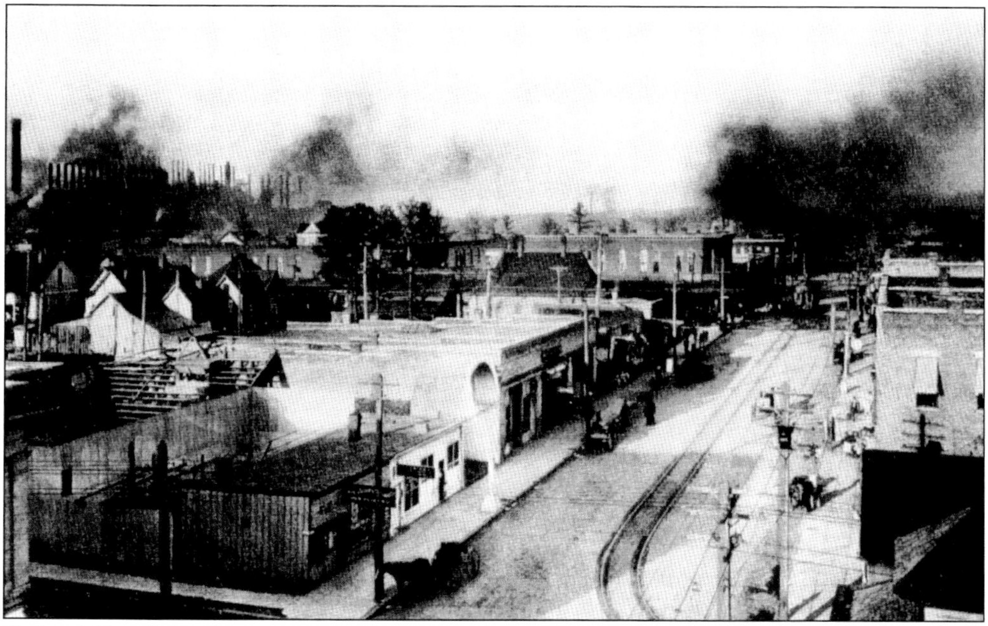

Colonel Enoch Ensley, a successful cotton planter from near Memphis, invested heavily in mining and manufacturing in the Birmingham District and in 1886 was named president of the Tennessee Coal, Iron and Railroad Company. Ensley dreamed of building a great industrial city, and founded the town bearing his name in 1888. (SG.)

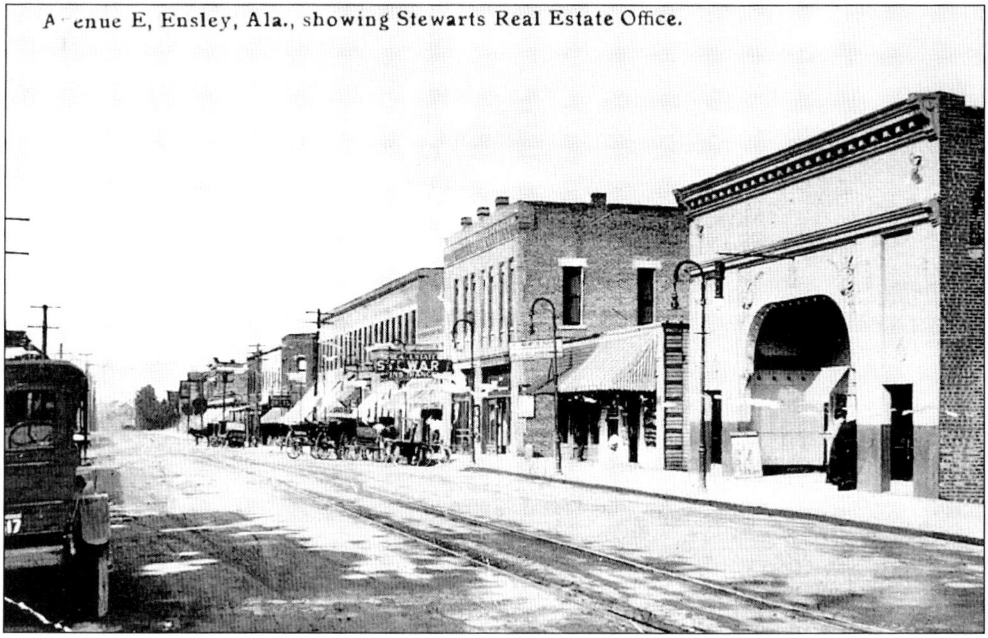

This card promoting Stewart's Real Estate was mailed from Ensley to Tennessee in 1911. During that year, the Stewart company shared this side of Avenue E's 1900 block with a number of other businesses including *The Ensley Enterprise*, a weekly newspaper issued every Saturday, Sam Loo Hand Laundry, which promised to "Make Old Shirts Look Like New," Nick DeNapple, a fruit vendor, and Killgore Furniture Company, a seller of "Fine Furniture, Stoves, Ranges, Rugs, Mattings and Linoleums." (BPLA.)

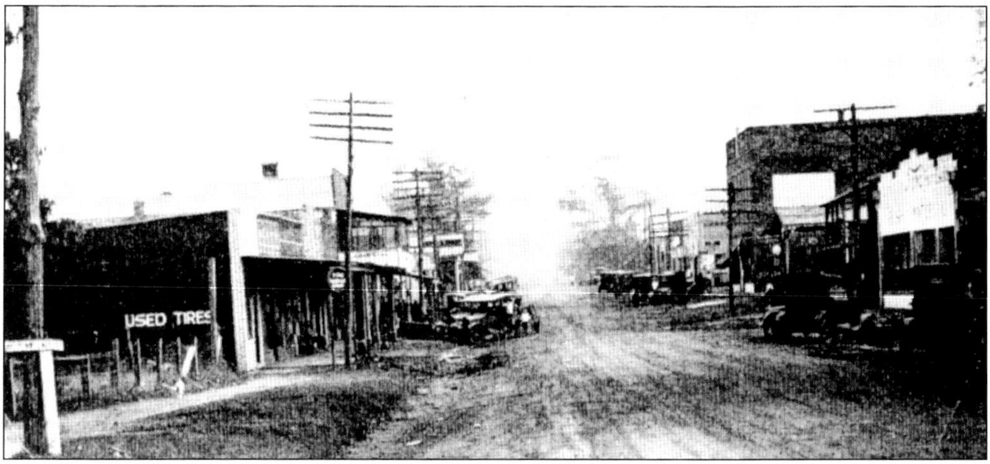

This is a rare early postcard of Leeds. Engineers building the Georgia Pacific Railroad (Southern) founded Leeds in 1881 and named the town for Leeds, England. By the time the card above was produced, *c.* 1915, Leeds was a thriving community. Looking east on muddy First Avenue (now Parkway Drive) is Bush Motor, the first white-faced building on the right. The tallest building on the right is the site where AmSouth Bank now stands. The number of automobiles parked on the street is worth noting. When postcard producers would visit small towns to photograph sites, town leaders often called everyone in the area who owned a car to come and park them on main street. The idea was to make the town appear thriving and cosmopolitan. (LCC.)

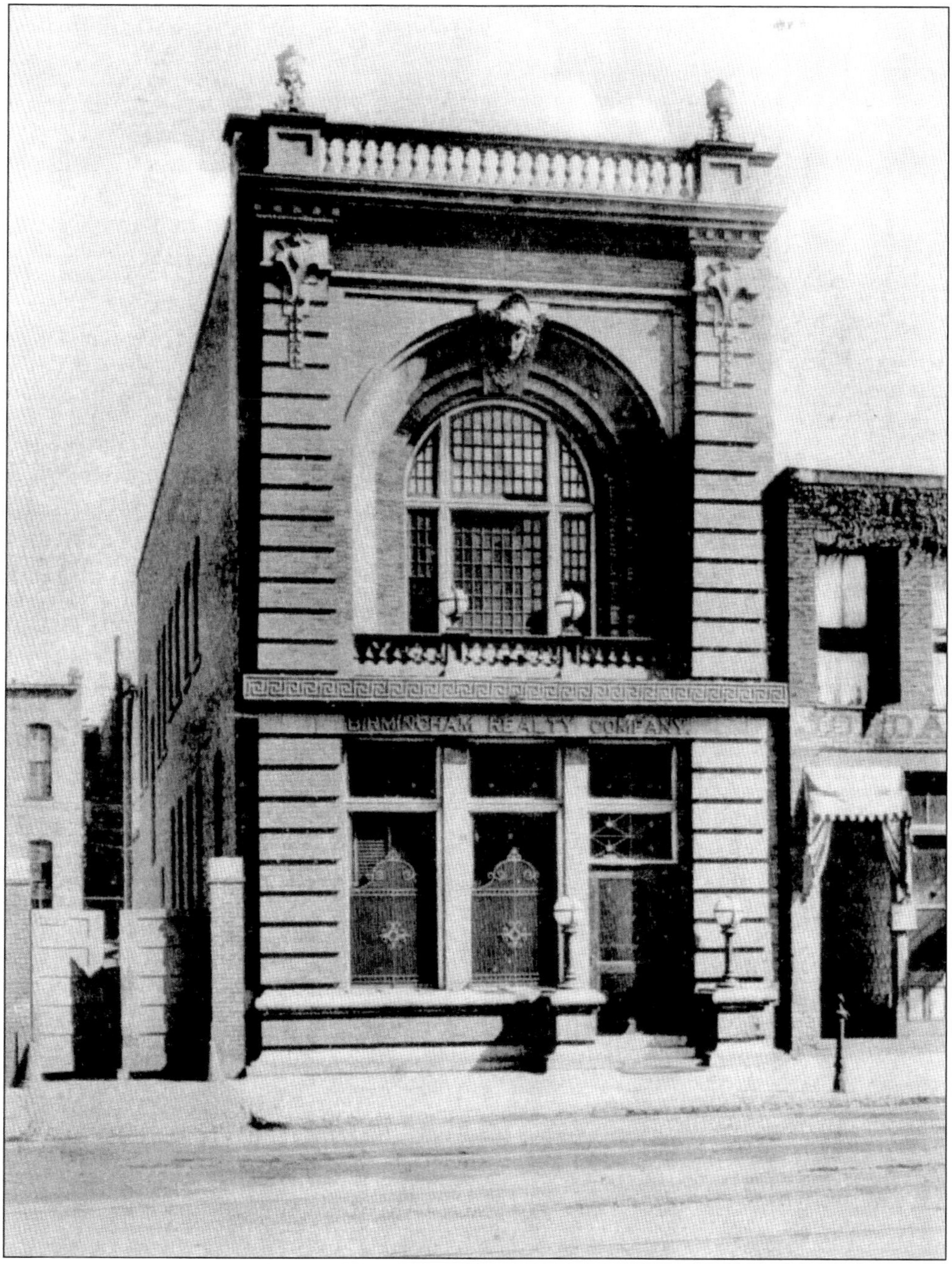

The Birmingham Realty Company is the successor to the Elyton Land Company, the concern that founded the city of Birmingham. The company office building shown here was completed around 1905 and is a fine example of the beaux-arts style of architecture. This postcard, mailed in 1907, is an early view of the building, which looks much the same today except that the balustrade between the two roof columns has been removed. (SG.)

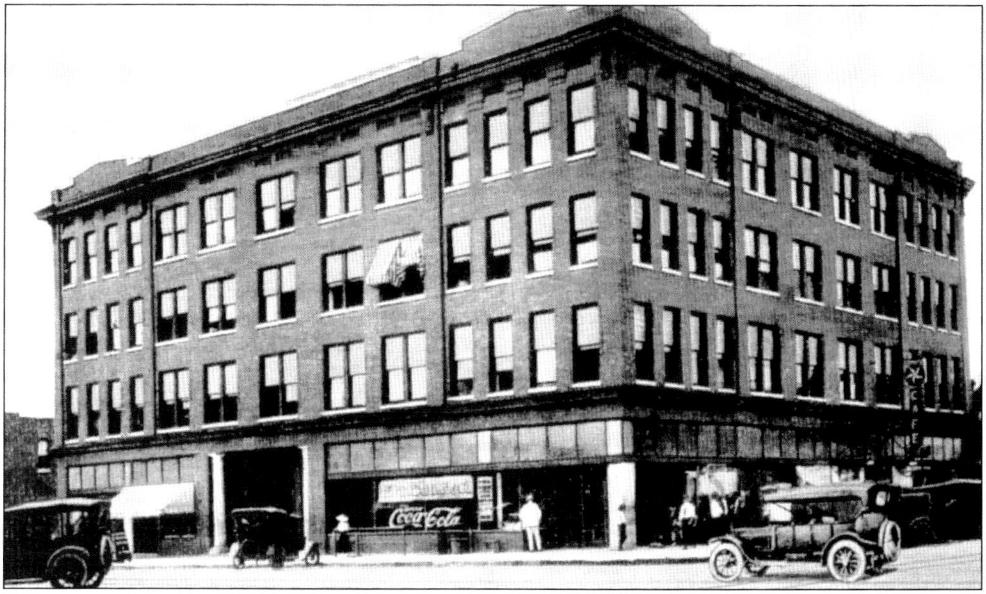

This view of Bessemer's Realty Building shows the Bright Star Café on the far right. When the building was constructed in 1915, space was provided for the restaurant, founded in 1907 at a different location. The man who would eventually become an owner of the Bright Star, Vasilios Demetrios Koikos, immigrated from Greece in 1920. He took a job at the restaurant as a bus boy, and within five years had purchased part ownership. The Koikos family still operates the Bright Star at the location shown above. (BHH.)

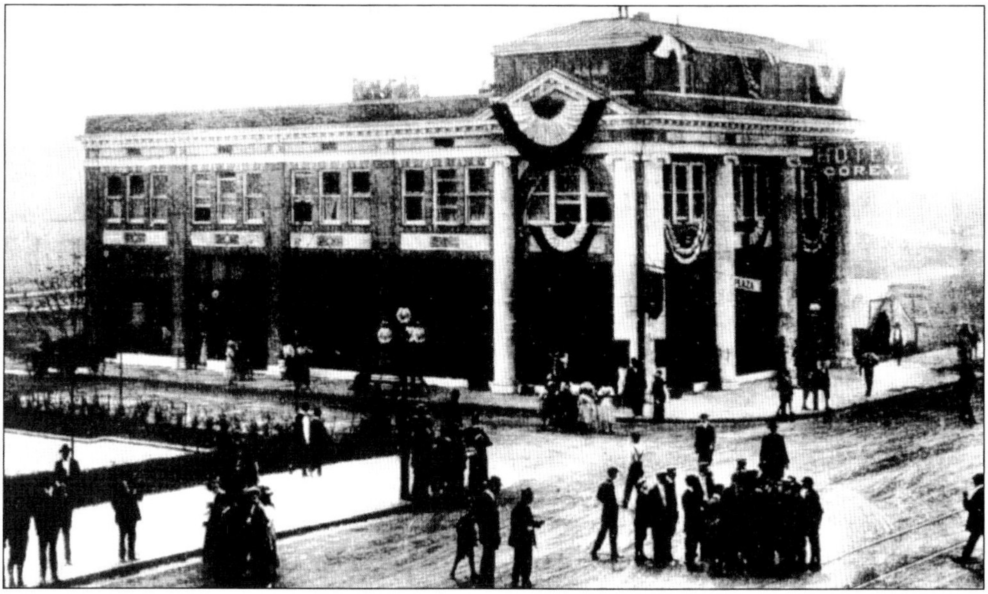

Planning for the town of Corey, later called Fairfield, began in 1909. The Tennessee Coal, Iron and Railroad Company, a subsidiary of United States Steel, developed Corey as a model town for its workers. Commercial buildings on the town plaza, including the bank and hotel pictured above, were designed by architect William Leslie Welton and opened in 1911. Theodore Roosevelt and early social worker Jane Addams visited Corey and praised the design of the town. (SG.)

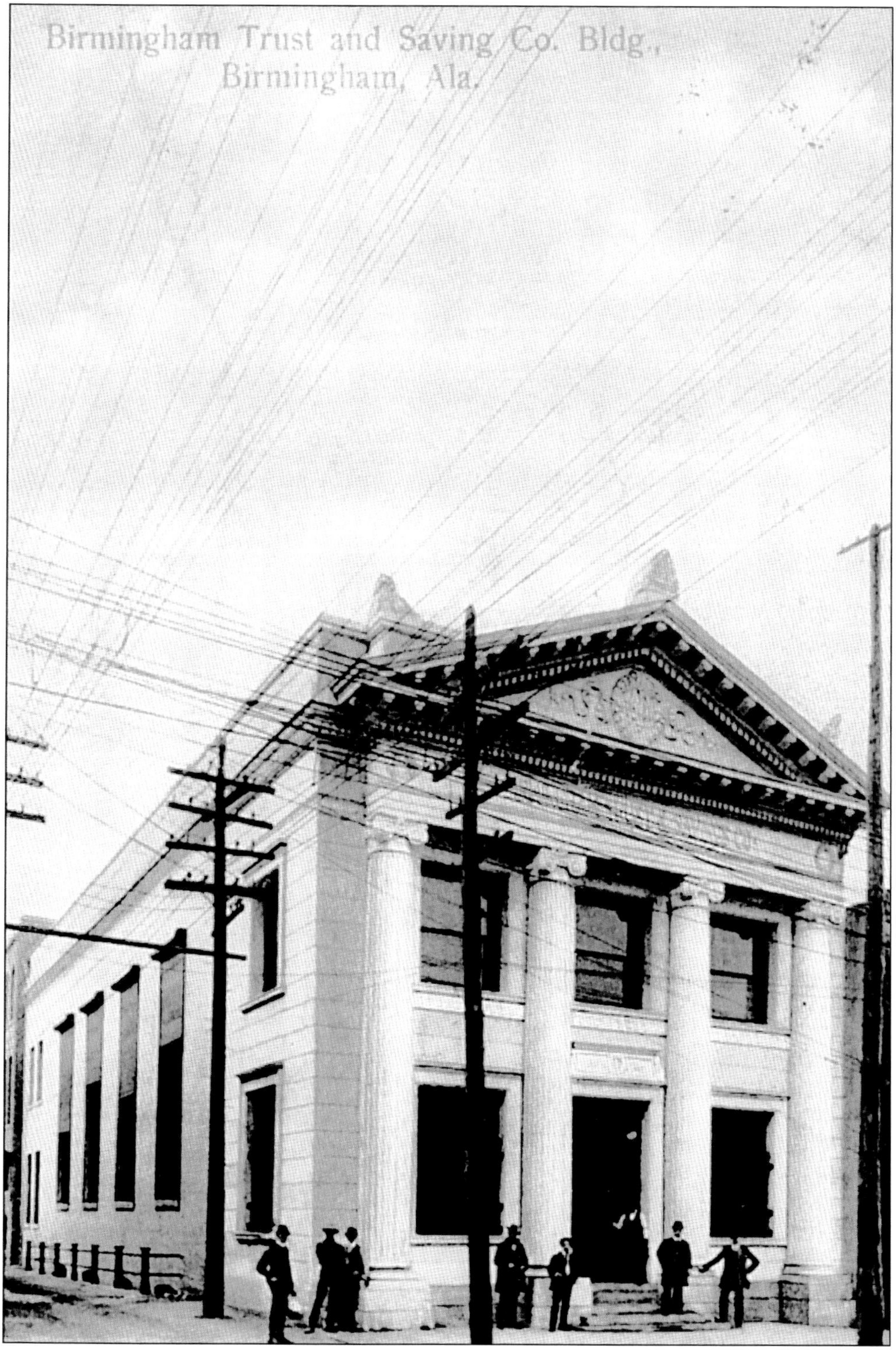

The Birmingham Trust and Saving Company became Southtrust Bank; the present company headquarters on Twentieth Street is located on the site of this earlier building. (BPLA.)

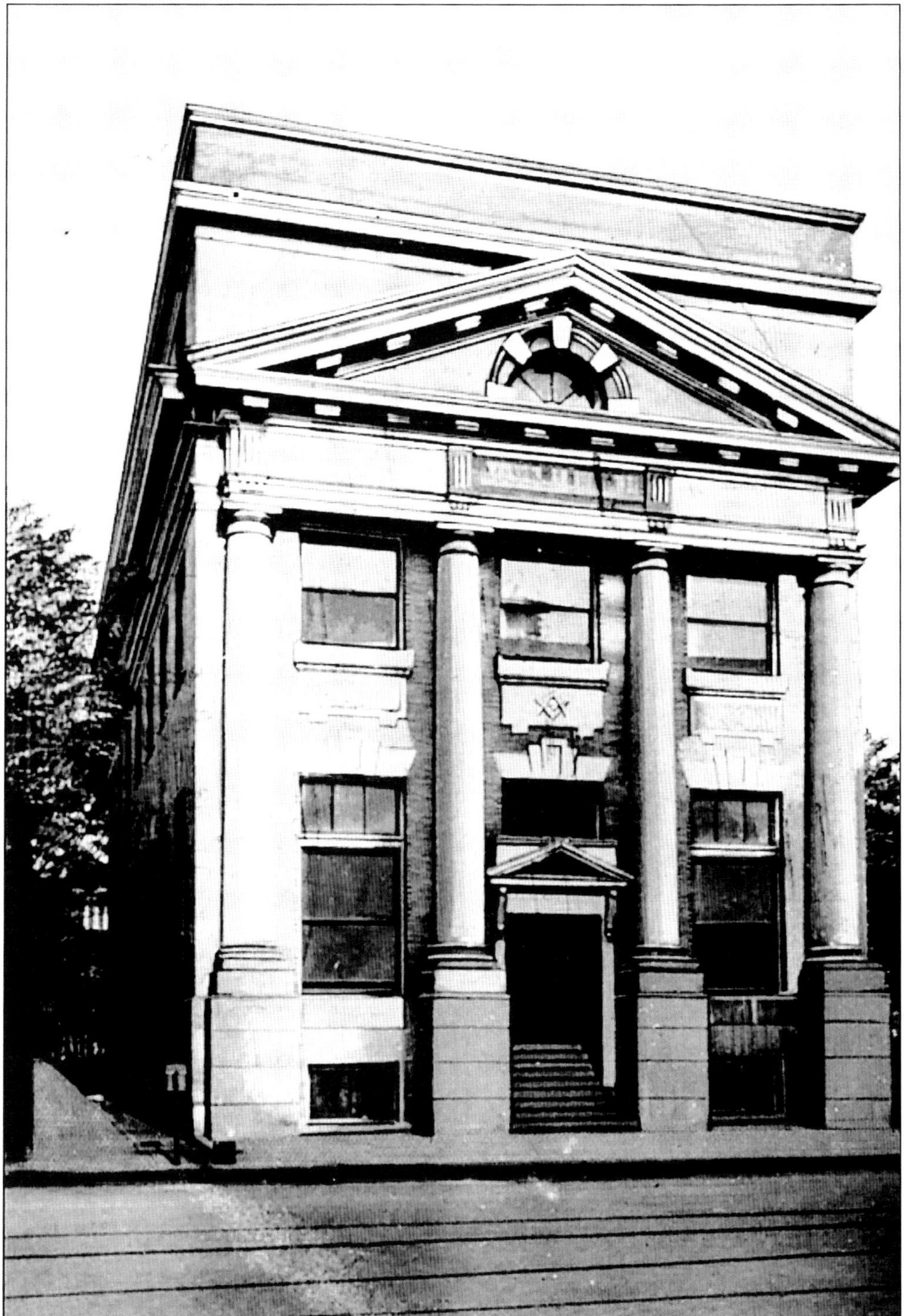

On this page and the facing page are two views of the old Masonic Temple located at the corner of Sixth Avenue and Nineteenth Street, North. This structure was replaced by a new, much larger Masonic Temple in 1922 (see p. 65). (BPLA.)

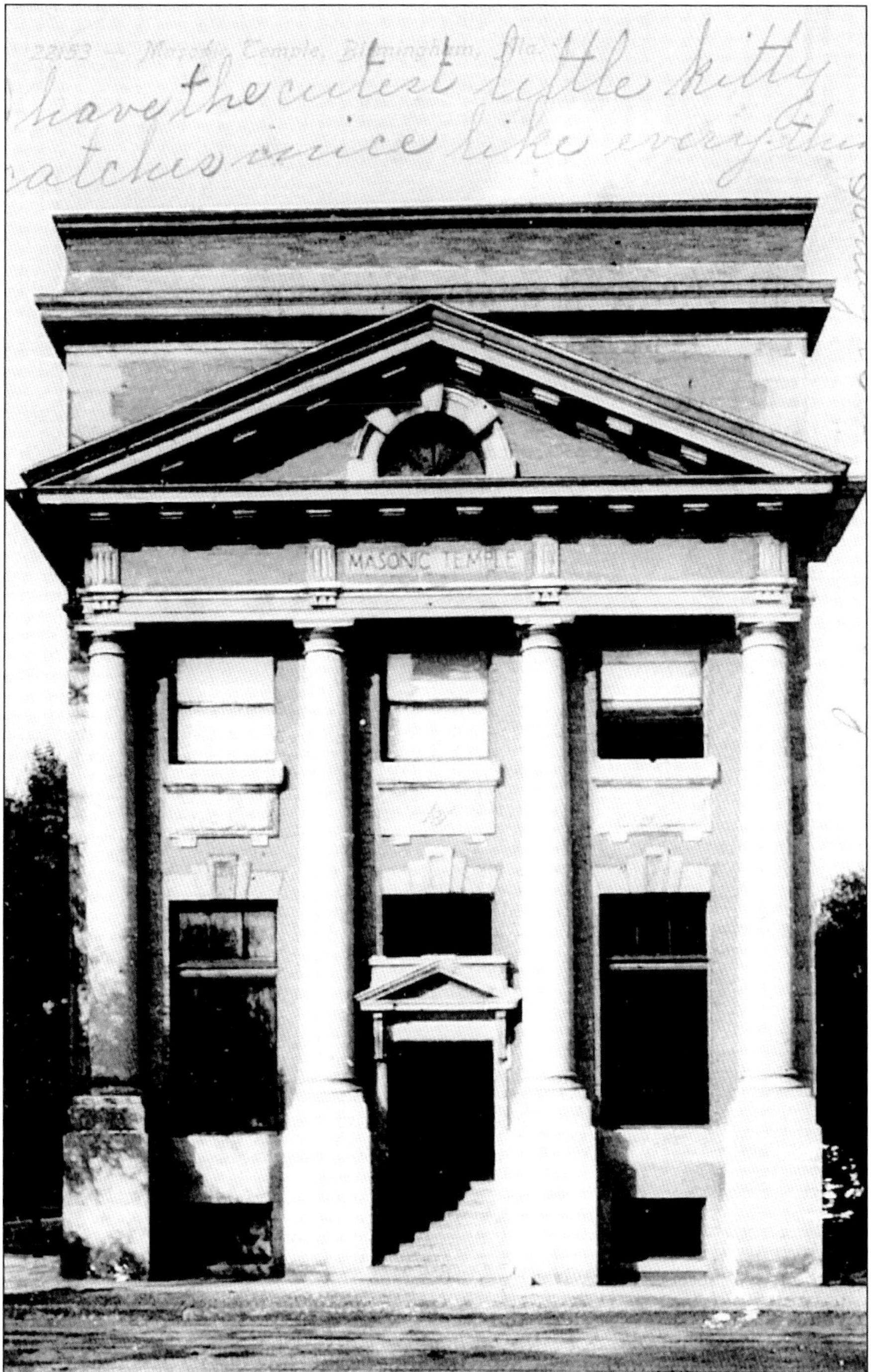

On the face of this card the sender writes, "I have the cutest little kitty catches mice like everything. Today is election day here." The card was mailed in 1928, at a time when postcards were often used for everyday communication, the way that telephones and e-mail would be used in later eras. The messages written on cards often have nothing to do with the image. (BPLA.)

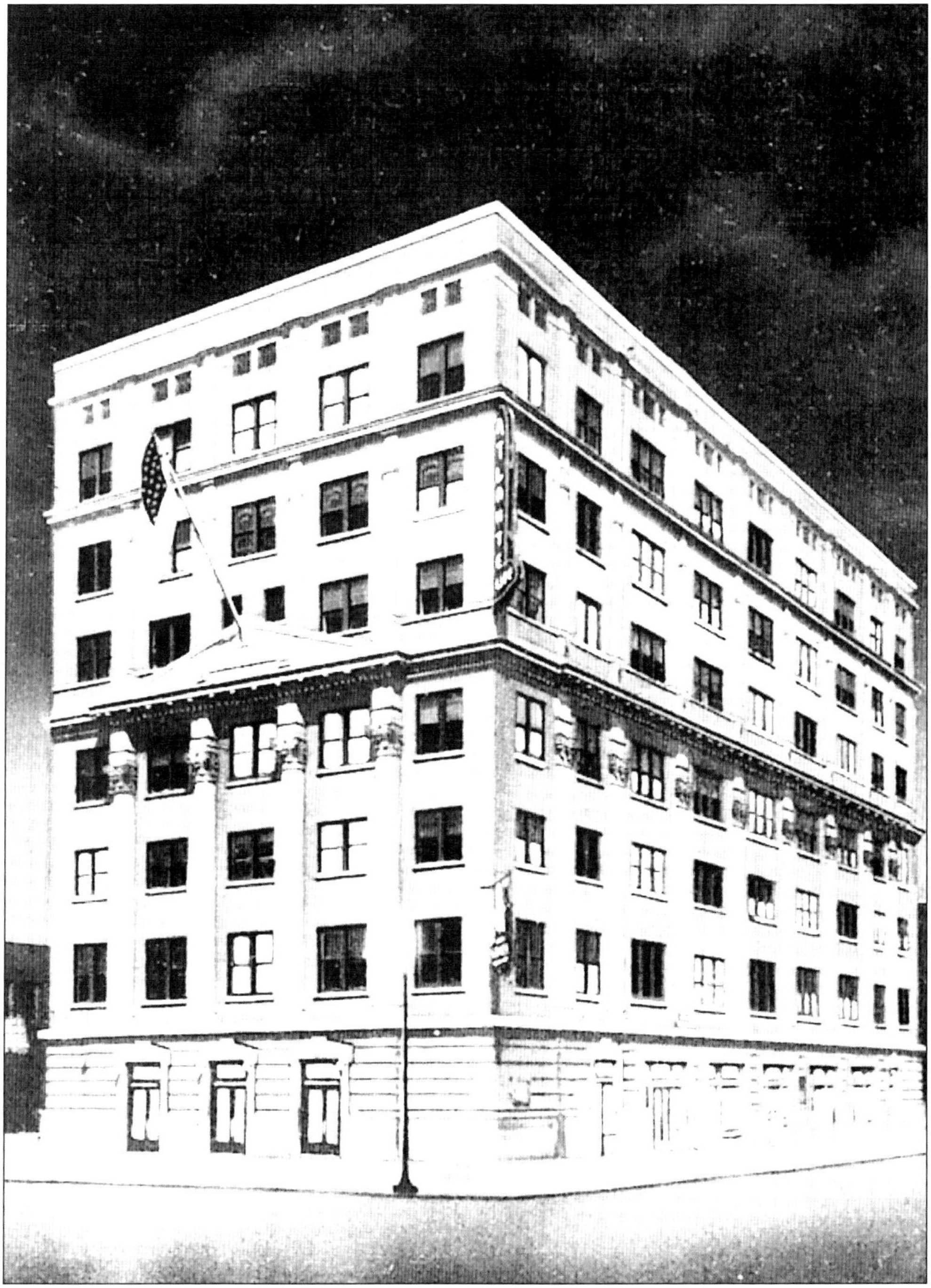

Located at 1630 Fourth Avenue, North, this neo-classic building has served Birmingham's African-American community since 1924 as a Masonic Temple (officially the Most Wonderful Prince Hall Grand Lodge F. and A.M. of Alabama) and office building housing attorneys, doctors, accountants, insurance companies, and headquarters of various labor unions. Designed by black architects Taylor E. Persley and Walter T. Woods, the building originally had only four floors. The three upper floors were added in two separate renovations. (BPLA.)

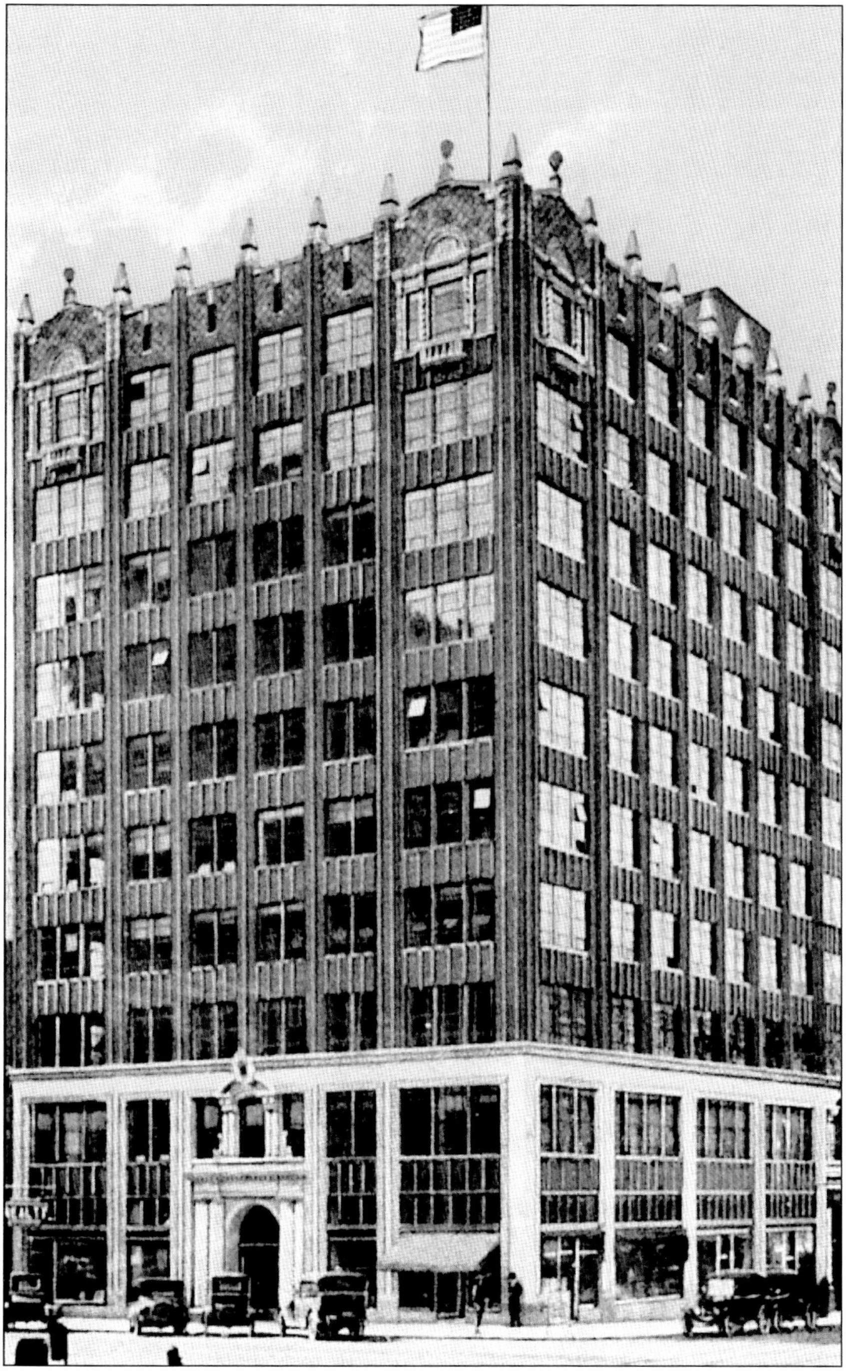

Birmingham entrepreneur and real estate developer Richard W. Massey originally planned a five-story building on this site at 2025 Third Avenue, North to house his business college. But the Banker's Bond Company convinced Massey to construct a ten-story building instead and lease the first five floors to them. Designed by architect William Leslie Welton, the building was completed in 1920 and was renamed the Massey Building after the Banker's Bond Company folded during the Great Depression. (BPLA.)

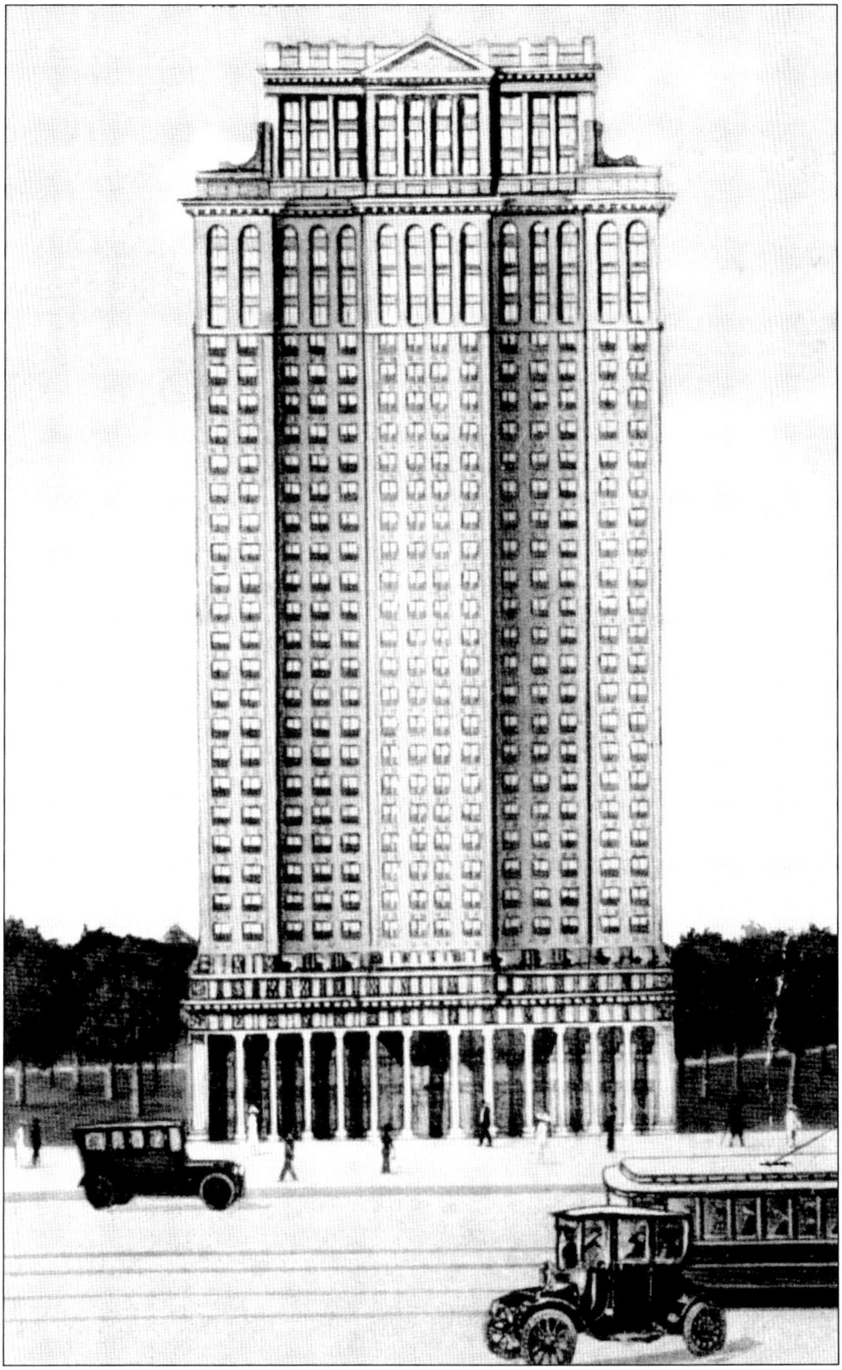

This postcard is a good example of the type card sometimes used by real estate developers (and sometimes by con men) to raise money for proposed projects. The verso of the card reads, "When erected its proceeds will be used to maintain and educate orphans, who have no means of support. The purchase of this card will be a sweet and lasting memory of your contribution to promote this worthy institution." The Grand Union's World's Orphan Building was never constructed. (SG.)

Two

Places of Residence

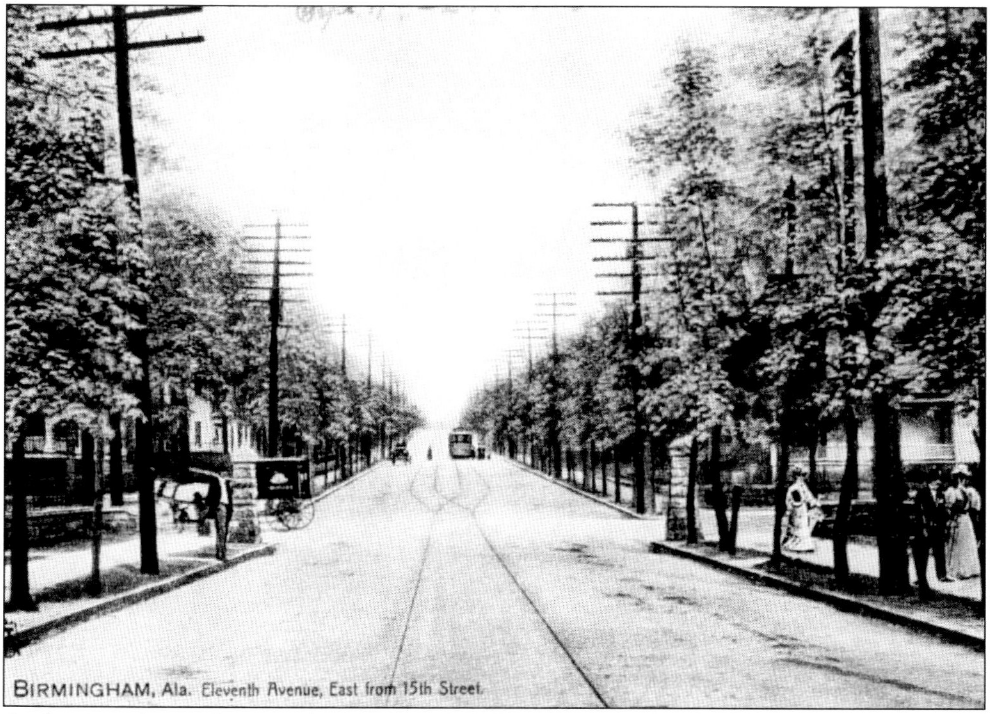

At the time this card was produced, around 1907, the streetcar line had been recently extended from the growing Five Points South community. The Idlewild Line connected Glen Iris with downtown Birmingham. Streetcars, like automobiles a few decades later, made it possible for people to live in bedroom communities miles from their place of work. Mule-drawn wagons like the one on the left side of the street were used to deliver a variety of goods including ice and coal, and to pick up and return laundry. (WS.)

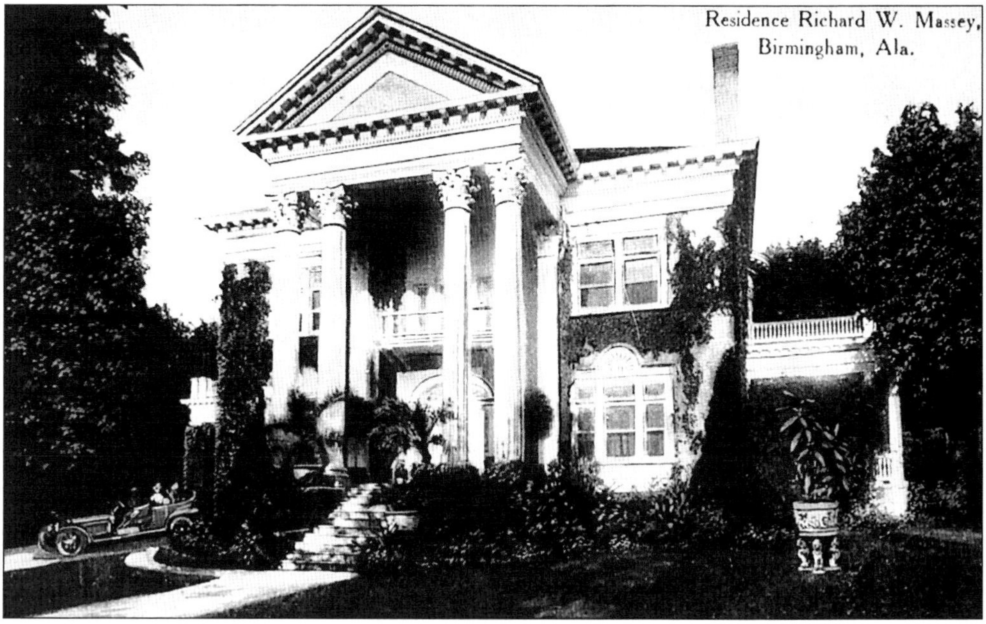

Businessman Richard W. Massey (see also p. 37) moved his family into this beaux-arts style mansion on Twenty-first Way, South about 1905. The touring car in the driveway appears to be a 1920s design. The presence of a toolbox on the car's running board gives testimony to the precarious nature of early automobile travel. The house and gardens were demolished to make way for the Red Mountain Expressway. (BPLA.)

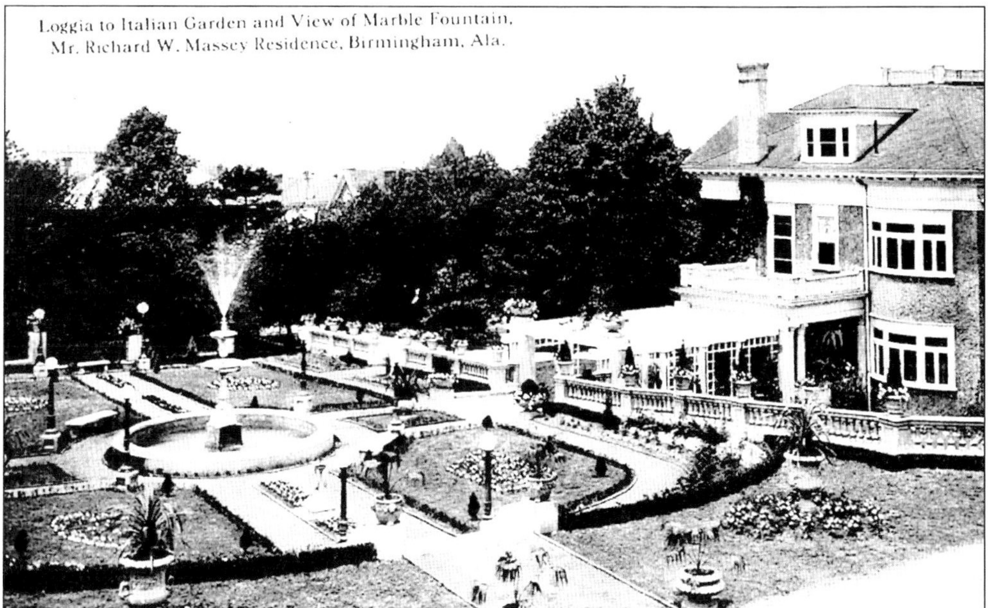

The Italian gardens pictured here and at the top of the following page were located on the east side of the Massey home. Richard Massey hired gardeners from Europe to care for his plants, fountains, and statuary. (BPLA.)

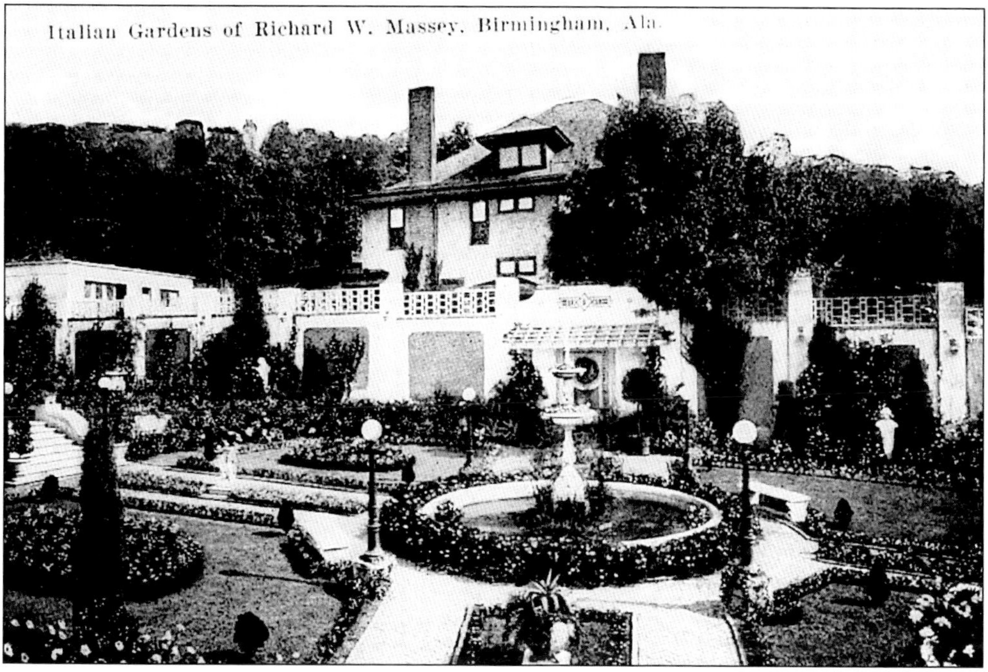

This is another view of Massey's impressive gardens. (BPLA.)

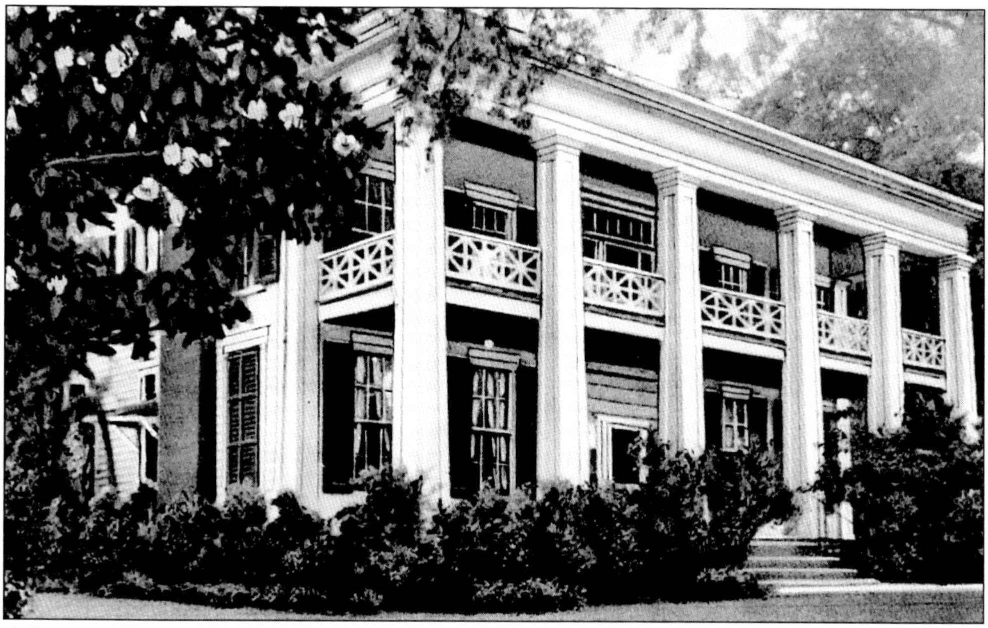

Arlington, located at 331 Cotton Avenue in Birmingham, is one of the oldest surviving structures in Jefferson County and was built by slave labor around 1842. According to various accounts the house served as headquarters for Union General James H. Wilson in the closing days of the American Civil War. During their raid through Alabama, Wilson's troops attacked and burned the cadet training school at the University of Alabama and the arsenal at Selma. This postcard shows Arlington after the house was restored and opened to the public as a museum by the Arlington Historical Society. (BPLA.)

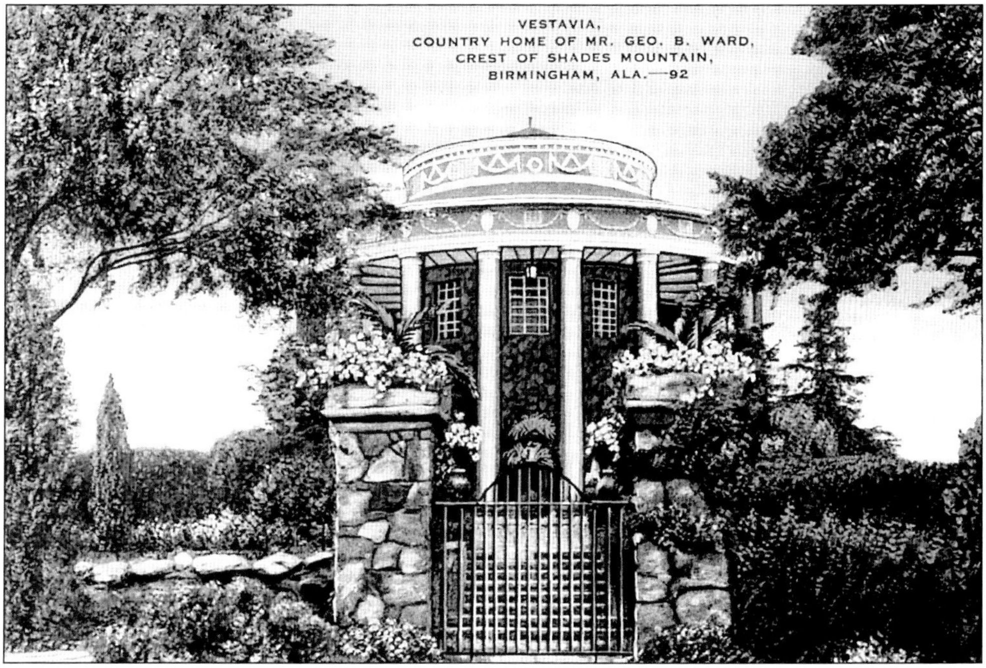

Above and below are two images of Vestavia. George B. Ward, mayor of Birmingham for many years, chose the crest of Shades Mountain to build this replica of the Roman Temple of the Vestal Virgins for his home in 1925. On special occasions Ward would open the house and gardens to the general public, and he was known for elaborate parties featuring young ladies dancing, guests in togas, and servants dressed as Roman soldiers. The doghouses at Vestavia were shaped like miniature Roman temples. Following Ward's death in 1940 the house was used as a restaurant and later became Vestavia Hills Baptist Church. The church demolished the house in 1971 to make way for a new sanctuary. (BPLA.)

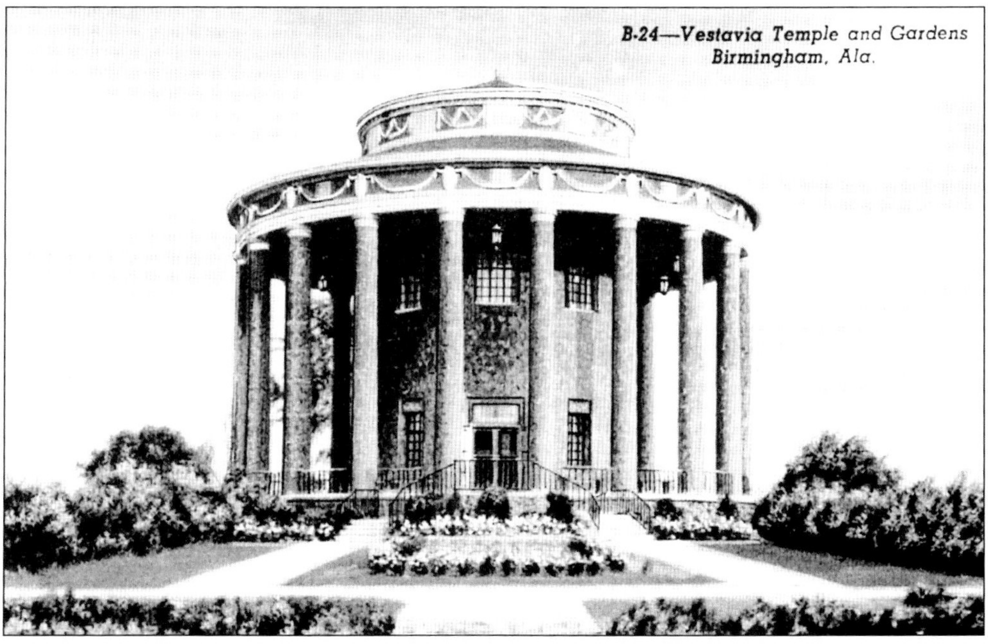

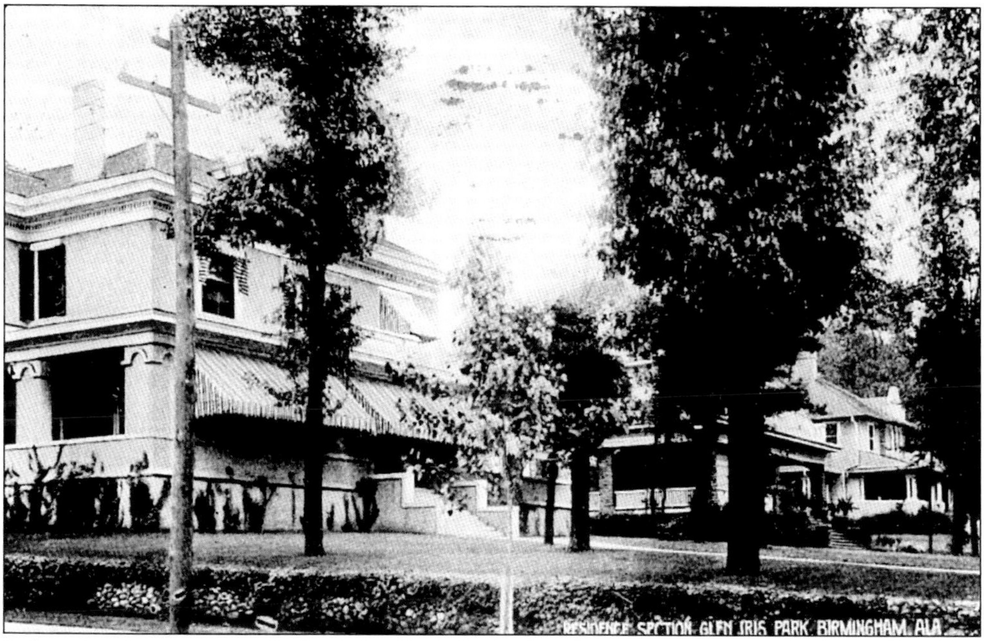

Robert Jemison Sr., who helped develop Birmingham's street car system, laid out Glen Iris, pictured above, as a residential park for his family and friends in the southwestern section of the city. Architect Thomas Walter III designed the neo-classical red brick home pictured below for Jemison. The house was completed in 1902. According to neighbor James Gillespy, who borrowed a spike-tailed coat for the occasion, the "swellest" affair ever in early Birmingham was the 1904 wedding reception given here by the Robert Jemisons for their daughter. (BPLA.)

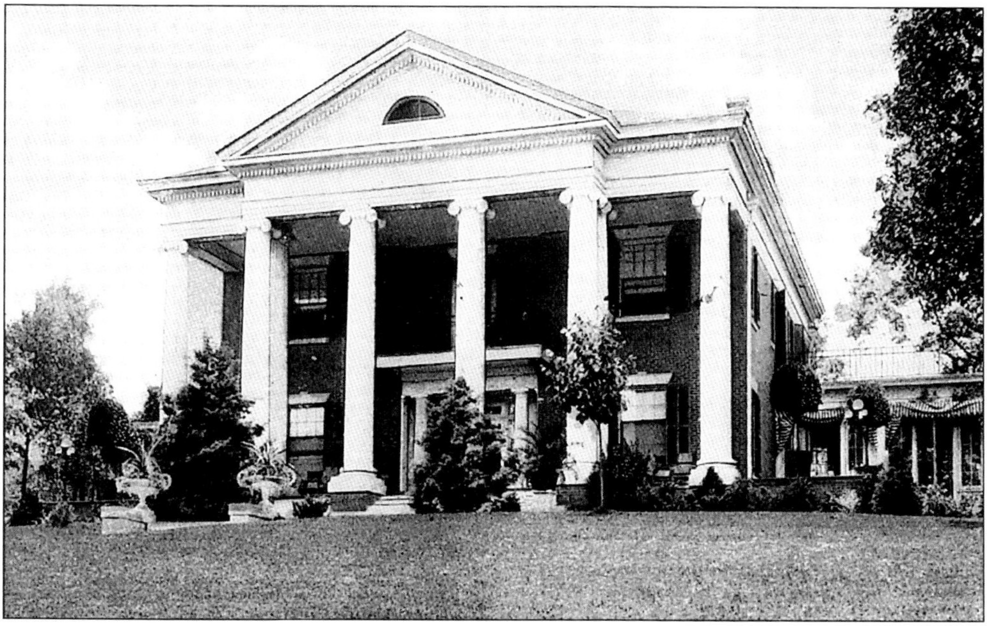

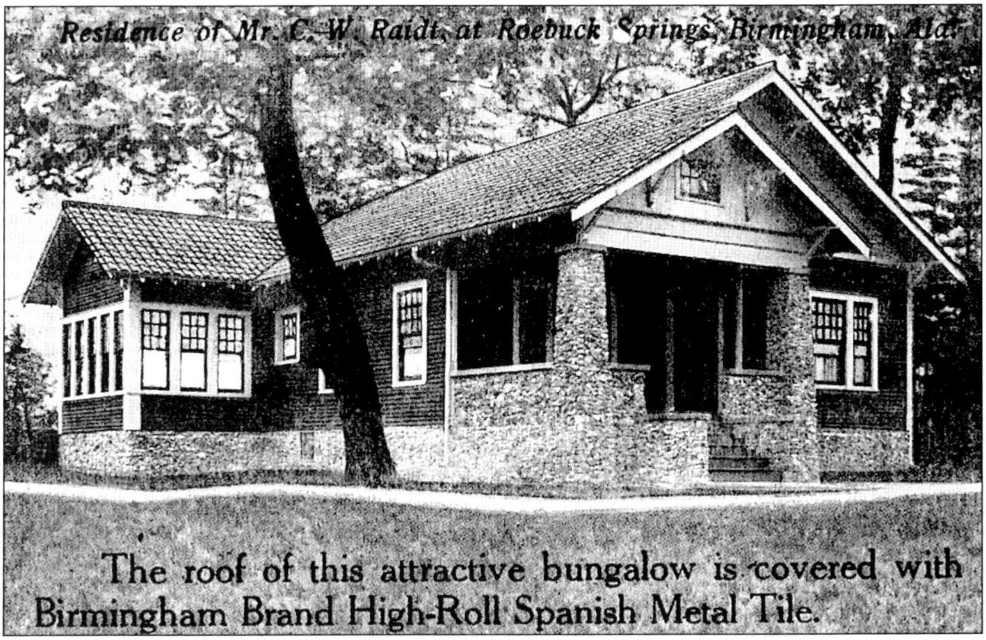

Companies often used postcards like this one to advertise their products, in this case a roofing material called Birmingham Brand High-Roll Spanish Metal Tile. The house was built in a bungalow style, which was popular in much of the United States during the early to mid-20th century, and many examples of the design have survived in Jefferson County. (BPLA.)

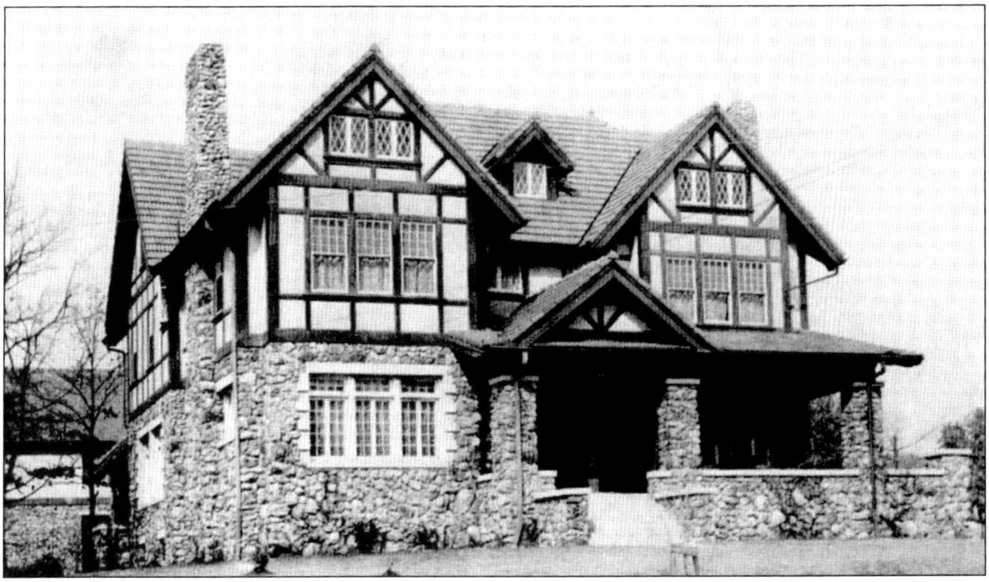

On the verso of this card, mailed in 1907, the sender writes, "Merry Christmas to you both. This is a photo of our house. We are enjoying it very much." Located at 2848 Highland Avenue, this house was designed for real estate developer S.E. Thompson and family by architect Dan Reamer, who also designed the Old Faithful Inn at Yellowstone National Park. A Tudor style that makes good use of rustic fieldstone, the house took several years to complete. Tragically, Thompson's wife, Anna, died shortly before the house was finished, and her funeral was held here. The house remained in the Thompson family until it was sold in 1998. (SG.)

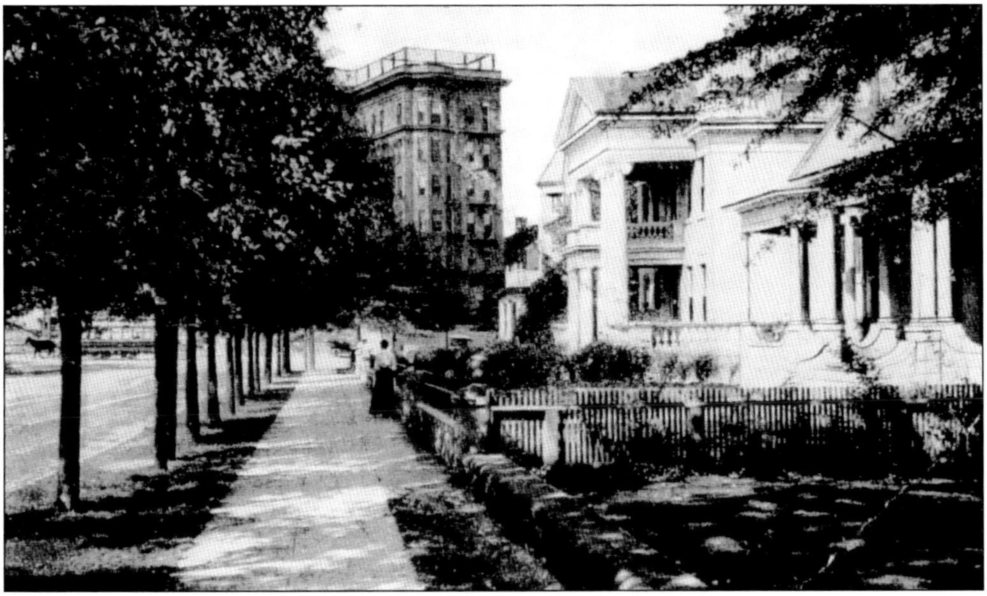

Highland Avenue was the fashionable place to live when this picture was taken about 1910. Fine homes lined the boulevard from Lakeview Park to Twentieth Street, South. In the far-left background a mule-drawn streetcar may be seen. The Terrace Court Apartments are visible in the center background (see p. 49). (SG.)

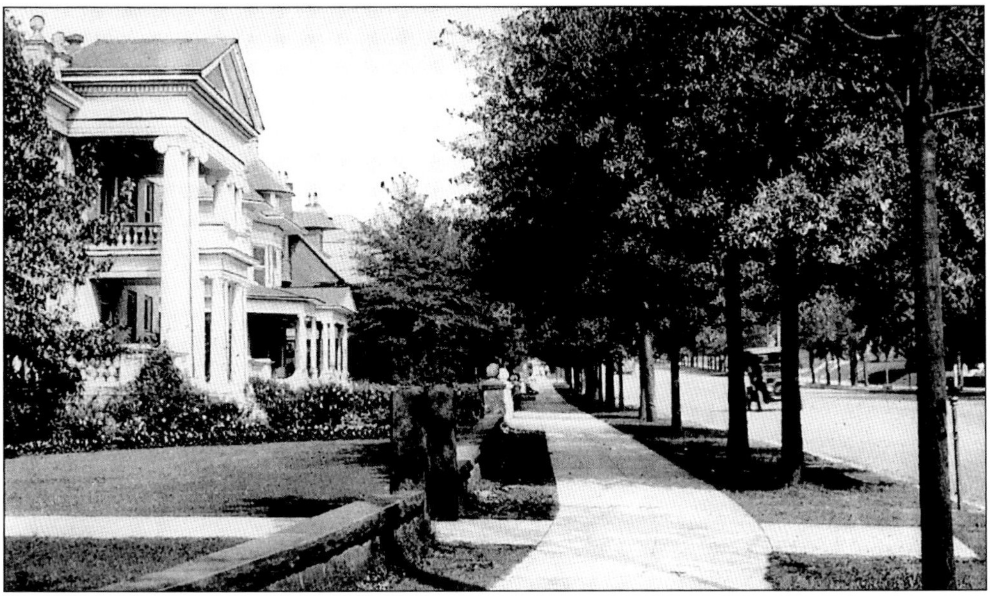

This view of Highland Avenue was made on the same block as the image above, but from the opposite direction. (BPLA.)

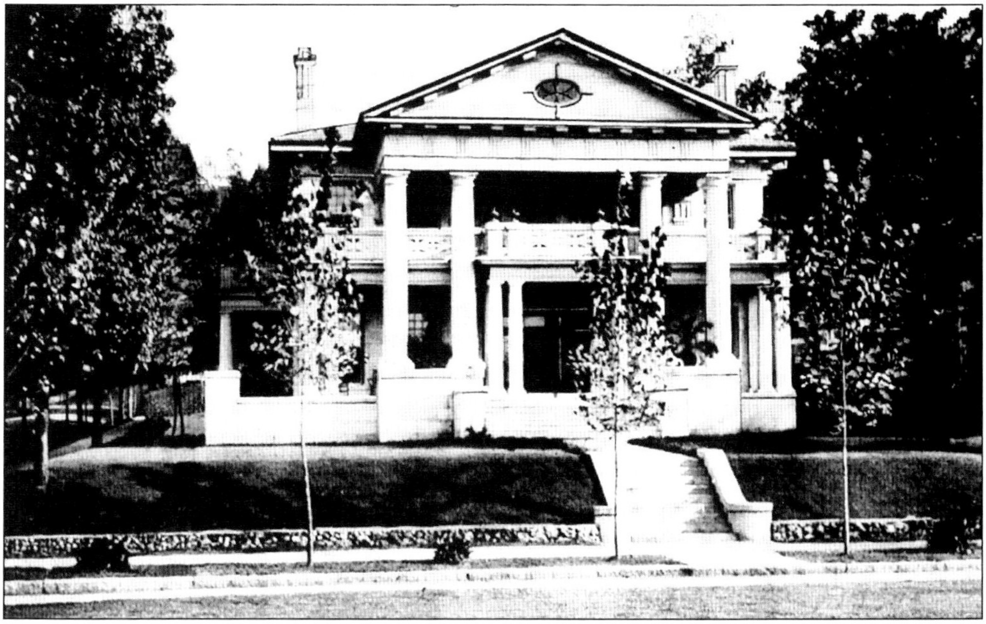

Completed in 1910, the Enslen House was one of the largest and most elaborate of the many imposing houses lining Highland Avenue. The exterior is faced with 2-inch thick Sylacauga marble. Eugene F. Enslen, president of the Jefferson County Savings Bank, used a spacious downstairs room as his home office. (BPLA.)

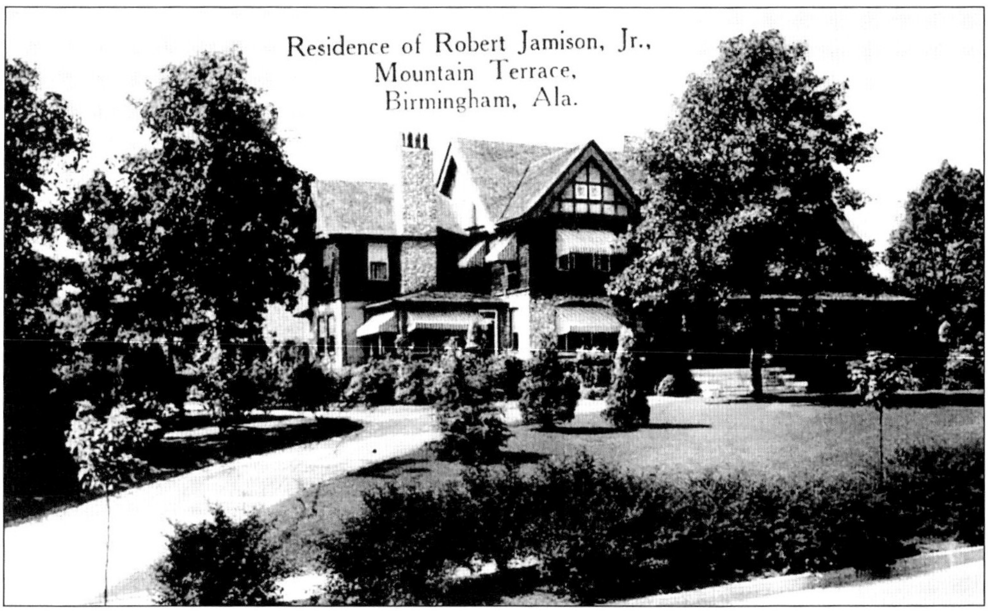

Robert Jemison Jr. could have used this card to promote his latest real estate venture, Mountain Terrace. Known as "Mr. Birmingham," Jemison's other real estate developments included Corey/Fairfield, Central Park, Redmont Park, and Mountain Brook. This card shows Jemison's Tudor-style residence, completed around 1907 at 4124 Crescent Road. Unusual features of the house included a wine cellar and an attic room for dancing. In 1915, banker Oscar W. Wells bought the house from Jemison, and lived there until his death in 1950. (BPLA.)

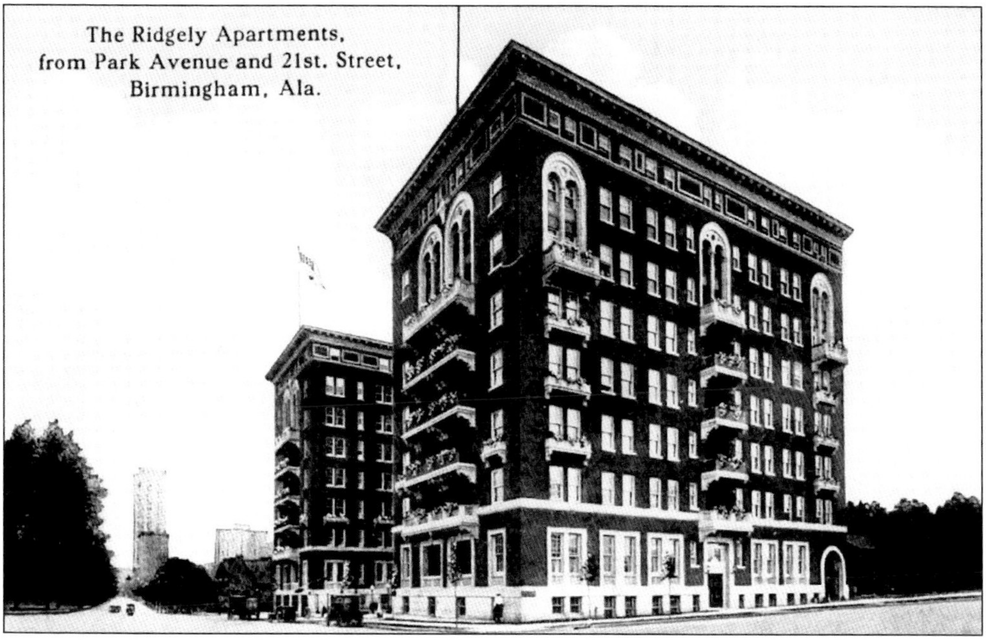

Located on the corner of Park Avenue and Twenty-first Street, North, the Ridgely Apartments building was designed by New York architect J.E.R. Carpenter and built by Robert Jemison Jr. in 1914 with financing from E.M. Tutwiler. About this same time Jemison and Tutwiler built the original Tutwiler Hotel on Twentieth Street (see p. 50). The original Tutwiler was demolished in 1974, and the Ridgley was renovated and became the new Tutwiler Hotel around 1985. During its decades as a luxury apartment building, the Ridgley was home to a number of prominent Birmingham figures, including newspaperman John Temple Grave II. Lila Mae Chapman, director of the Birmingham Public Library from 1926 until 1947, occupied a fifth-floor apartment from which she could keep an eye on her library just across the street. (BPLA.)

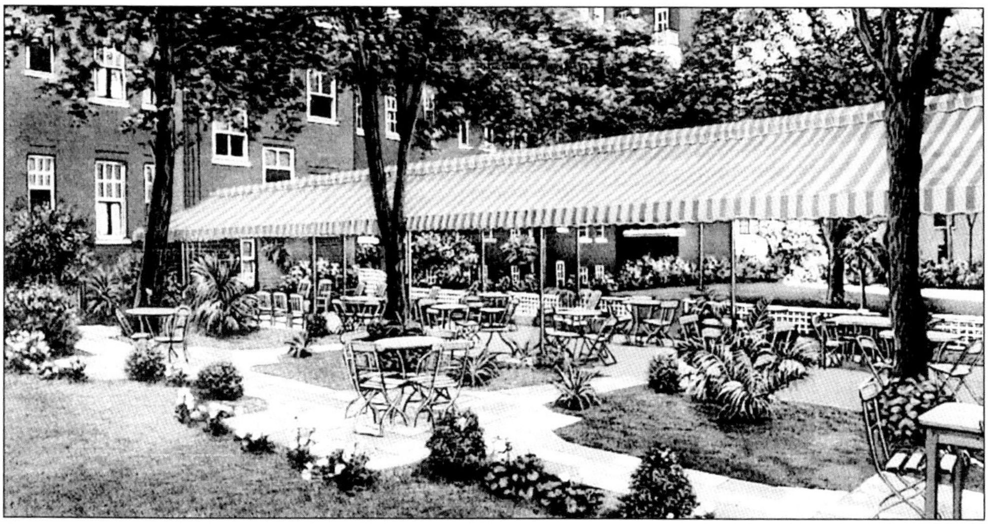

The terrace garden pictured here is gone. This spot is now occupied by the Tutwiler Hotel parking lot, which is behind the hotel and on the side of the Birmingham Board of Education building. (BPLA.)

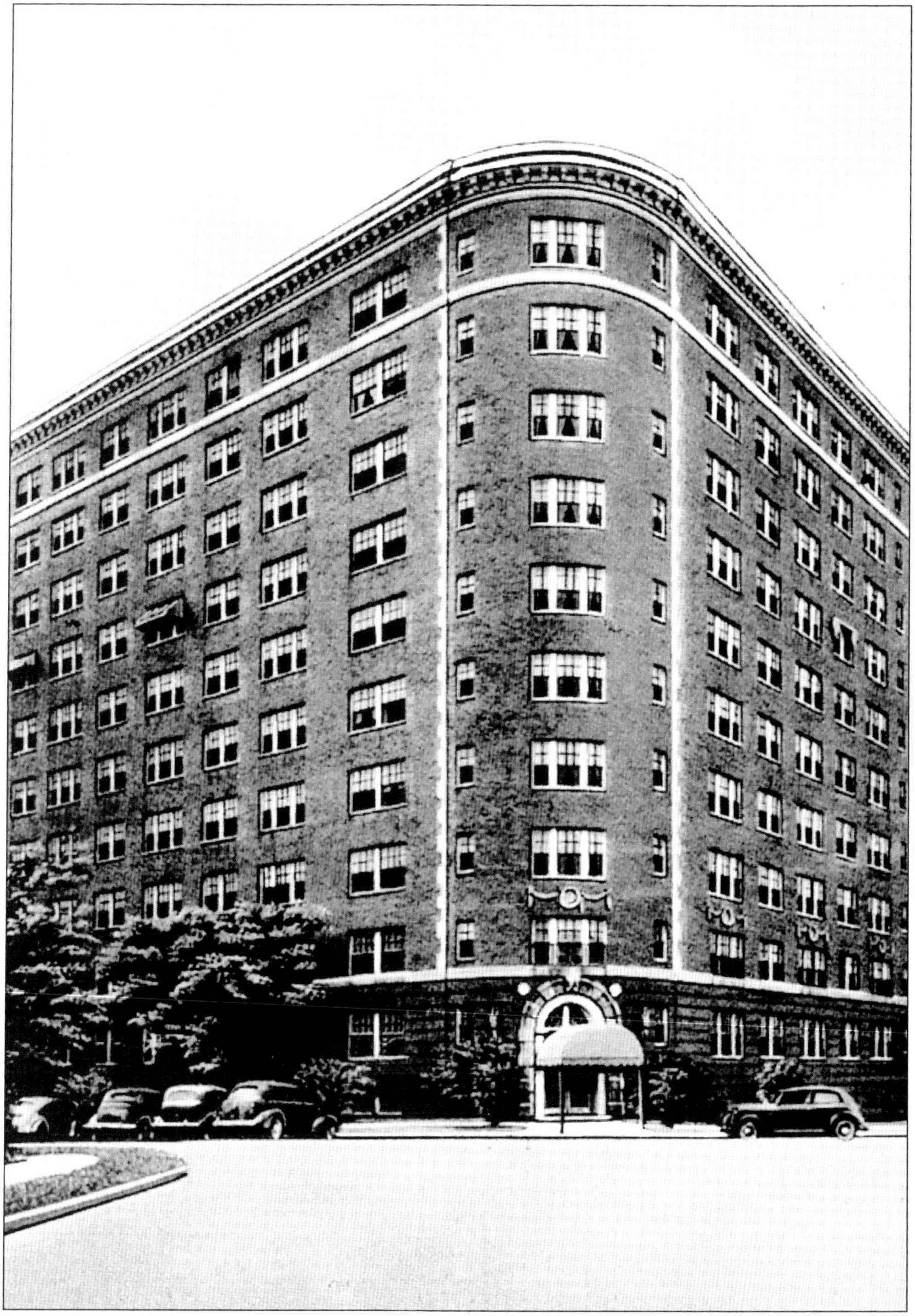

Located at 1101 Twenty-seventh Place, South and built in 1924, early tenants of Claridge Manor Apartments included Titus L. Bissell (an employee of Alabama Power) and his wife, Blanche; a traveling salesman named Benjamin Cox; and Florence Deuel, a dental hygienist. (BPLA.)

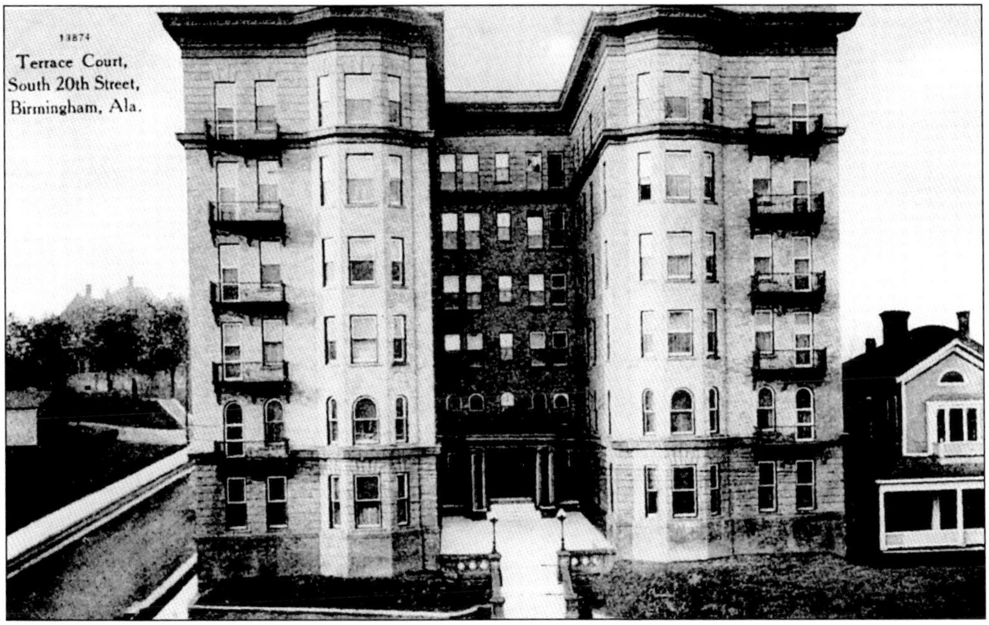

On November 6, 1907, builder Richard Massey opened Terrace Court Apartments with an elaborate "christening" ceremony. Located in the Five Points South area on the corner of Twentieth Street and Twelfth Avenue, South, Terrace Court was promoted as the first high-class apartment building constructed south of Washington, D.C. When opened, the building contained 24 apartments, and as advertised, rent would not exceed $8 per month. Early residents included J.F. Leary, president of Avondale Land Company; T. Ashby Weller, a land agent for the Bessemer Coal, Iron and Land Company; and Robert McLester, a wholesale grocer. Leary, Weller, and McLester were neighbors on the fourth floor. (BPLA.)

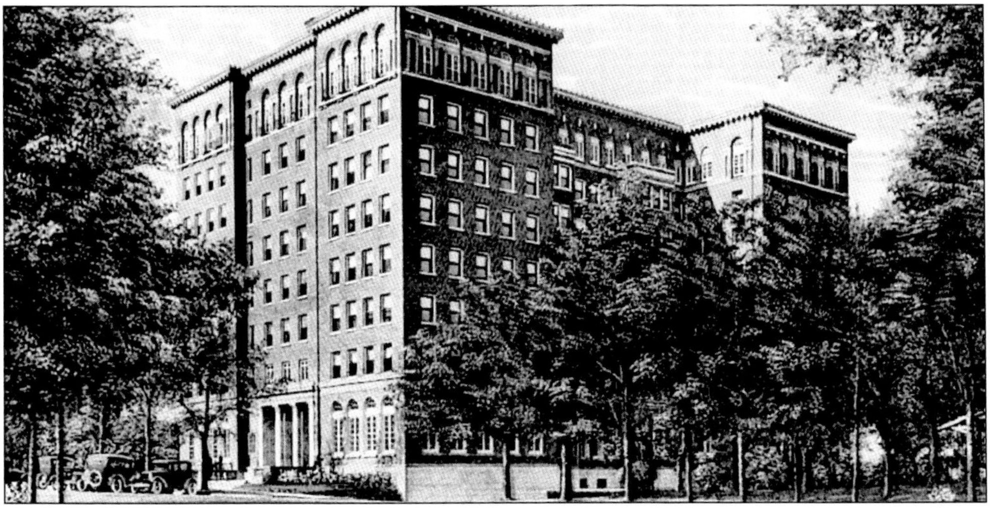

Located at 2250 Highland Avenue and designed by the architectural firm of Denham, Van Keuren and Denham, Highland Plaza Apartments is shown above, soon after its completion in 1924. The Plaza offered amenities often associated at the time with hotels, including a switchboard and game rooms. Some of the building's first tenants included dentist Henry H. Fairfax and his wife, Julia; Pattie P. Robinson, a widow; and Thomas A. Lambert, an engineer at Connors Steel Company, and his wife, Margaret. (BPLA.)

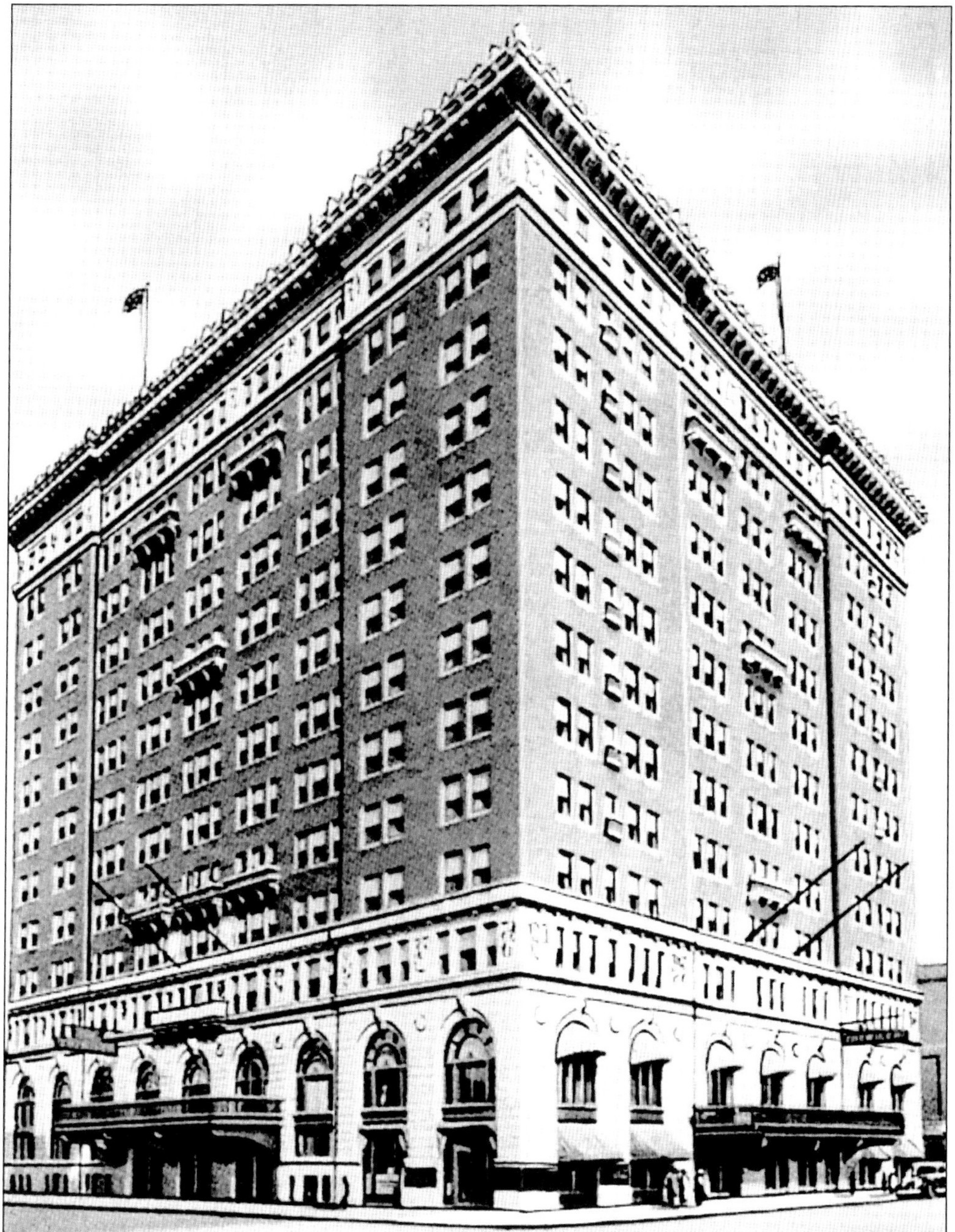

Built in 1914, the Tutwiler was Birmingham's premier hotel for decades. Located on the corner of Fifth Avenue and Twentieth Street, North, the Tutwiler played host to national conventions, servicemen of two world wars, and visiting dignitaries including United States senators, screen actors, and at least one Miss America. When the hotel was demolished in 1974, it took two blasts to implode the structure and bring it down. The site is now occupied by the headquarters of Regions Bank, formerly First Alabama. (BPLA.)

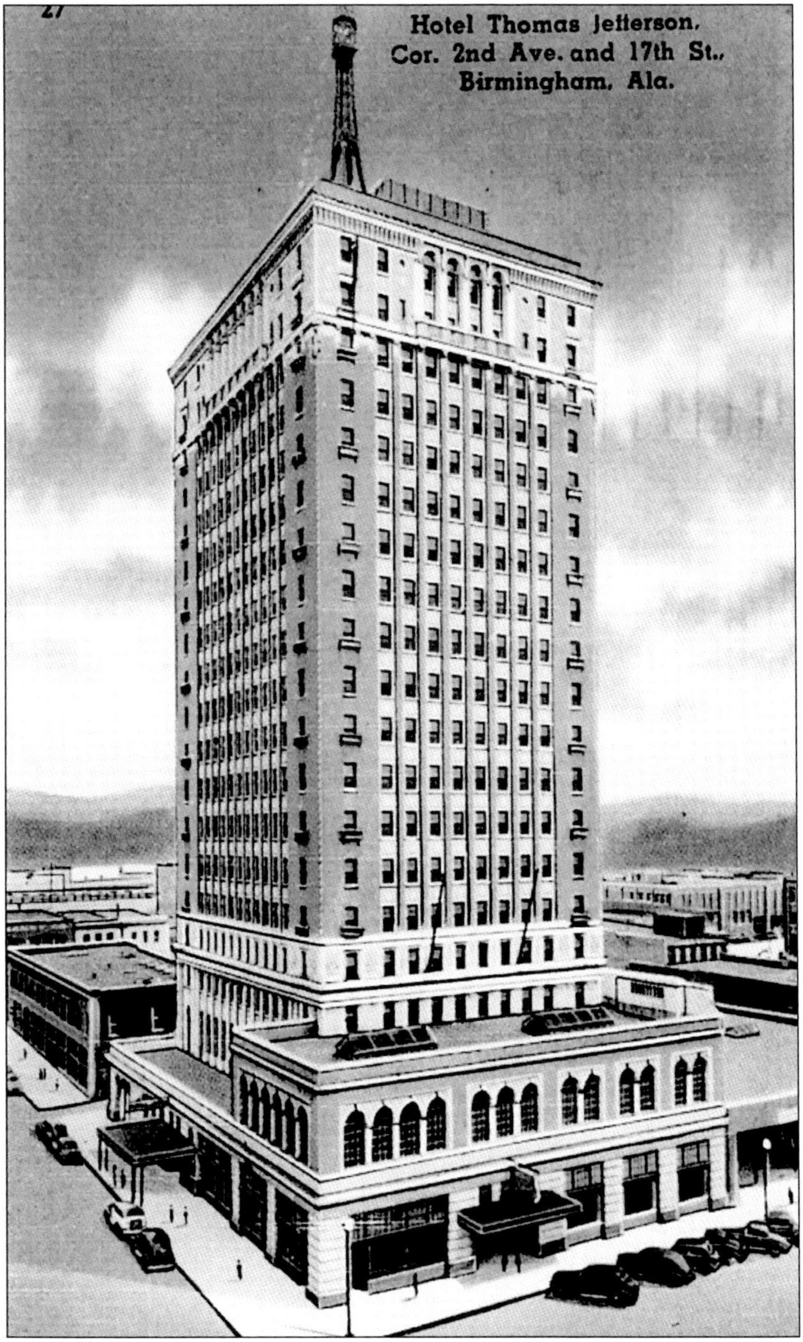

On the verso this card reads, "Birmingham's newest twenty story fireproof hotel. One of the city's outstanding structures. From the roof gardens may be seen a wonderful panorama of the city, viewing the skyscraper district to the east, and the steel mill industries at Bessemer and Ensley to the west. Cost approximately two million dollars." Located at Seventeenth Street and Second Avenue, North, the Thomas Jefferson opened in the 1920s, a decade that saw the construction of three major hotels in Birmingham. The name was later changed to the Cabana. The building no longer operates as a hotel, but is used for storage. (BPLA.)

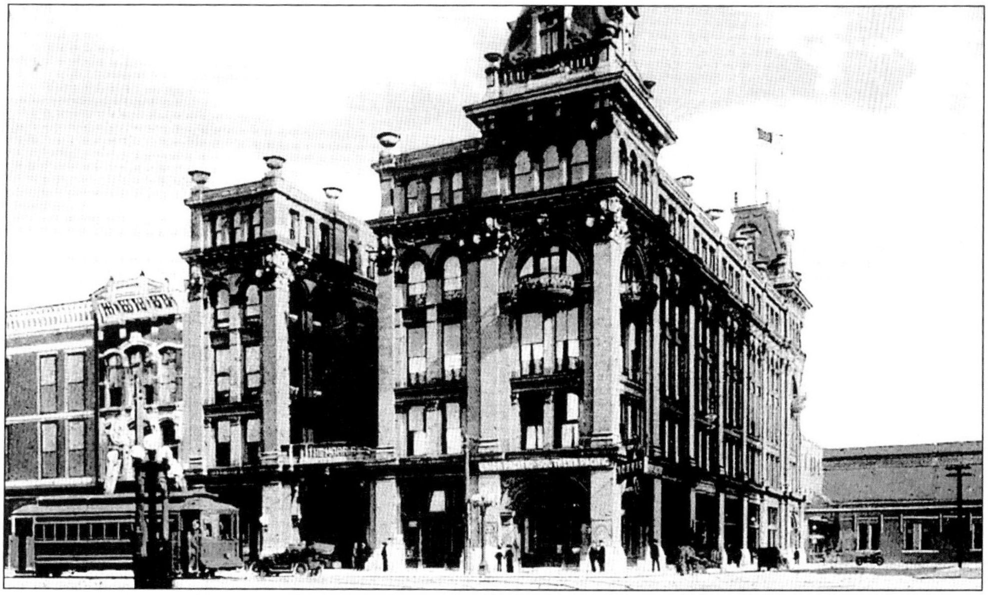

The Morris Hotel, built originally for business offices in 1888, became for a time Birmingham's premier place to stay after the Caldwell Hotel burned in 1894. Designed by a French architect, the ornate building was a fine example of the Renaissance style popular in the late 19th century. Named for Josiah Morris, an early Birmingham developer, the hotel was located on the corner of First Avenue, North and Nineteenth Street. Morris Avenue and the railroad reservation run behind the building. The Morris Hotel was demolished in 1959. A parking deck now occupies the site. (BPLA.)

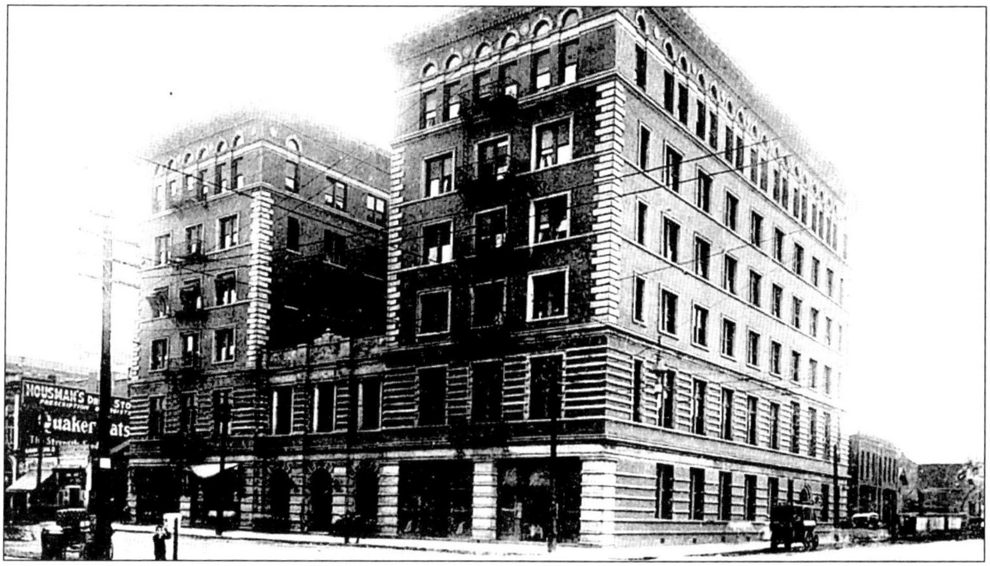

Recognizing the need for a better hotel in Birmingham to succeed the Morris, a group of investors that included Robert Jemison Sr., E.M. Tutwiler, Frank Nelson Jr., and W.J. Milner formed the Hotel Hillman Company in 1900. By 1902 the Hillman, located on the corner of Nineteenth Street and Fourth Avenue, North, was popular for local banquets and out-of-town guests. President Grover Cleveland stayed at the Hillman during his visit to Birmingham in 1909. The building was demolished in 1967. A parking lot now occupies the site. (BPLA.)

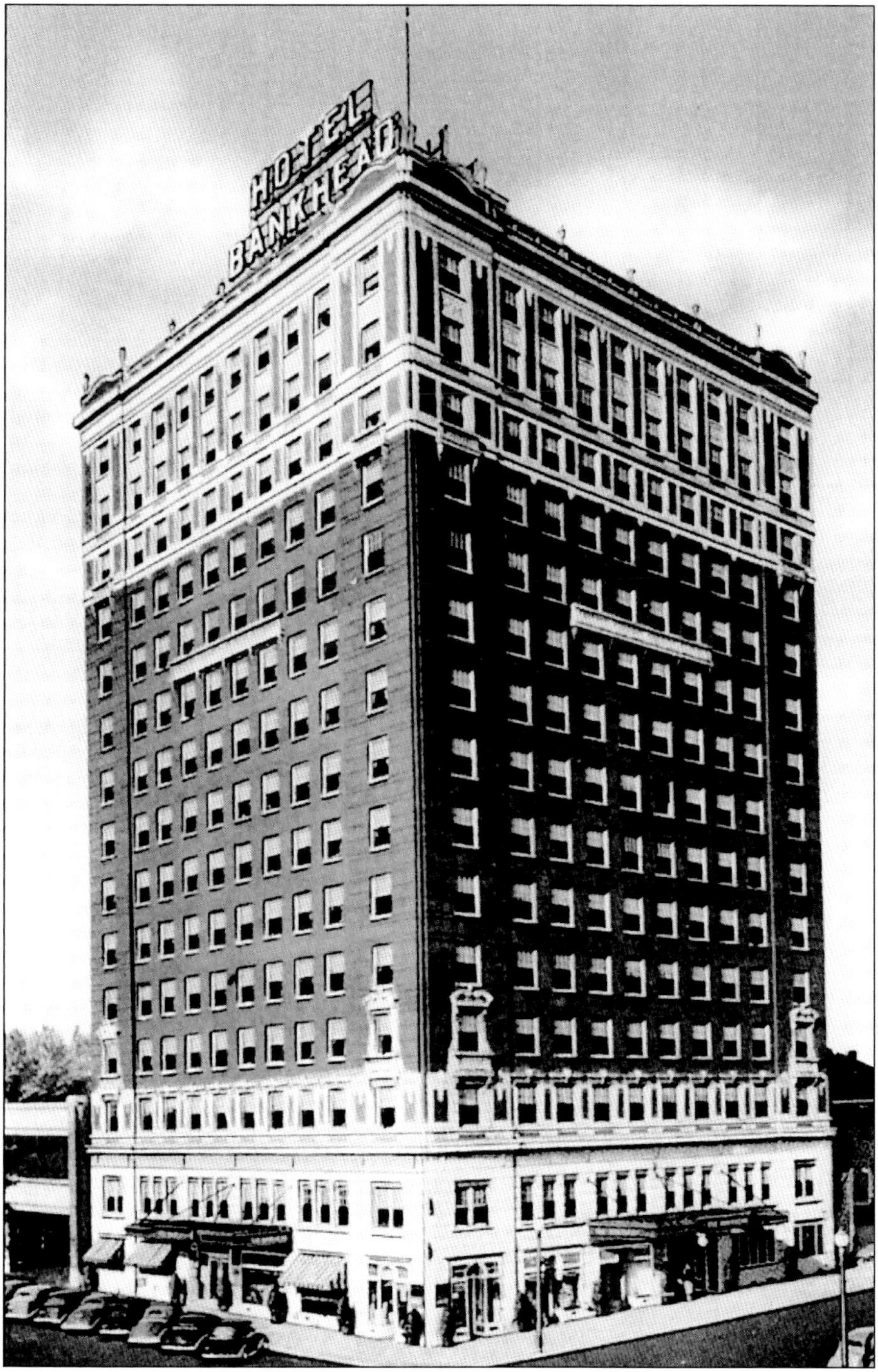

Built in 1926 on the corner of Fifth Avenue and Twenty-third Street, North, the Bankhead Hotel was located close to Birmingham's Terminal Station. Designed by the Chicago architectural firm of H.L. Stevens and Company, the Bankhead no longer functions as a hotel but is a success story in the area of adaptive reuse. In 1977 a 15-story addition was built, and the entire structure remodeled into a living facility for the elderly and handicapped. (BPLA.)

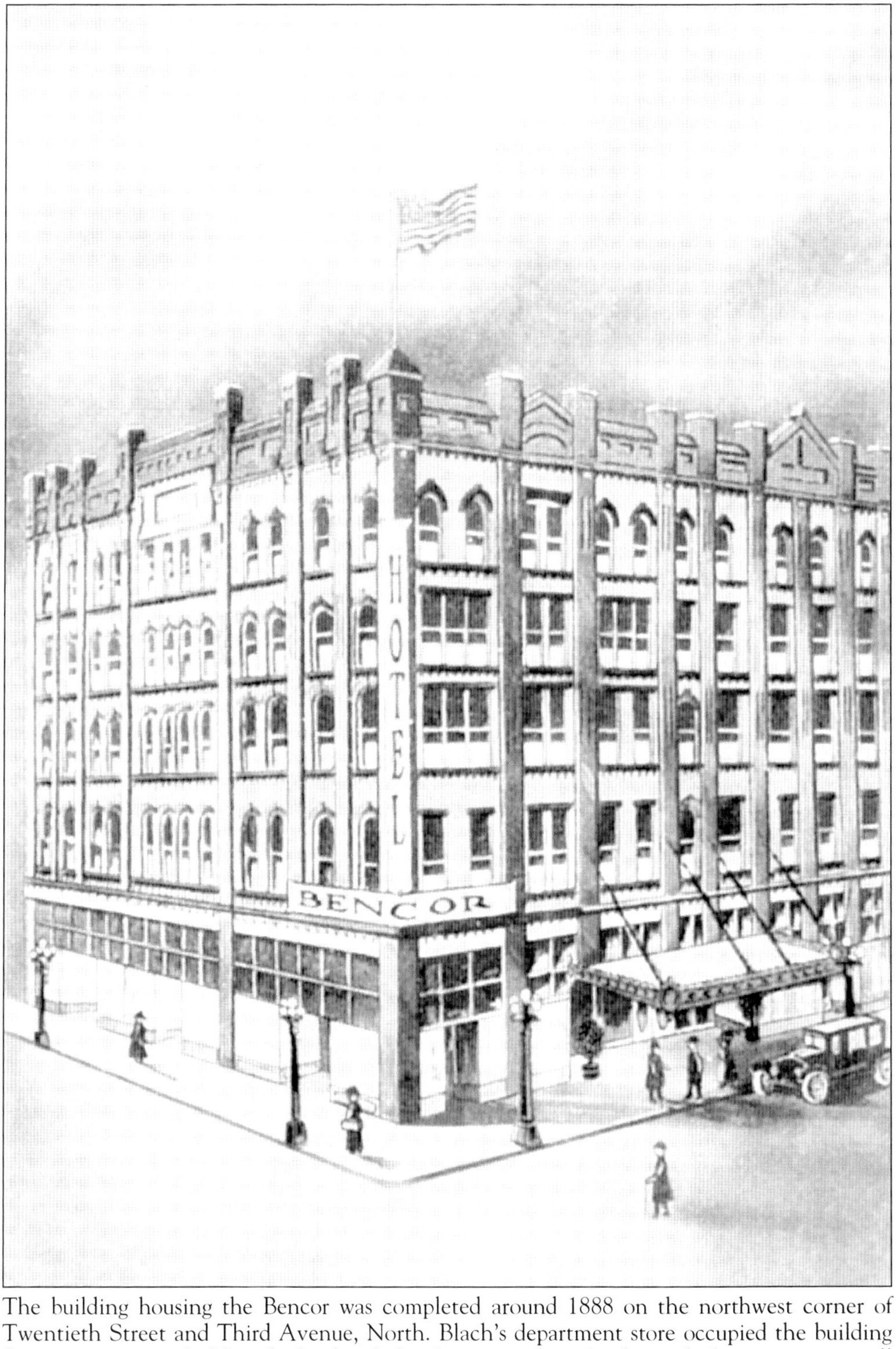

The building housing the Bencor was completed around 1888 on the northwest corner of Twentieth Street and Third Avenue, North. Blach's department store occupied the building for many years, and although the façade has been significantly changed, the structure is still standing. (SG.)

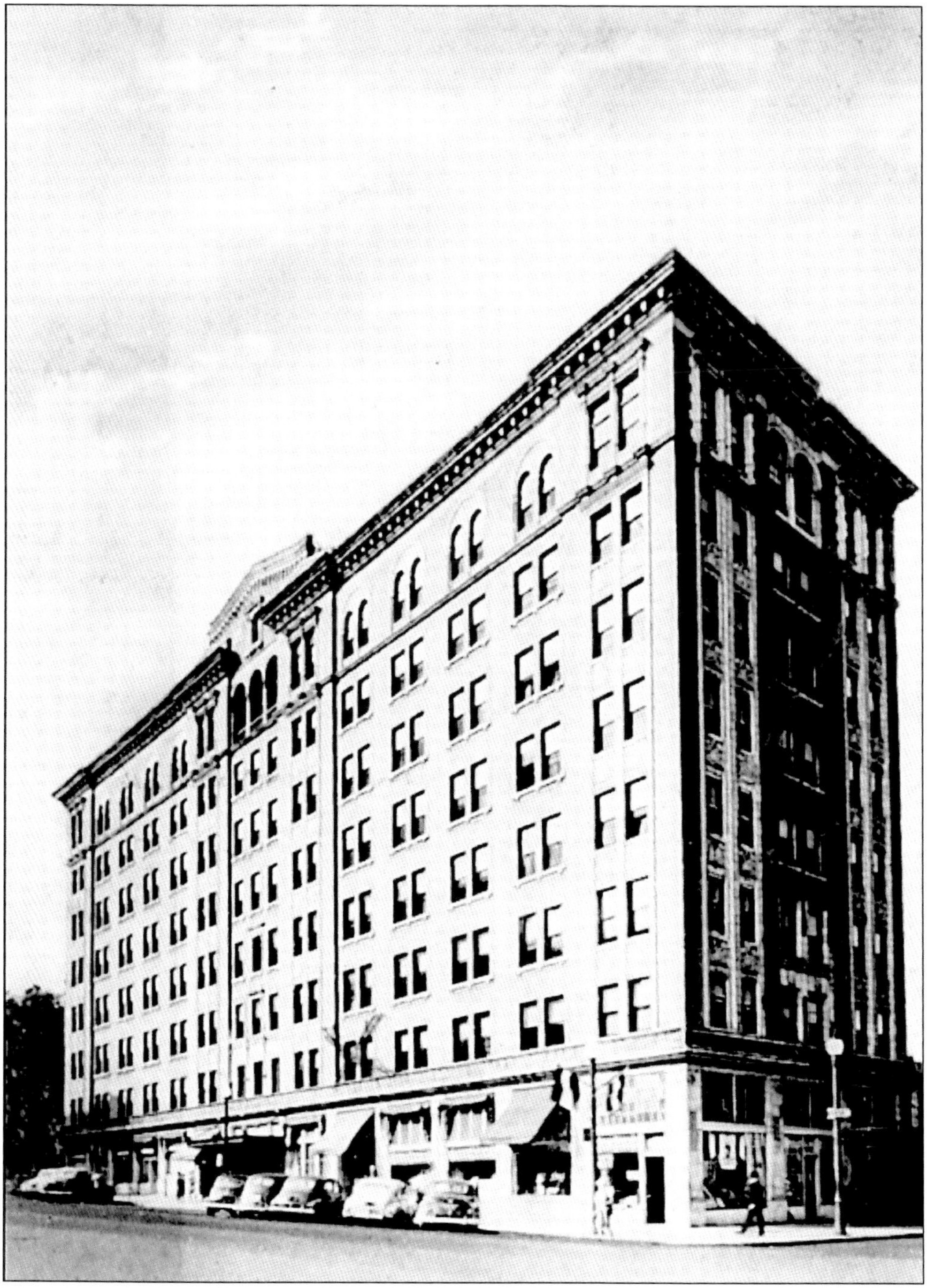

The Molton Hotel was a downtown landmark for 65 years. T.H. Molton constructed the hotel in 1913 on choice land given to his wife by her father, Charles Linn, who built the First National Bank of Birmingham in 1873. Located on the northeast corner of Twentieth Street and Fifth Avenue, North, the hotel's coffee shop was famous for its icebox pies. Politicians considered the Molton to be a lucky campaign headquarters. The structure was demolished in 1979 to make way for the Financial Center Building. (BPLA.)

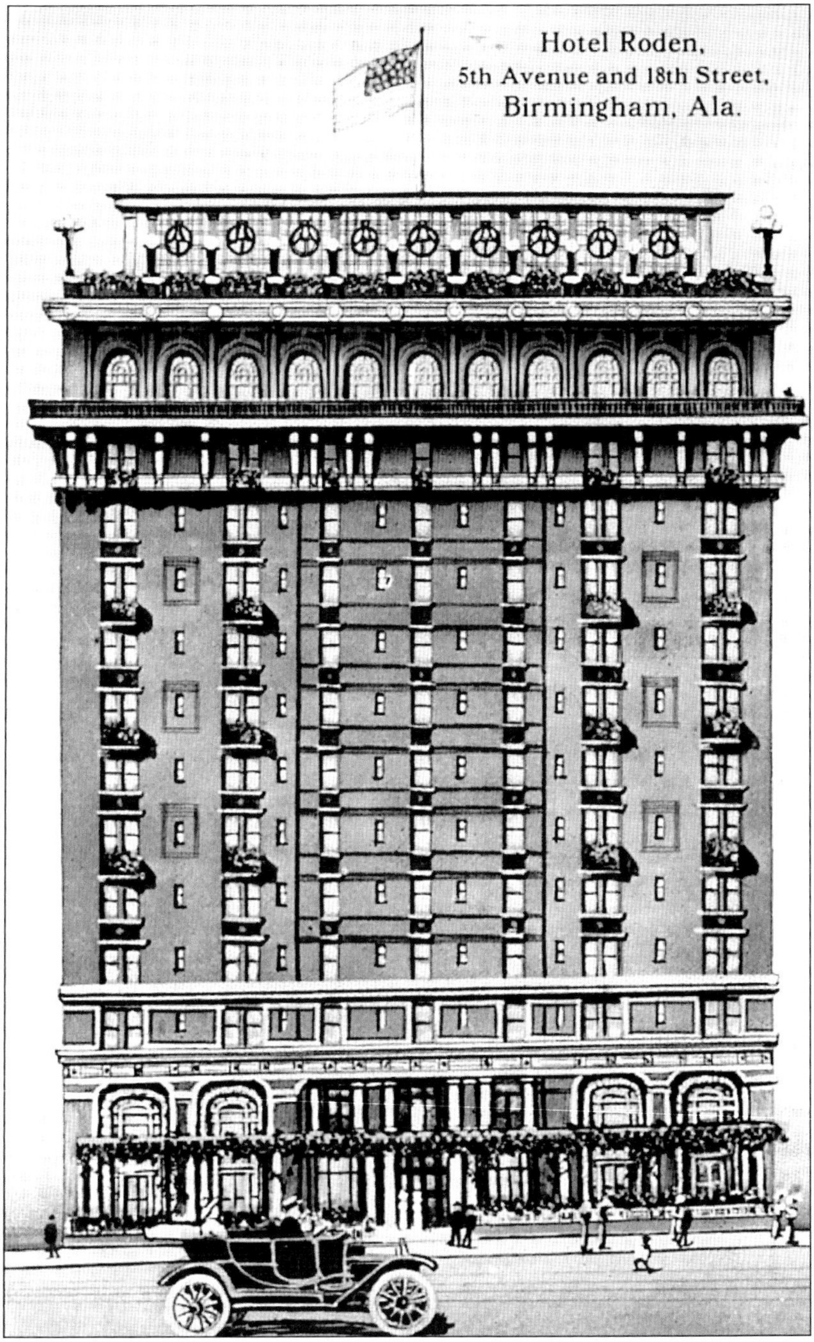

This postcard shows one conception of how the Roden Hotel might have looked, had it been completed. Another drawing by architect William C. Weston shows a very similar but less ornate structure. Construction began on the Roden in February of 1913, and by the following summer the 12-story steel frame was complete. At this point financing fell through and no more work was done. Local jokesters referred to the Roden, which had no walls, as the "best ventilated hotel in America." After the United States entered World War I, the hotel's frame was dismantled and sold for scrap. (BPLA.)

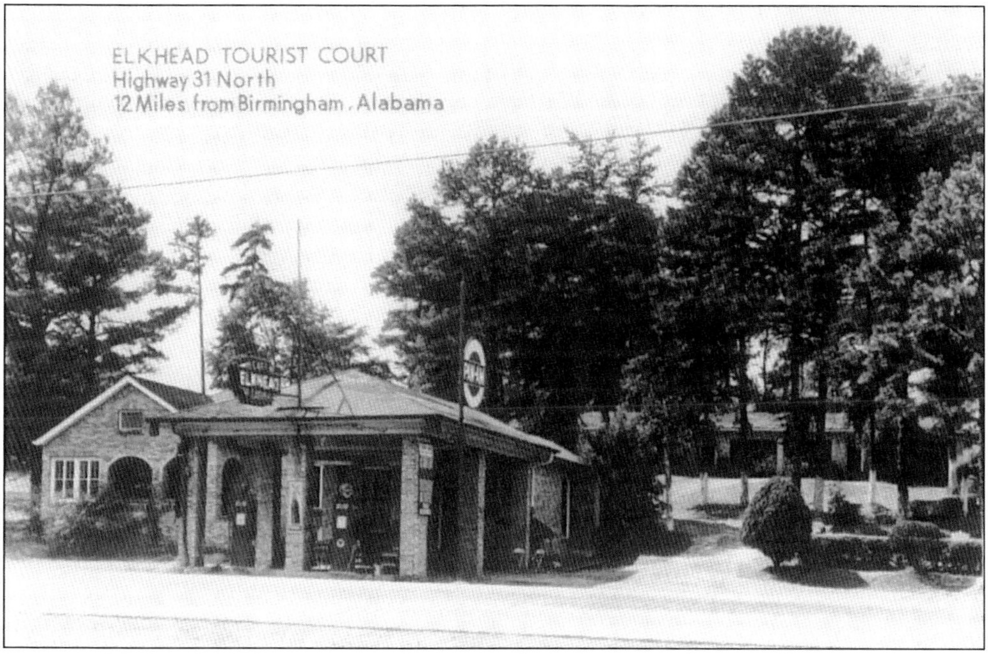

Between 1910 and 1945 vacationing by automobile, known early on as "gypsying," grew in popularity throughout the United States. The large increase in tourists traveling by car led to the development of "tourist courts" and "tourist camps," small motels often with detached cabins. The postcards on this page show two such motels, the Elkhead and the Fulton Springs, that operated on Highway 31 north of Birmingham. As these images show, tourist courts often included gas stations and small restaurants. (SG.)

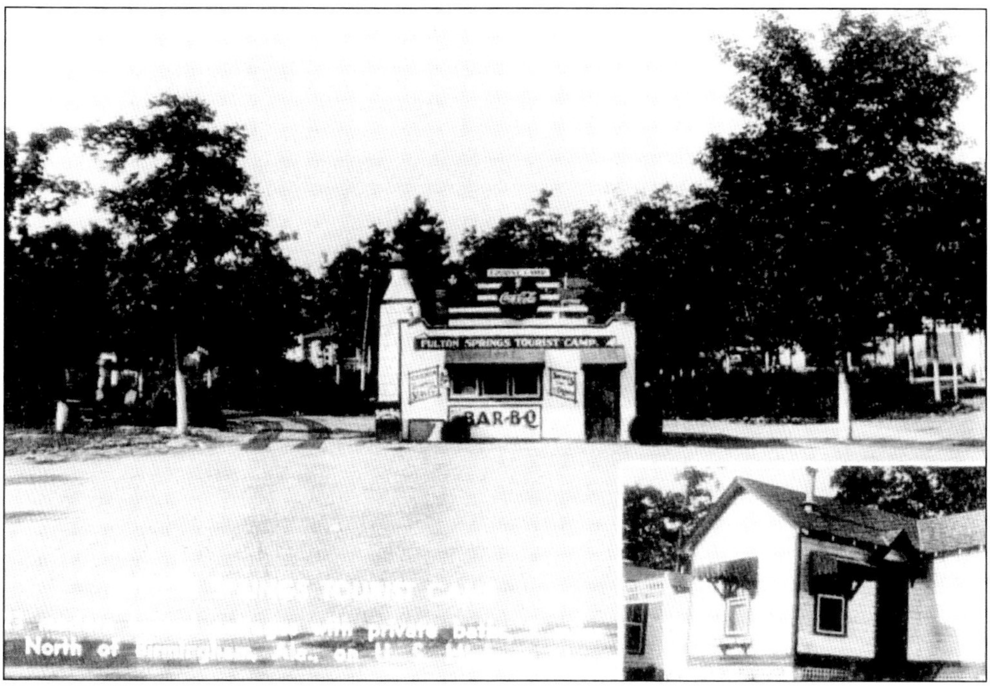

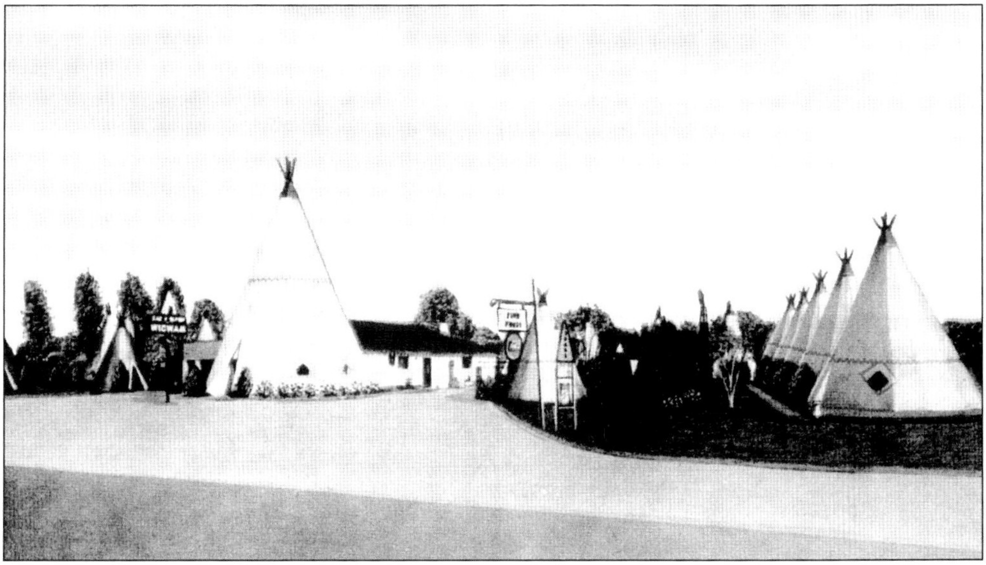

Few tourist camps anywhere, and certainly none in Jefferson County, could match the Wigwam Village for originality (or audacity). The verso of this card reads, "Eat and Sleep in a Wigwam. The South's finest food, Indian Wigwams. Real Southern Hospitality. Located on Birmingham, Bessemer Super Highway (U.S. 11) 10 Miles South of Birmingham, Ala. TRAVELERS ONLY." (SG.)

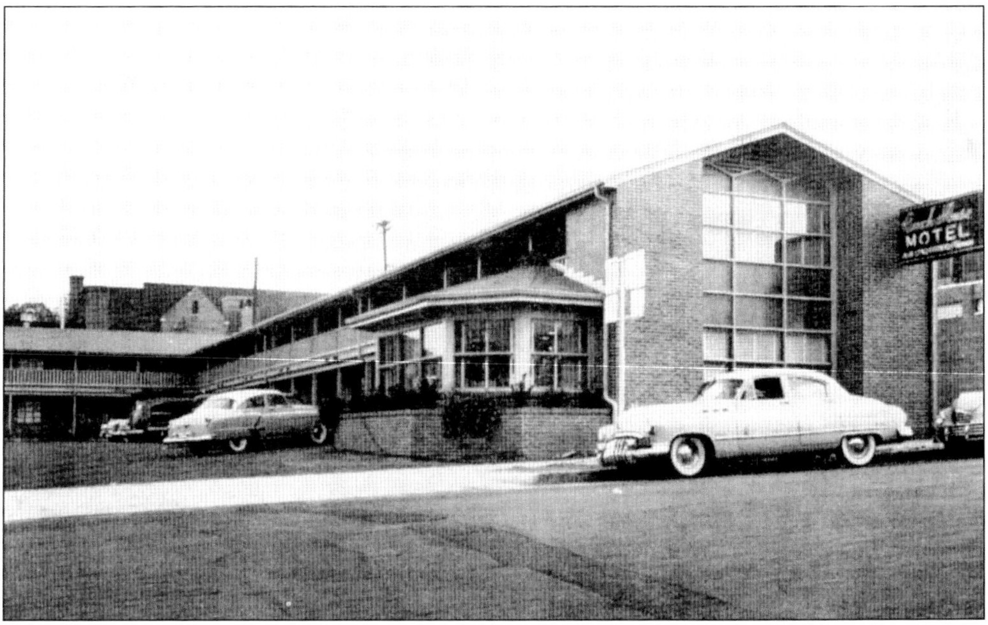

By the mid-20th century, motels were evolving into establishments that were less colorful than the earlier tourist camps. But these newer establishments, such as the Ranch House Motel on Birmingham's Southside, offered comforts and amenities attractive to travelers. The verso of this card reads, "On U.S. 31 & 91 in Downtown Birmingham. 1 1/2 blocks from Medical Center. Circulating Ice Water—Air Conditioned—All Tile Baths and Showers—Ample Parking and every Comfort of your own home." (SG.)

Three

PLACES OF AMUSEMENT

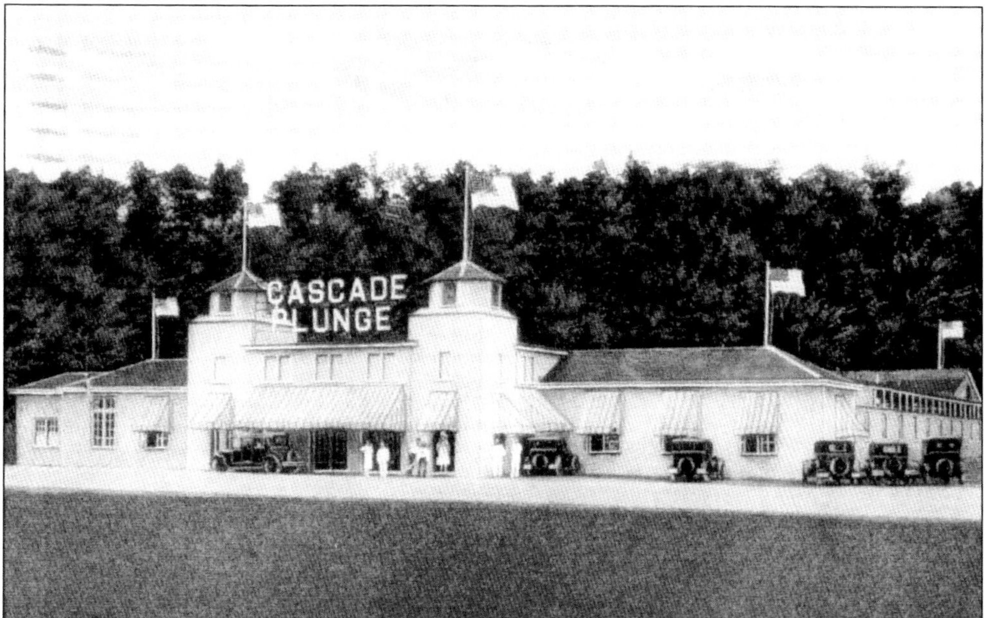

The swimming pool and dance hall at Cascade Plunge, which opened in the Wahouma (East Lake) area in 1923, were popular summertime destinations for decades. At one time a special streetcar served the site. The building pictured above, which includes a dance floor, surrounds a swimming pool and "wading pool for the little fellows." In the 1940s adults could swim for an admission of 45¢, children for 25¢. Monday was "Ladies' Day," when women received a 15¢ discount. The building still stands and is now operated as Elks Lodge No. 79. (SG.)

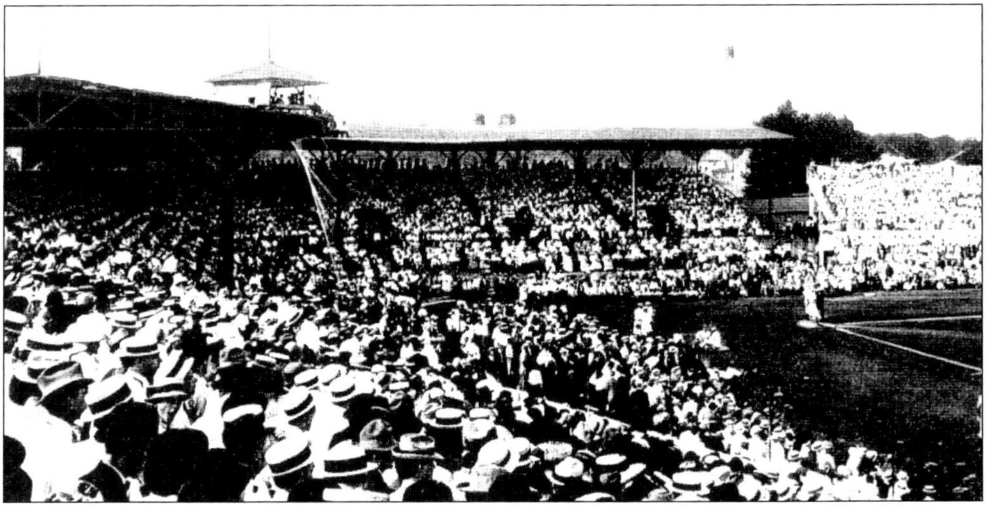

Rick Woodward had a passion for baseball and was heir to the Woodward Iron Company fortune. He built Rickwood Field, pictured above, in 1910. Two years later Woodward, who liked to dress in his own uniform and practice with the team, was ejected from a game for punching an umpire in the nose. The stadium served as home for the Birmingham Baseball Club, the Birmingham Barons, the Birmingham Black Barons, and the Birmingham A's. Baseball stars who played at Rickwood included Babe Ruth, Ty Cobb, Willie Mays, Dizzie Dean, and Piper Davis. Today, Rickwood is the oldest standing ballpark in the United States. (SG.)

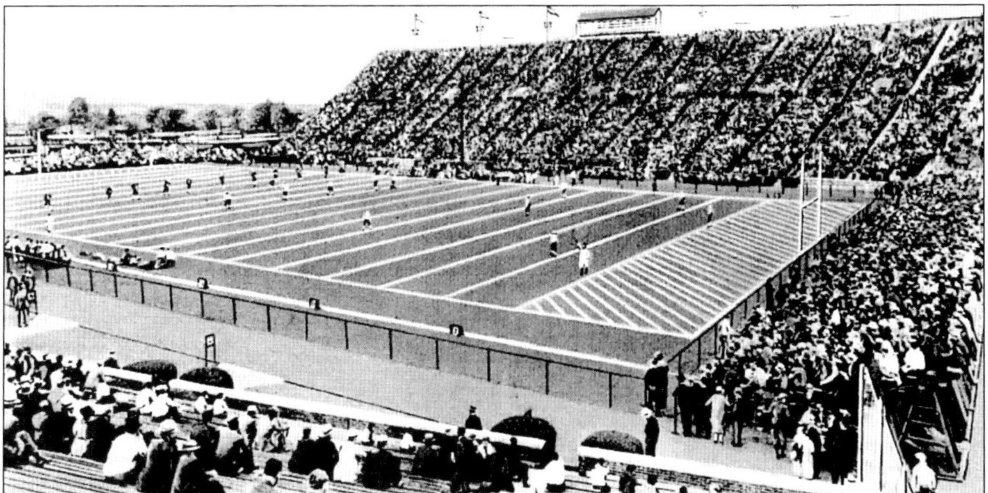

Constructed in 1927 at Birmingham's McLendon Park, Legion Field was long considered one of the finest football stadiums in the South. Named Legion Field as a tribute to Birmingham's war dead and to veterans of the First World War, the stadium—which now seats more than 80,000—was originally built to hold 21,000 spectators. Legion Field was designed to host track meets, boxing matches, and other events as well as football games. In 1928, after the image above was produced, "flood lamps" were installed to allow for night games. To keep the field in shape during those early years, one man labored year-round mowing the grass with a hand mower. "He begins at one end," the Birmingham Park Board reported, "works down the field, then starts back again." (BPLA.)

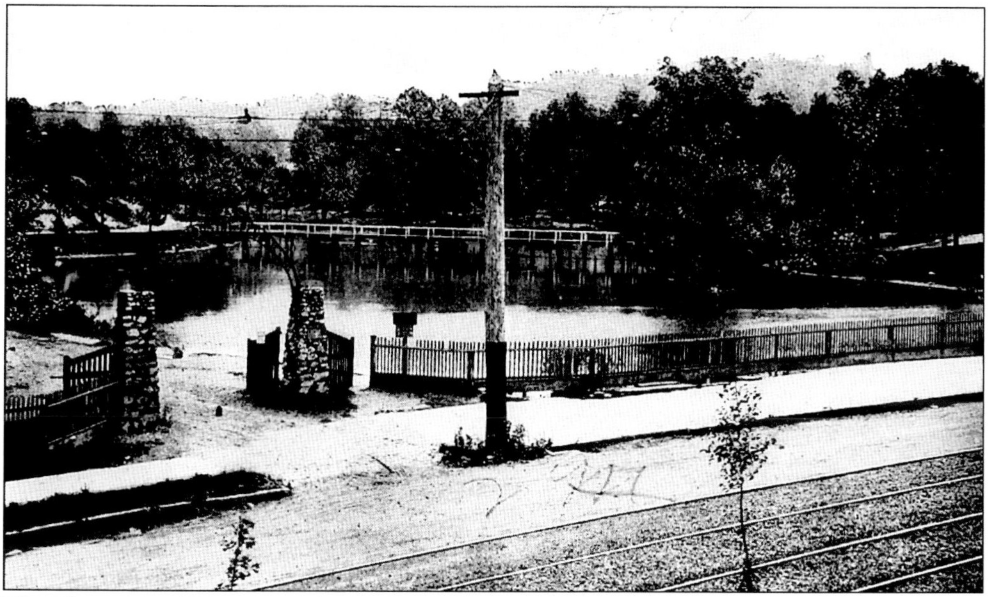

The Elyton Land Company, the company that founded Birmingham, built Lakeview Park at the end of Highland Avenue and opened a hotel there in 1887. Served by two streetcar lines, Lakeview was a popular summer resort, just a short distance from downtown but far enough away to escape the heat and smoke of industrial Birmingham. In addition to swimming, visitors could enjoy boat rides, a skating rink, and a bowling alley. Unable to sustain itself, the hotel closed and the building was converted to a college before burning in 1893. In 1903 the park was leased to the Country Club of Birmingham, and later became the property of the city and was operated as a golf course. (BPLA.)

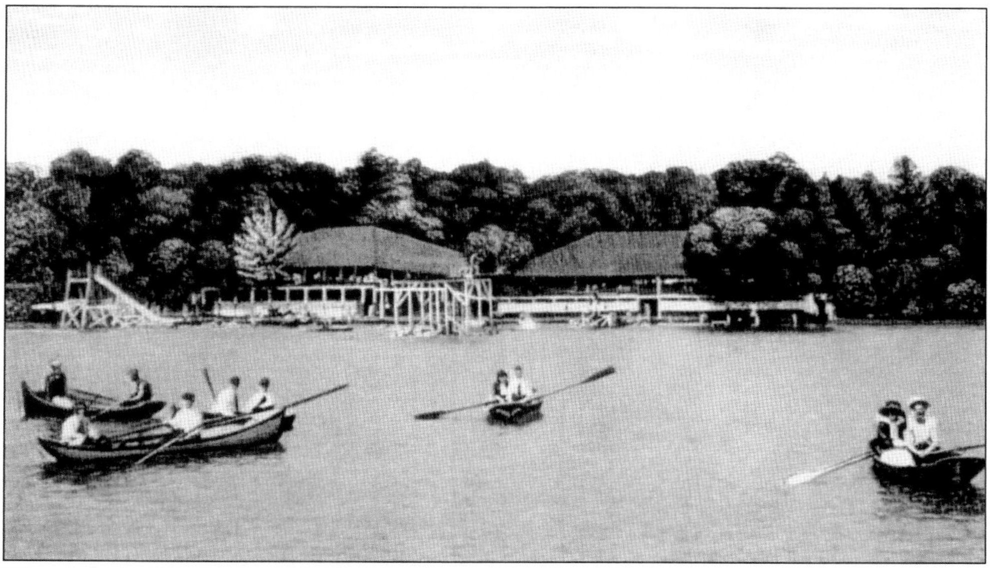

West Lake Mall now occupies the site shown here, but in the early part of this century West Lake, with its pavilion and boat rides, was a major source of recreation for area residents. One historian writes that, "Roebuck Spring produced the coldest swimming water in the county while West Lake, near Bessemer, had warmer water and a better beach."

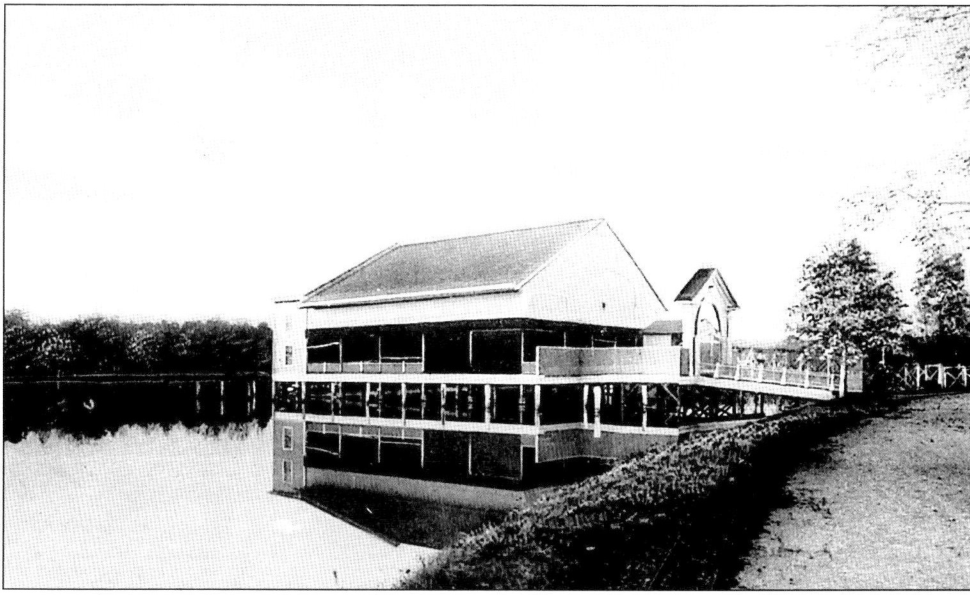

In 1887 the East Lake Land Company, which was developing a new suburb near Birmingham, constructed a 34-acre artificial lake 6 miles from downtown. Originally called Lake Como, East Lake and the surrounding park have offered a variety of attractions over the years, including a hotel, boat rides, a dance pavilion (the "casino," shown above), a roller coaster, a swimming pool, and a zoo. In 1892 the East Lake Zoo menagerie included two pelicans, two deer, a groundhog, two white rabbits, a kangaroo, and a "South American anteater." On the verso of the card below, mailed in 1907, the sender writes, "Here is where the Birmingham youngsters 'bill and coo' and yours truly sits and looks and wonders why." The City of Birmingham purchased East Lake Park in 1917 and continues to operate it as a place for boating, fishing, and exercise. (BPLA.)

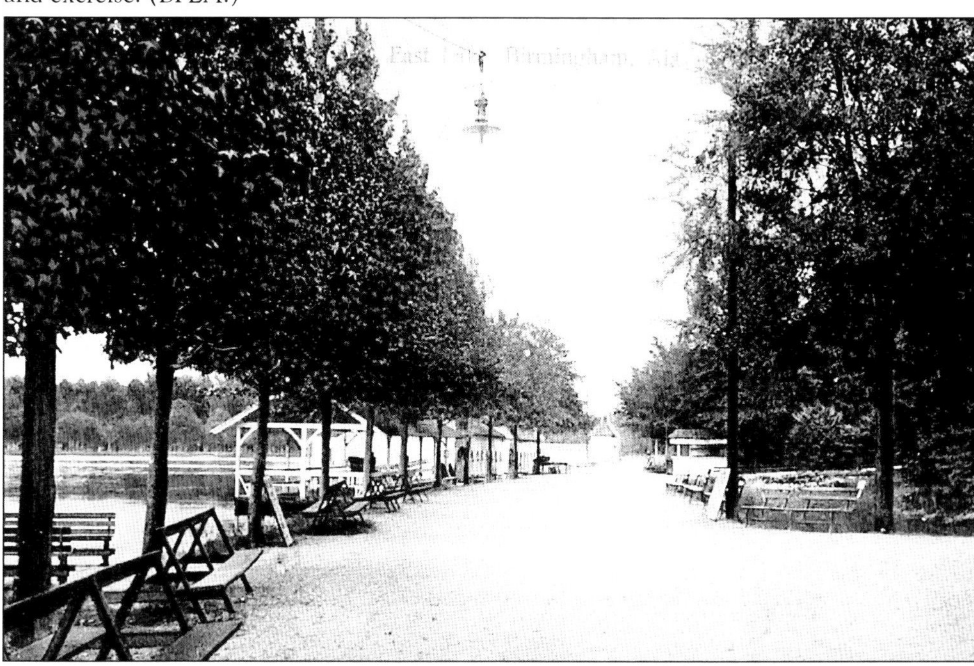

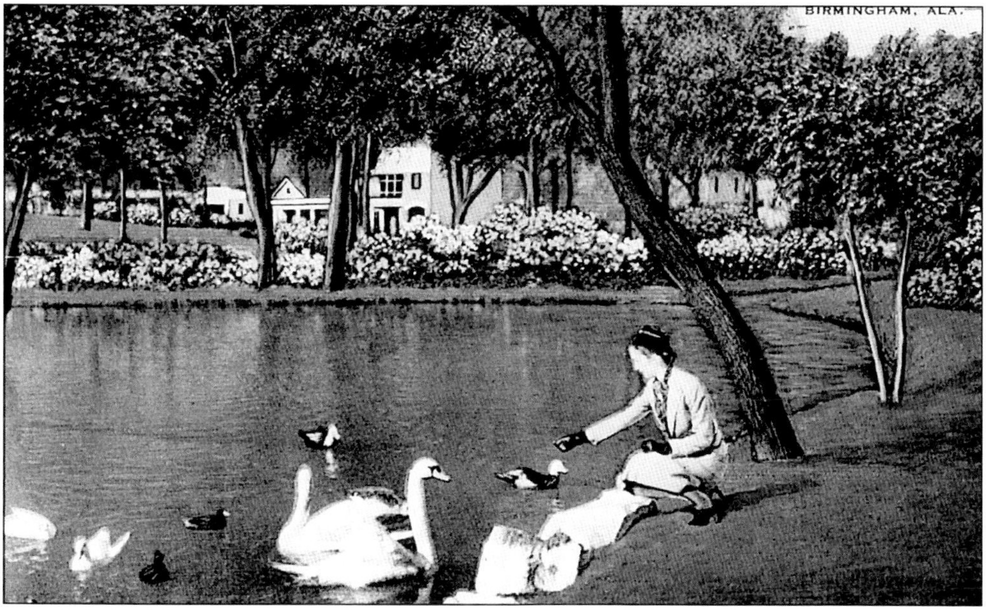

Avondale Park has long been a favorite recreation spot in Jefferson County. The spring once provided fresh water for area farms, and since the 1880s there have been free band concerts and plays in the park. In 1921 Birmingham's semi-centennial pageant was held at the Avondale amphitheater. Avondale Park has also been popular for its rose gardens and wading pool. Like East Lake Park, Avondale was once home to a zoo. The main attraction was "Miss Fancy," an elephant who was either purchased by the city or left by a traveling circus (it depends on whom you ask). A former employee of the park remembered that Miss Fancy would occasionally escape, but she could always be found nearby at Avondale School, where the delighted children would share their lunches with the runaway elephant. (BPLA.)

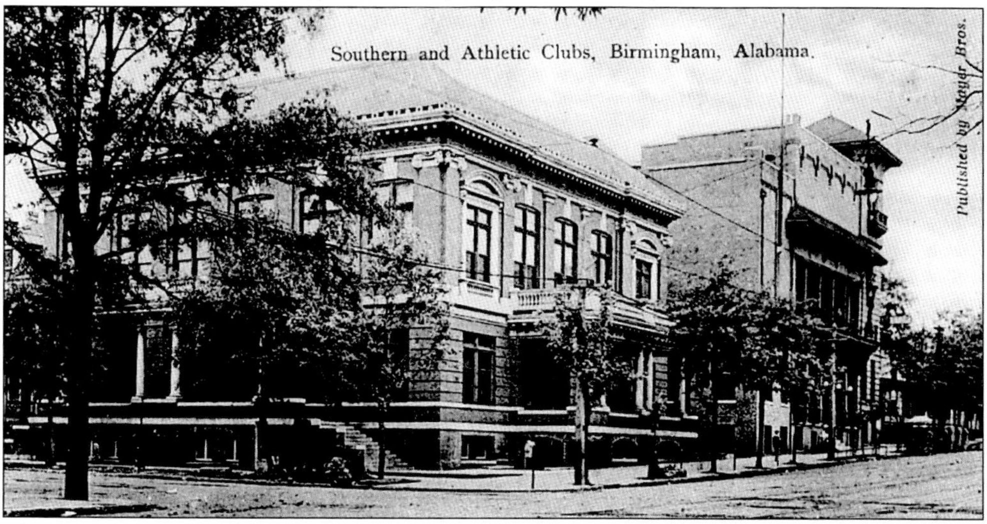

The Southern Club, located on the corner of Twentieth Street and Fifth Avenue, North, played an important role in the social life of Birmingham from the 1890s to the 1920s. The club was the scene of debutante balls, lectures, and receptions. Membership in the Southern Club, as well as the adjoining Athletic Club, marked one's social prominence in early Birmingham. (BPLA.)

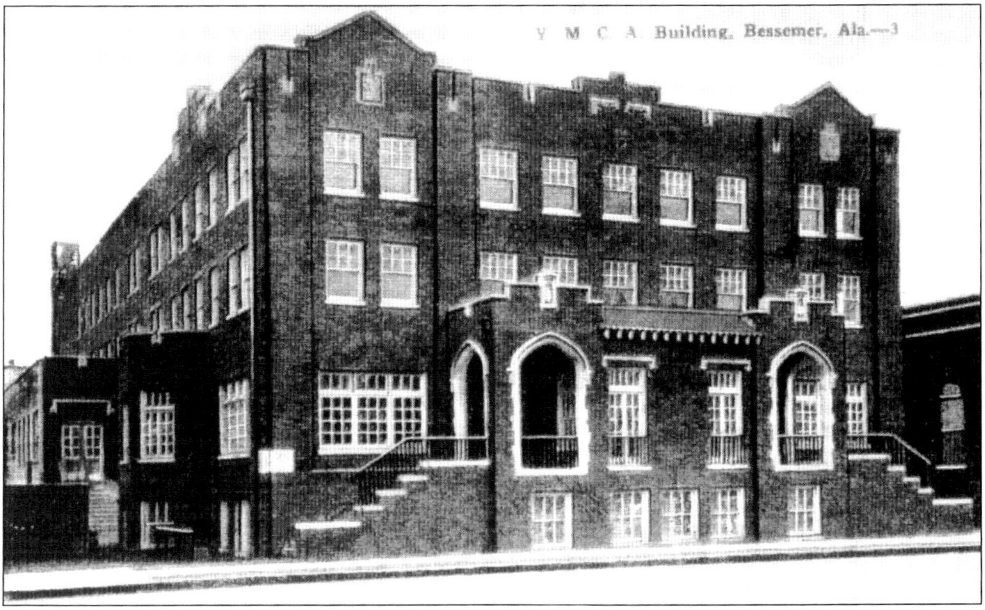

The old Bessemer YMCA was located on Fourth Avenue, behind the present Chamber of Commerce building. This structure was razed in 1976 when a new "Y" was constructed. A parking lot now occupies the site. (BHH.)

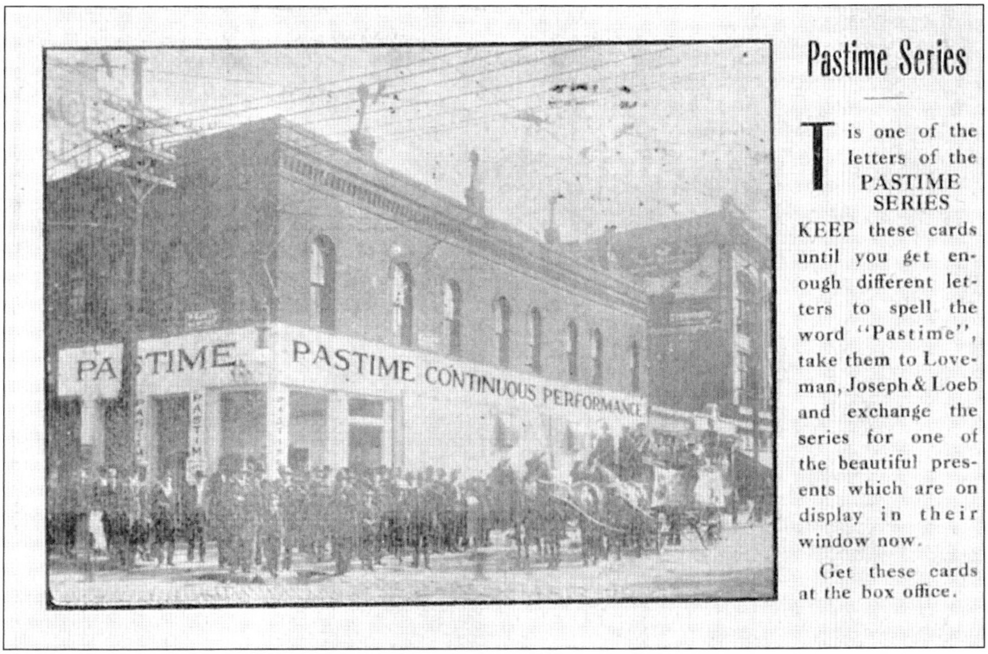

The Pastime Theater was located on the corner of Nineteenth Street and Second Avenue, North from 1909 to 1912. As the card explains, patrons of the theater could collect enough cards with individual letters (this card is a "T") to spell "Pastime," and then exchange the cards for a gift at the Loveman, Joseph and Loeb department store. This was an earlier version of the soft drink bottle caps that spell out brand names or messages, or the fast food restaurant game boards. (SG.)

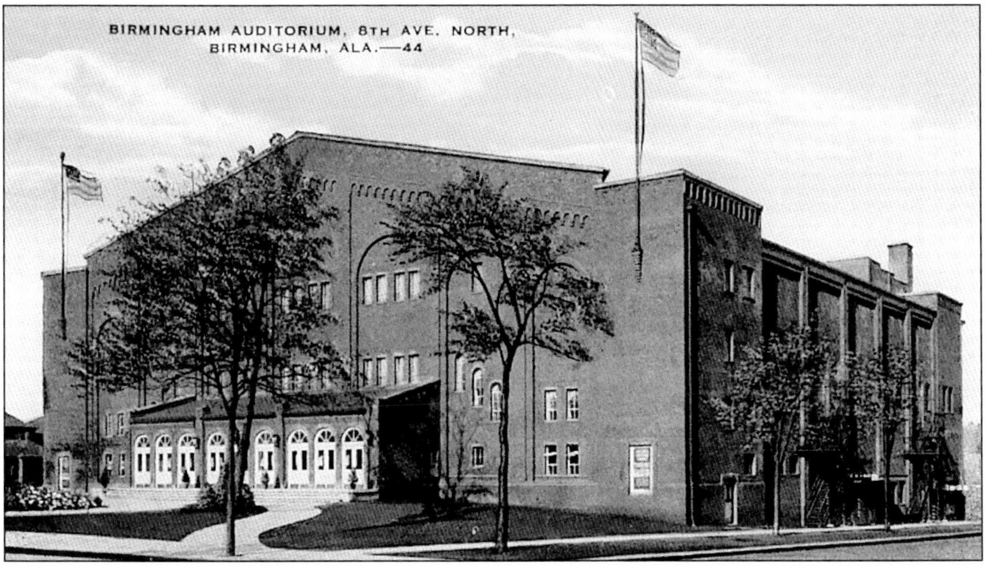

Miller, Martin and Lewis, architects, had a difficult time in the 1920s designing a new multi-purpose auditorium for Birmingham. The facility had to accommodate a variety of events, from car shows to grand opera. The postcard above shows the auditorium as it appeared shortly after construction. Originally called Municipal Auditorium, the name was later changed to Boutwell Auditorium to honor Birmingham mayor Albert Boutwell. A large entranceway and exhibition hall was added to the front of the building in the 1950s. Over the years the auditorium has hosted symphony concerts as well as performances by Nat "King" Cole, B.B. King, and others, political conventions, Ku Klux Klan rallies, Broadway shows, and professional wrestling. (BPLA.)

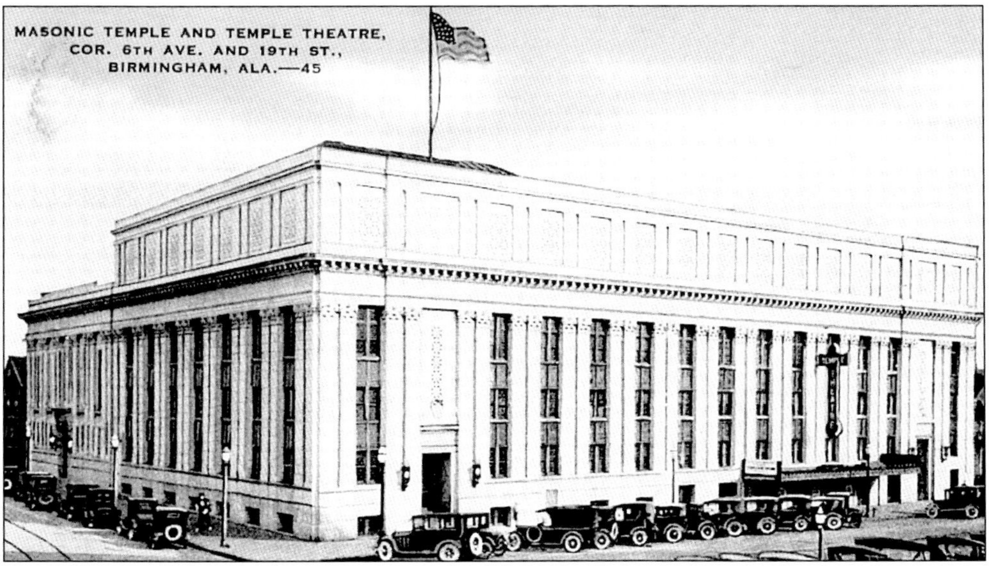

Not a single empty parking place is visible around the Temple Theatre in this photo taken about 1925. The Temple was Birmingham's premier entertainment place for vaudeville, silent movies, operas and concerts, and plays. Alabama's own Tallulah Bankhead performed here. The building was demolished in 1970, and the site is now occupied by the AmSouth-Harbert Plaza. (BPLA.)

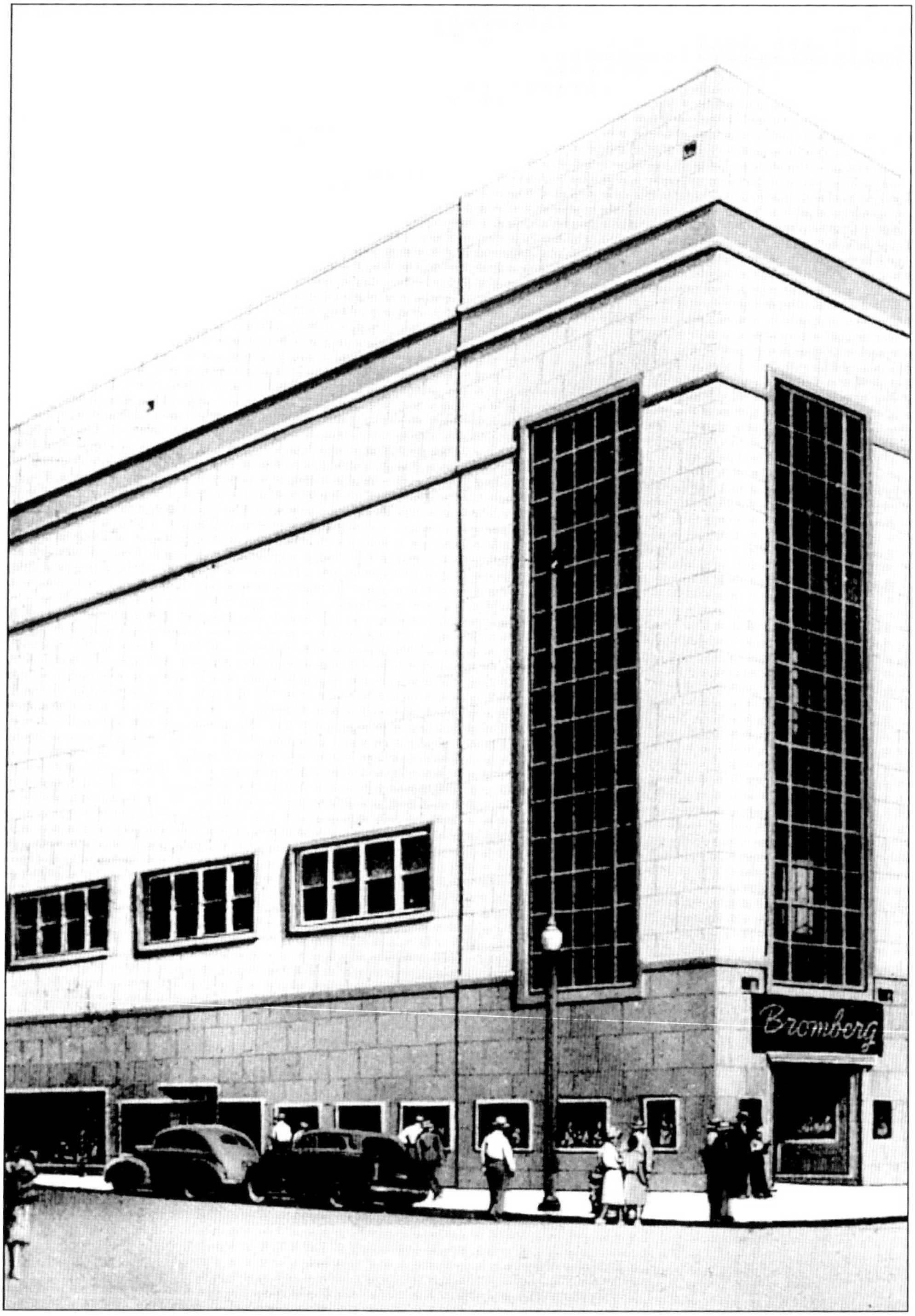

Bromberg and Company held the "formal opening" of its new downtown store, located on the corner of Twentieth Street and Second Avenue, North, on July 22, 1946. This store is still in business. An earlier building on the site, which housed Stein's All Wool Clothes and a billiard hall, burned in 1944. (BPLA.)

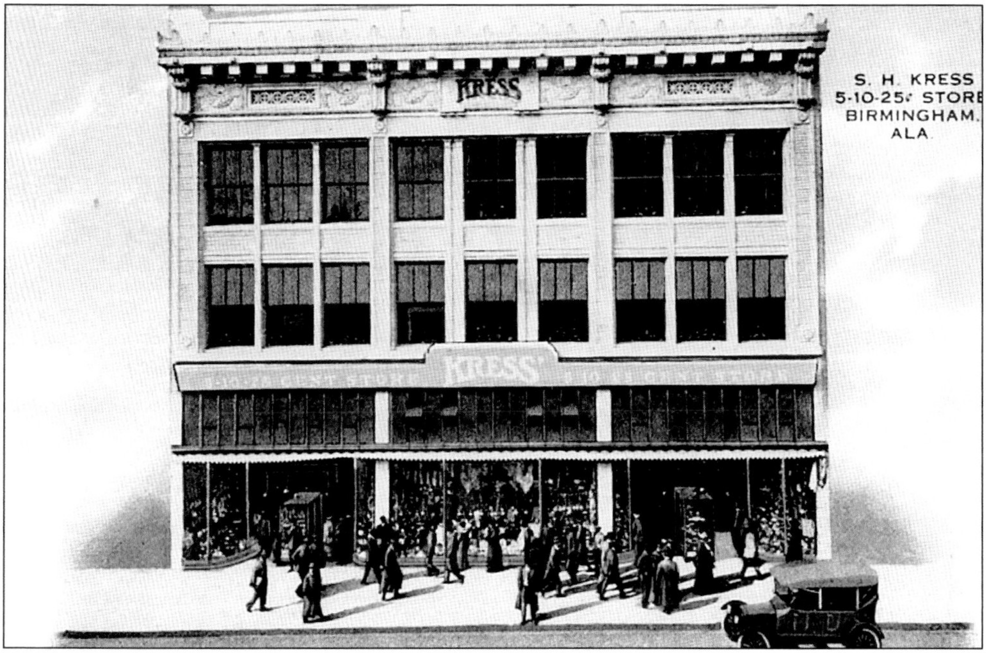

Between 1896 and 1980, S.H. Kress and Company opened approximately 400 of its five and ten cent stores throughout the United States. Along with Woolworth's and Alabama chains like V.J. Elmore, Kress offered customers a wide variety of goods at low prices. The company operated one store in Bessemer and three in Birmingham. The image on the card above shows Birmingham's first Kress store, on the 1900 block of Second Avenue, North. This elaborately decorated store opened in 1915 and was closed in 1937. The card below shows the Kress store located on the corner of Nineteenth Street and Third Avenue, North. Along with Woolworth's, Loveman's, Newberry's, and others, Kress made downtown the place to come for shopping. Designed by a Kress Company architect, Edward F. Sibbert, this Art Deco-style store opened in 1937 and remained in business until 1981. The building, which is listed on the National Register of Historic Places, still stands. (BPLA.)

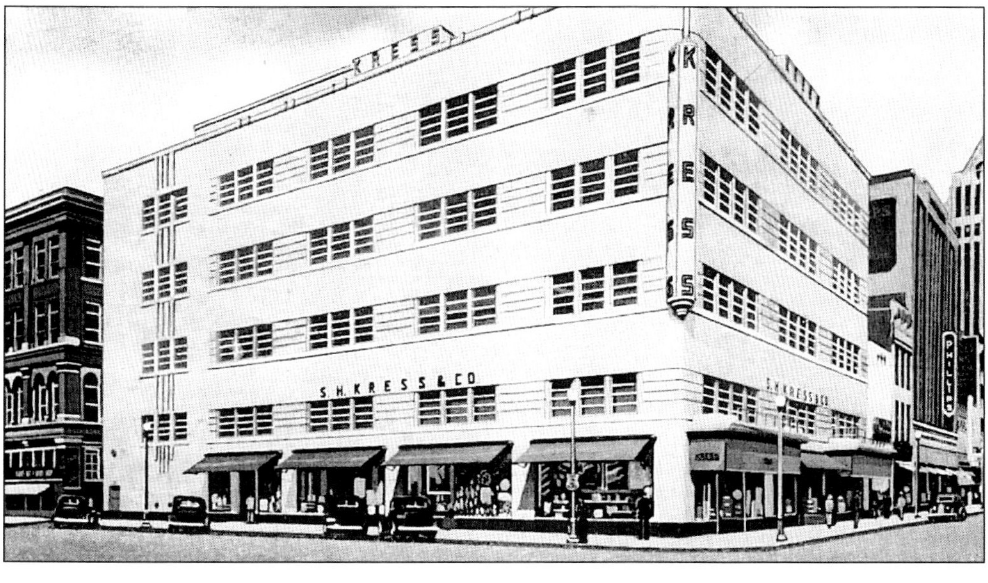

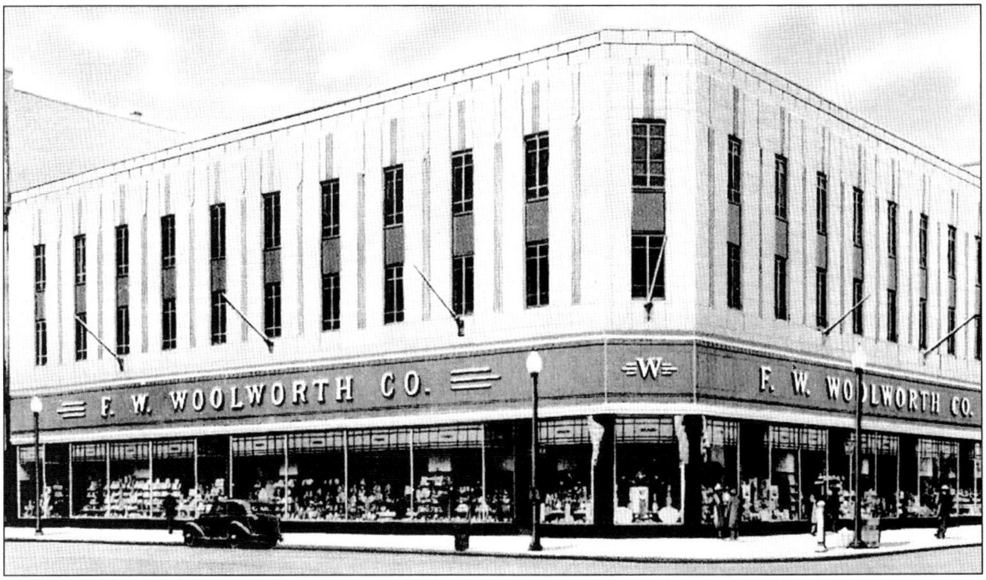

Frank W. Woolworth opened his first store in New York in 1879, and eventually the Woolworth chain operated more than 1,000 stores in the United States, Canada, Great Britain, Germany, and Cuba. The F.W. Woolworth pictured above opened in 1930 on the southeast corner of Nineteenth Street and Third Avenue, North. (BPLA.)

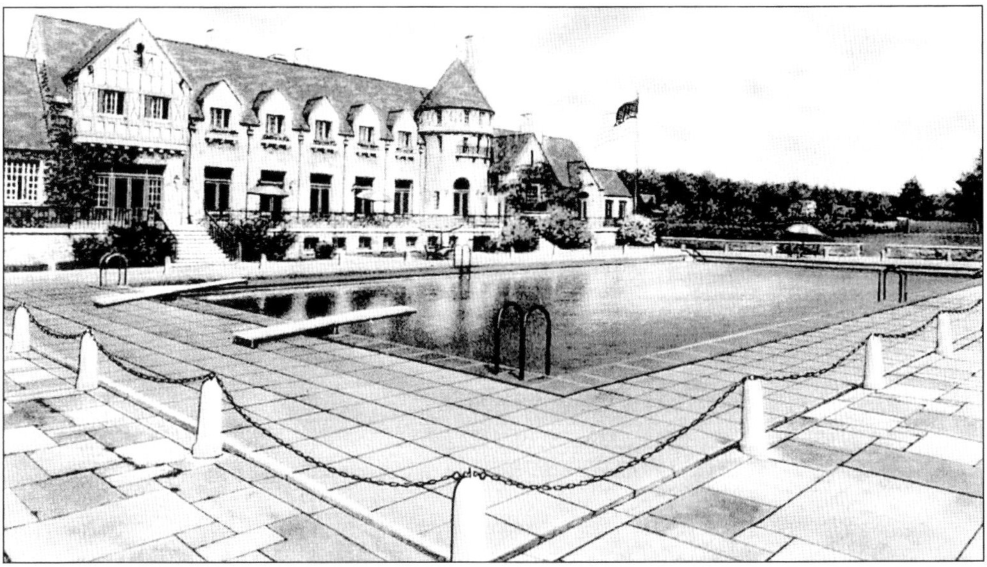

The Country Club of Birmingham began as an exclusive driving club with a clubhouse and restaurant in North Birmingham. The driving club later merged with the Birmingham Golf Club and relocated, in 1904, to Lakeview. In 1927 the Lakeview facility (pictured on the bottom of the facing page) was sold to the City of Birmingham and the club moved again, this time to Shades Valley. The clubhouse pictured here, built in 1928, was designed by the architectural firm of Warren, Knight and Davis. Johnny Weissmuller, Olympic athlete and star of several Tarzan movies, gave a swimming exhibition in the pool in 1931. (BPLA.)

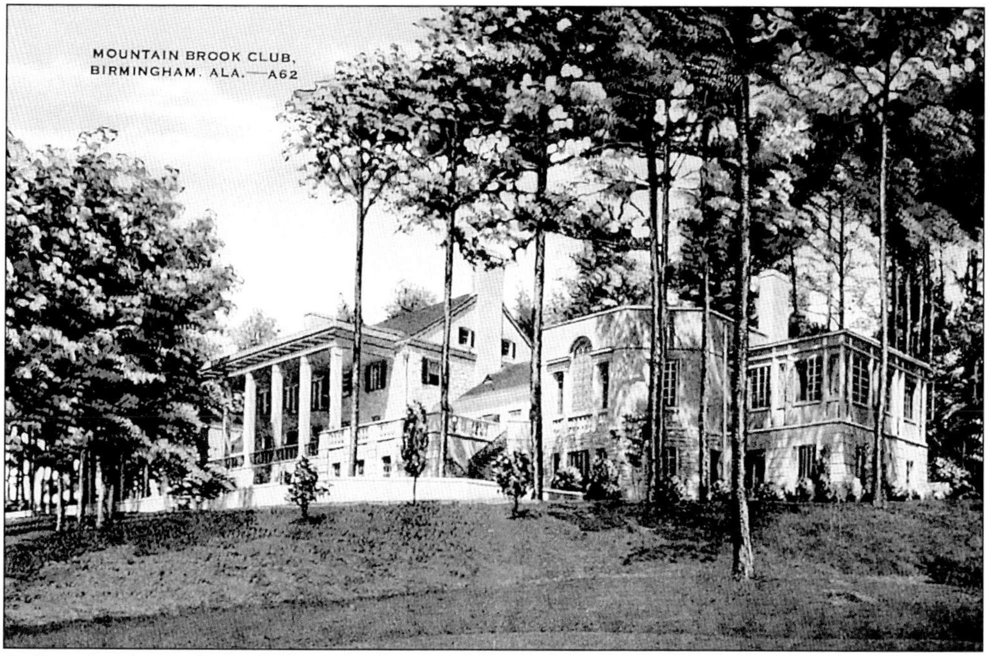

Golfers on the 18th green have this view of the white brick-and-stone Mountain Brook Club. Built in 1929, with Aymar Embury II as the architect, the Colonial-style clubhouse was the final achievement of Robert Jemison Jr. in developing Mountain Brook. (BPLA.)

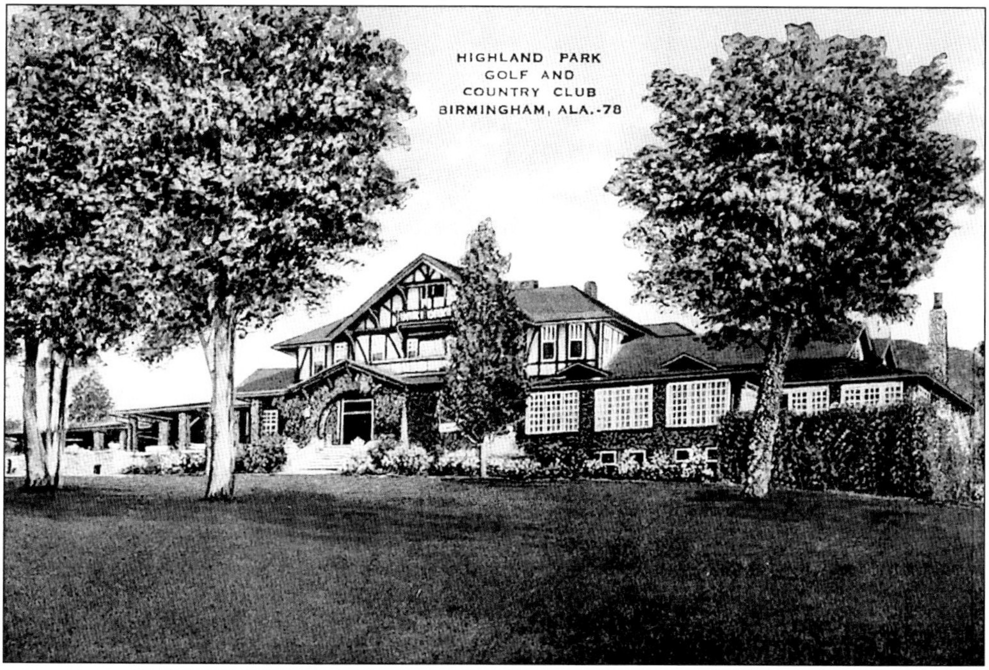

Located at Highland Avenue and Thirty-third Street, the rustic Tudor-style clubhouse of the Country Club of Birmingham, and later of the Highland Park Golf and Country Club, was designed by architects John A. Miller and Hugh Martin. This building burned in 1973. (BPLA.)

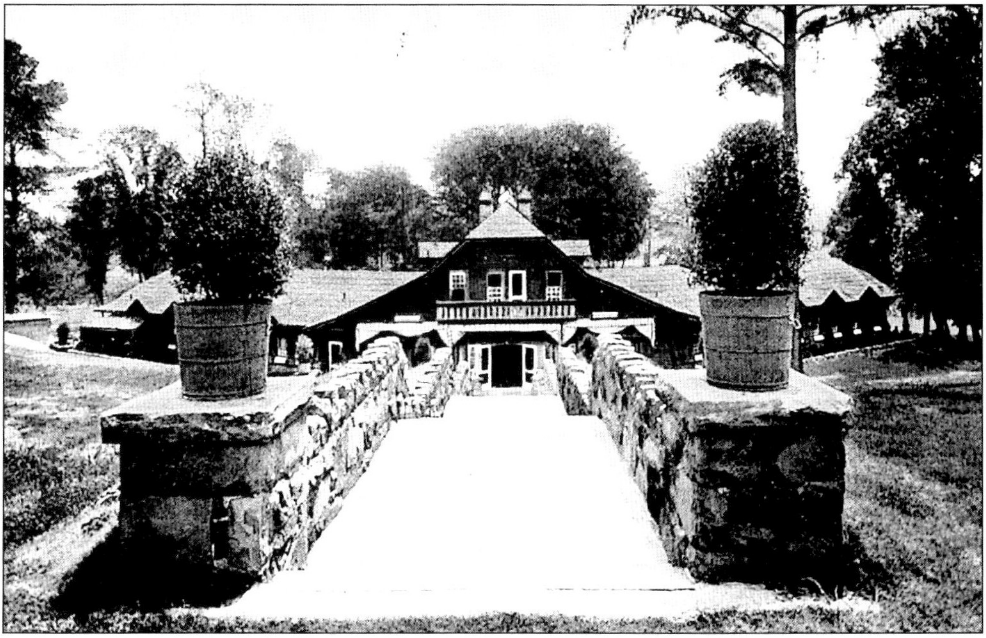

The Roebuck Springs Country Club was started in 1911 by a group of Birmingham businessmen who wanted a place "out in the country" to play golf. The course became one of the finest in the South, and golf great Bobby Jones won his first Southern Golf Association championship here as a teenager. Roebuck ceased to be a private club during the Great Depression. The clubhouse and pool are gone, but the golf course, now operated by the City of Birmingham, is open to the public. (BPLA.)

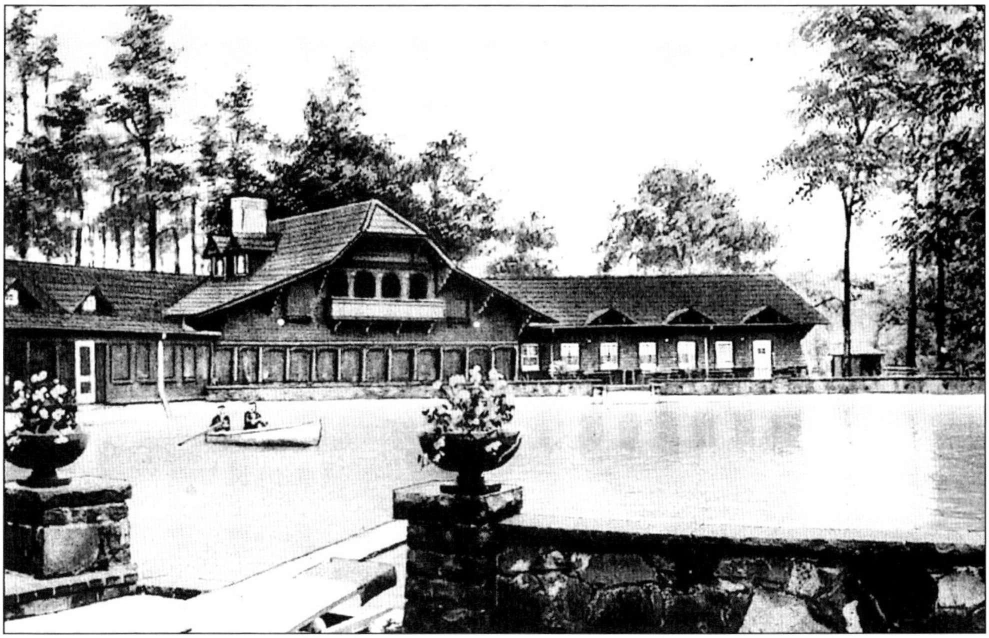

Four

PLACES OF WORK

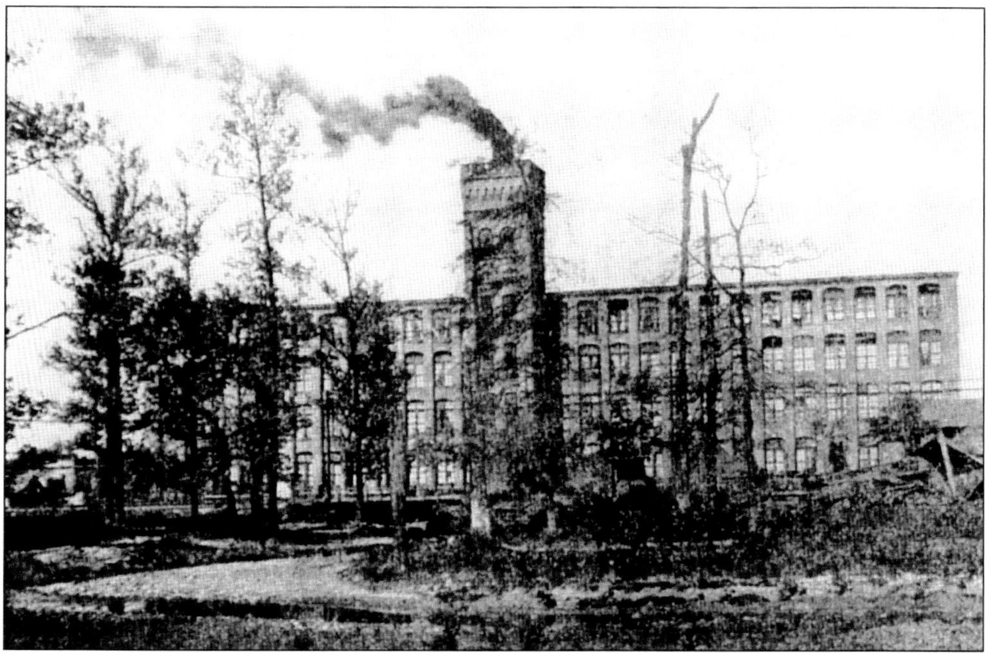

Braxton Bragg Comer, who would eventually be elected governor of Alabama, founded Avondale Mills in 1897. By 1920 Comer had built a mill village of 120 houses, and his company provided its workers with a gymnasium, swimming pools, and physicians. The Avondale Mills Band was well known and highly regarded. Eventually Avondale Mills grew into one of the nation's largest textile manufacturers, operating mills in a number of Alabama towns. A changing economy and international competition led to the closing of the Birmingham operation in 1971. The mill building pictured above was demolished in 1975. (SG.)

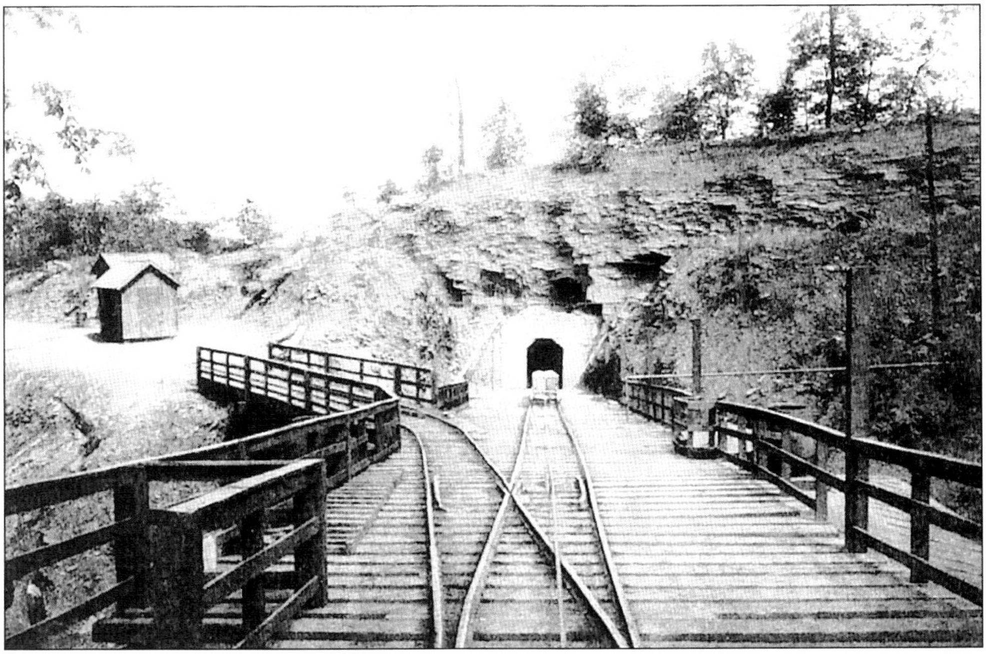

Work in the Birmingham District's mines was dirty and dangerous, but ore mines like the one pictured above provided the raw materials that drove Birmingham's industrial economy. (JM.)

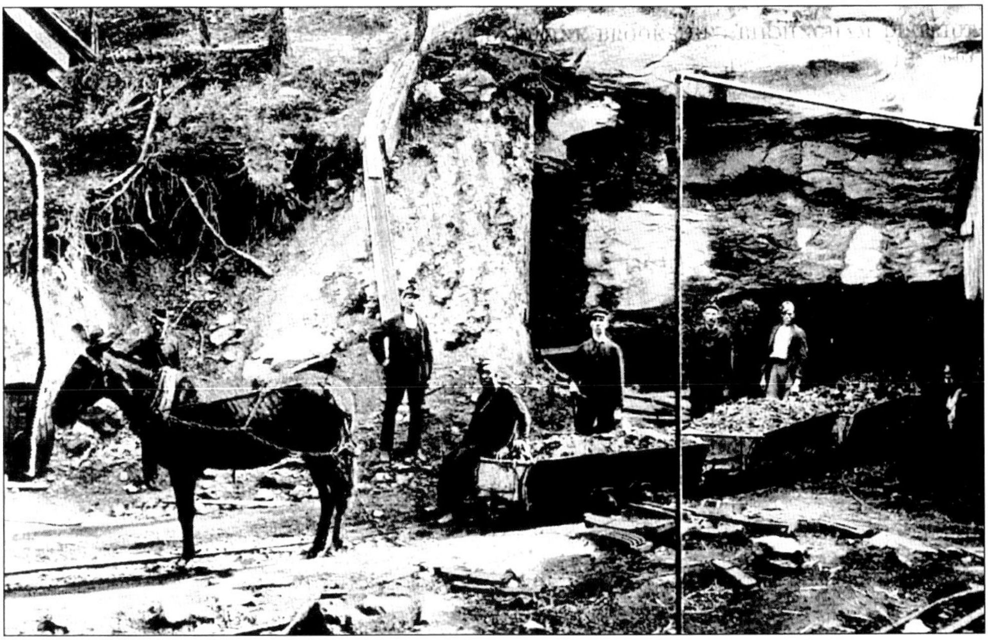

The coal mine pictured on this card is identified as being at Brookside, a small community in northwest Jefferson County between Gardendale and Graysville. Coal was discovered in the area in the 1880s. Numerous families from eastern and southern Europe, including Poles, Czechs, Slovaks, Hungarians, Austrians, and Italians, immigrated to Brookside to work in its mines. Today the community is home to the only Russian Orthodox Church in Alabama. (BHH.)

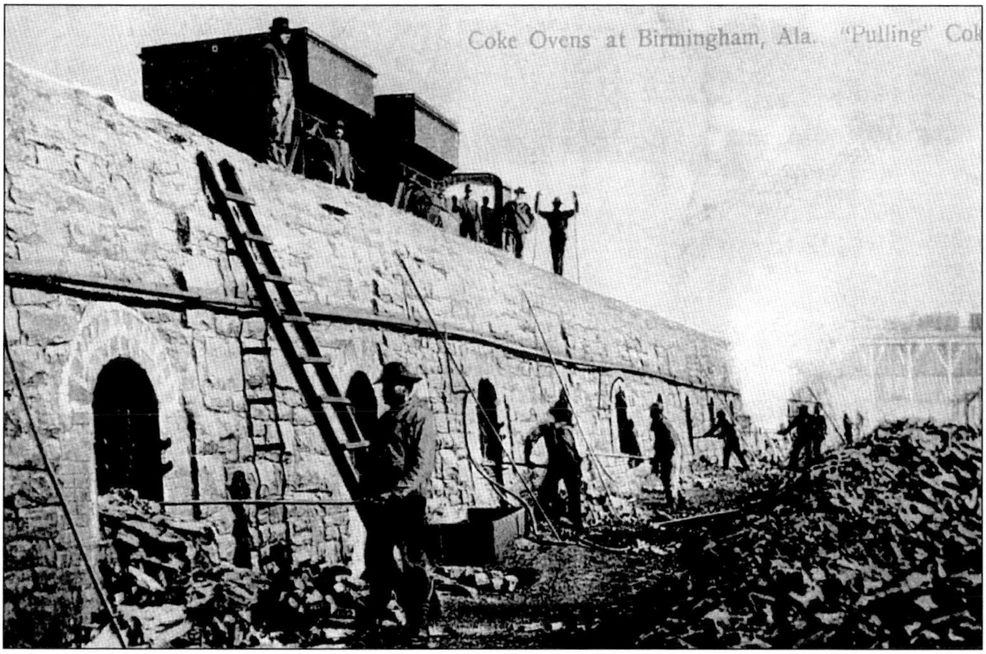

Prior to World War I, beehive ovens, like those pictured above, were used to turn coal into coke, a necessary ingredient in iron making. The first coke from Birmingham coal was produced at the Oxmoor Furnaces in 1878. (JM.)

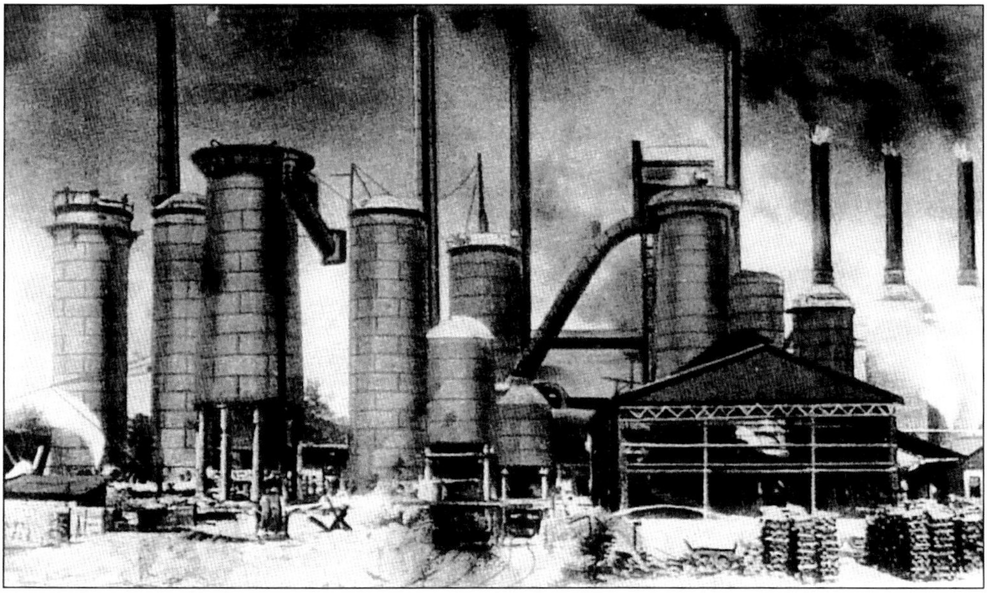

Henry F. DeBardeleben built the city of Birmingham's first iron furnace, called "Little Alice," at Fourteenth Street and First Avenue, North, in 1880. DeBardeleben named the furnace for his eldest daughter. "Big Alice" furnace opened three years later. The first pig iron using Birmingham coke was produced at the Alice Furnaces. According to legend the Alice Furnace had its own ghost. In 1887 Theophilus Jowers, a worker at the facility, fell into the furnace and was killed. From that time until 1927, when the furnace was dismantled, workers reported periodic visits from Jowers' apparition. (JM.)

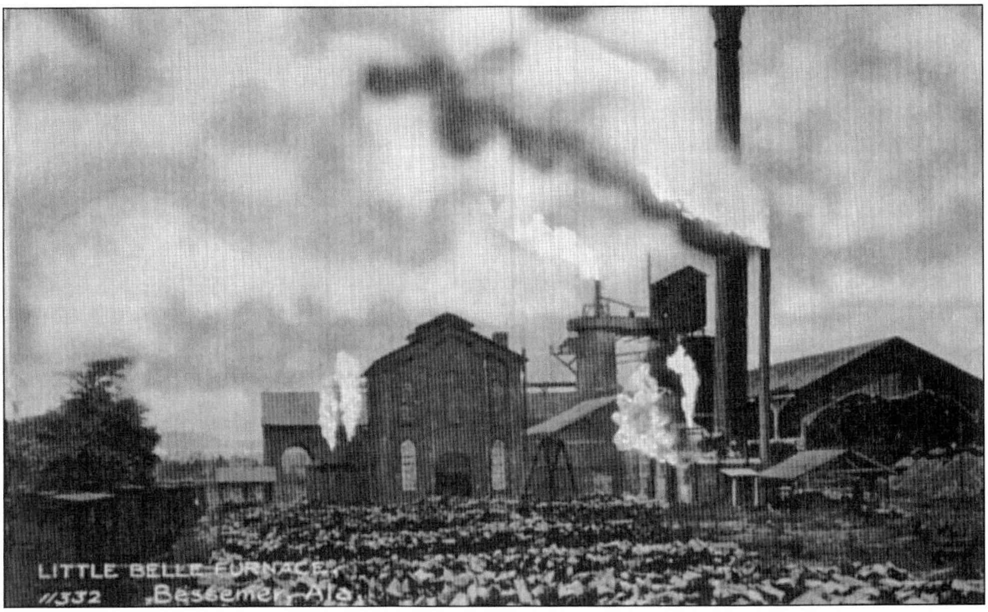

In 1889 three Bessemer-area iron companies consolidated to form the DeBardeleben Coal and Iron Company. Henry DeBardeleben had by this time turned his attention to building the new industrial city of Bessemer. Little Bell Furnace (the name is misspelled on the card) was the smallest of the company's three furnaces. Little Bell operated from 1890 until 1906. It was brought back into service during World War I, but ceased operation again in 1919, and was dismantled in 1927. It is barely visible in the center background in the postcards of downtown Bessemer (see p. 27). (JM.)

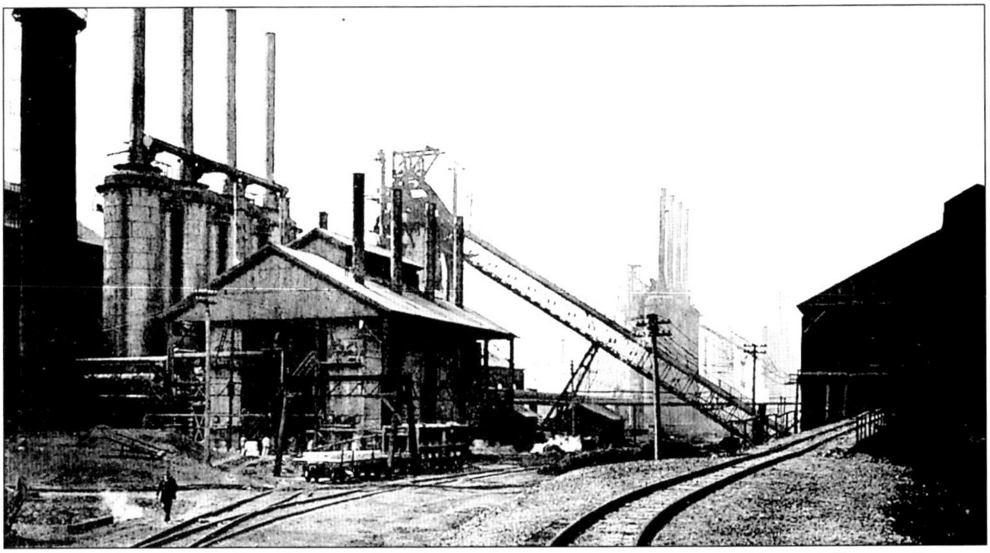

David Thomas, the son of a Pennsylvania iron family, purchased land in Jefferson County shortly after the Civil War. Thomas and a group of investors formed the Pioneer Mining and Manufacturing Company in 1868, and in 1888 the company's first furnace was put into blast at Thomas. A second furnace went into operation two years later. In 1899 the Pioneer Company was taken over by the Republic Iron and Steel Company, which opened Thomas Furnace No. 3, then the largest furnace in the Birmingham District, in 1902. (BPLA.)

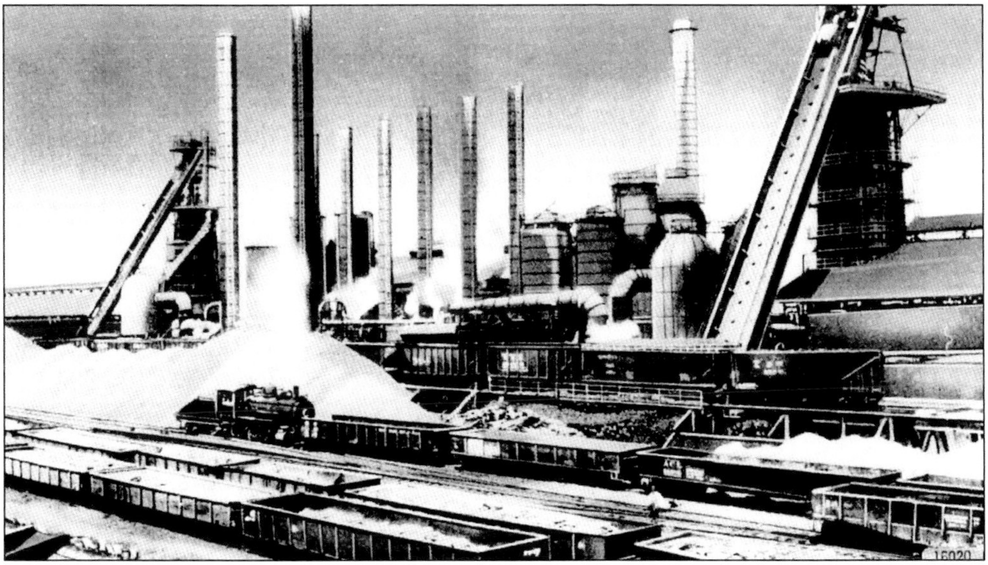

Encouraged by Henry DeBardeleben, James Withers Sloss and a group of investors formed the Sloss Furnace Company in 1881. The company opened its first furnace in 1882, and a second a few years after. Sloss became a major producer of pig iron, and in 1927 the old furnaces were dismantled and a new pair constructed. Later acquired by the United States Pipe and Foundry Company, which became the Jim Walter Corporation, the facility shut down in 1971. Sloss sits beside the First Avenue, North viaduct, and for many years families on outings and couples on dates would watch from the viaduct as the furnaces were tapped, releasing an impressive light show of fire and molten iron. The Walter Corporation donated Sloss Furnaces to the City of Birmingham, and despite calls for its demolition, the site opened to the public in 1983 as the Sloss Furnaces National Historic Landmark, a museum of industry and iron making. If reports can be believed, Theophilus Jowers, the ghost of Alice Furnace, moved his residence to Sloss after Alice had been demolished. (BPLA.)

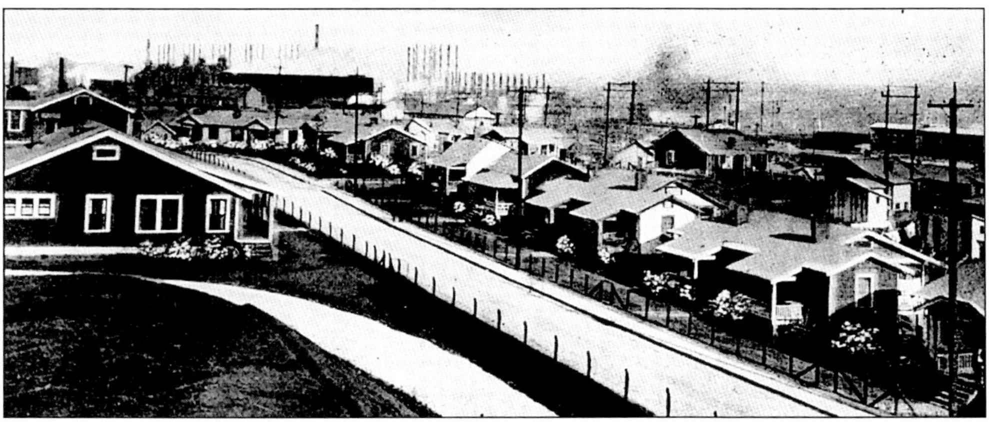

Consolidated by Enoch Ensley of Tennessee in 1884, the old Alice Furnaces, Linn Iron Works, and the Pratt Coal and Coke Company became the Pratt Coal and Iron Company. By 1885 the company was the largest holder of coal lands in Alabama and furnished most of the coke used in the Birmingham District. The town of Ensley was founded near the furnaces, a few miles southwest of Birmingham. In 1886 the Pratt Company was acquired by the Tennessee Coal, Iron and Railroad Company (TCI). The United States Steel Corporation purchased TCI in 1907 for just over $35 million. (JM.)

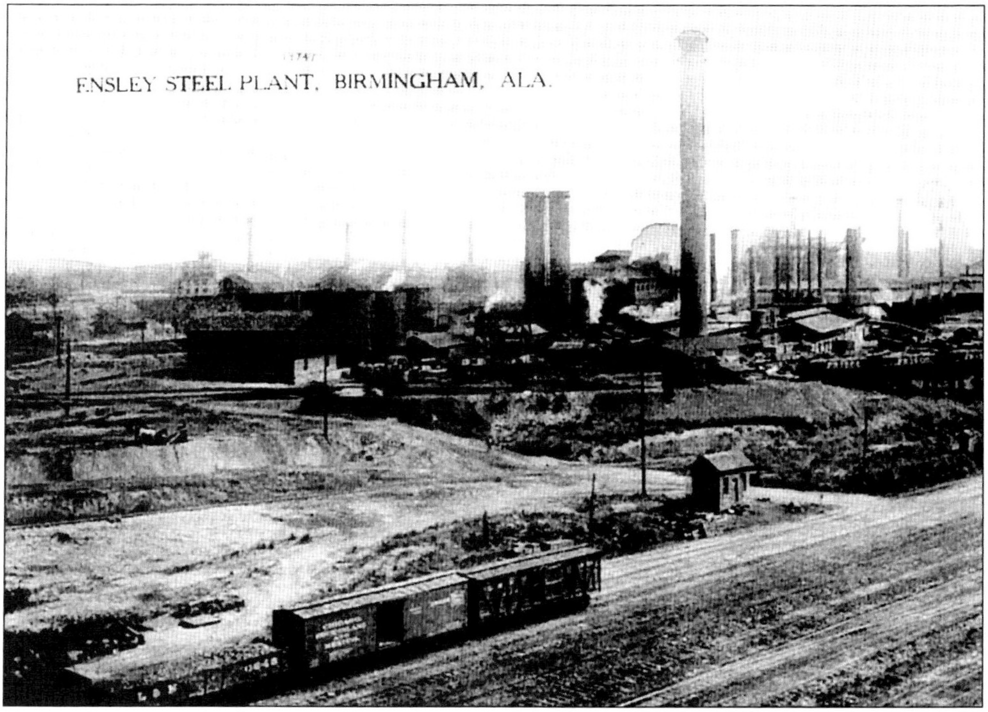

The six furnaces at Ensley owned by U.S. Steel were rebuilt and remodeled several times. (JM)

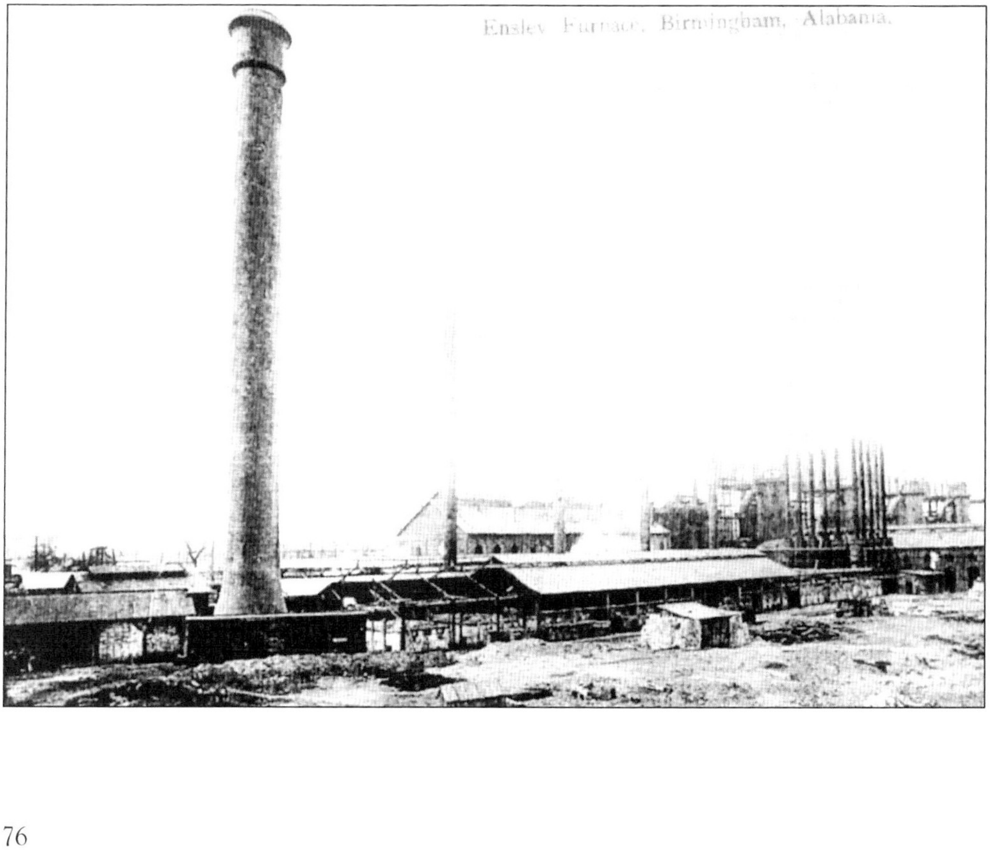

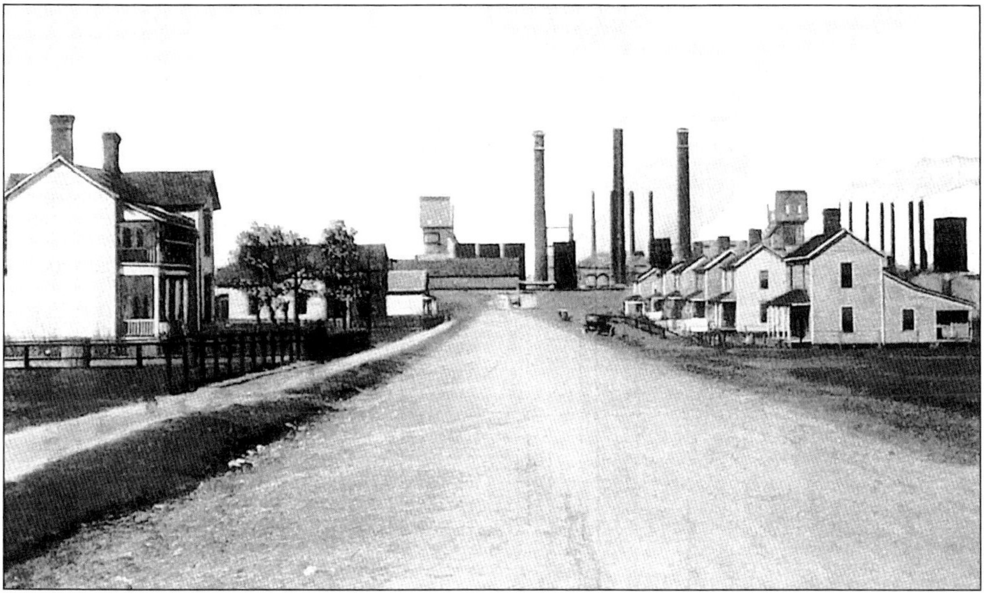

The Pratt Coal and Iron Company began construction of four new blast furnaces at Bessemer, and TCI completed work on them. The four stacks were 80 feet high and had a daily capacity of 200 tons each. Furnace #4 went into blast on April 9, 1888, #3 on June 5, and #2 on December 1. The fourth furnace, #1, was blown into operation on March 9, 1889. This card shows the close proximity of worker housing to the mills. Most iron and steel makers in the Birmingham District provided living quarters for their workers, but employers kept their employees close at hand. This arrangement was convenient for the workers, but it also made it easier for the company to monitor the workers' activities and to call the employees to work with horns and whistles. (JM.)

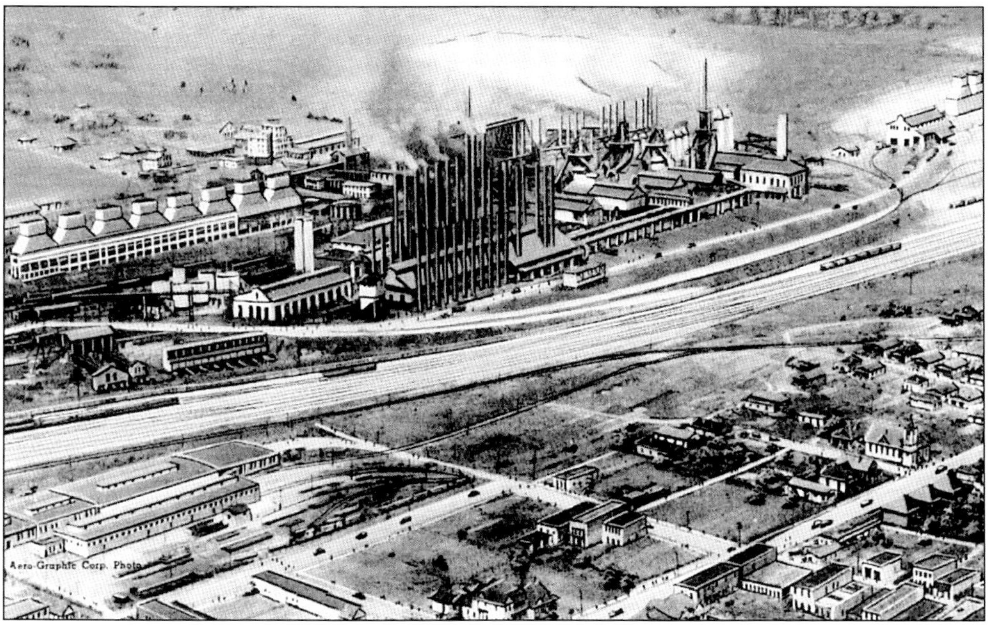

The tin plate mill at Fairfield, pictured above, was owned by TCI and was among the many manufacturing operations associated with the Birmingham-area steel industry. (BPLA.)

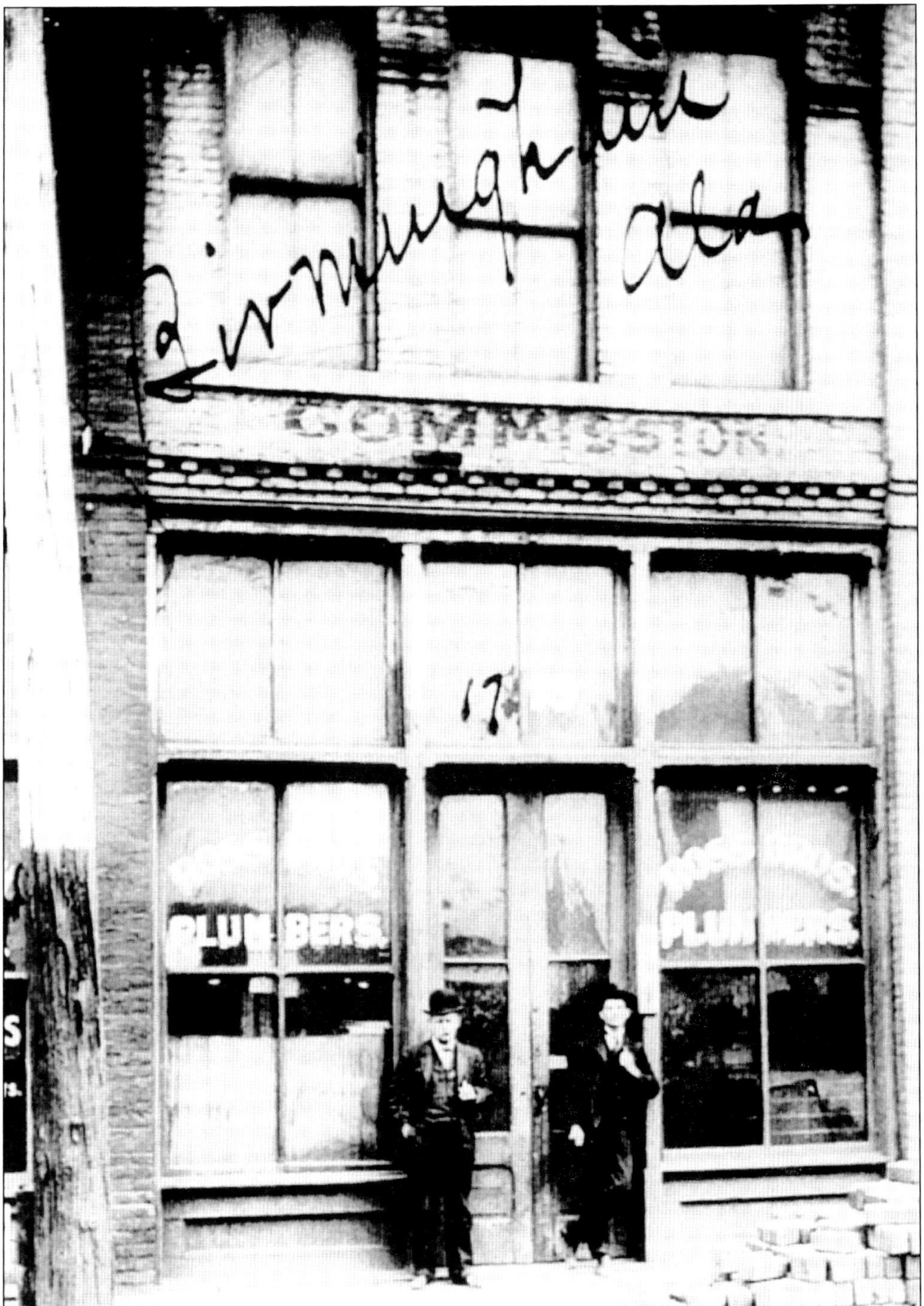

The two gentlemen posing proudly on this card may be Charles and George Ross, owners and operators of Ross Brothers Plumbers. Early in this century the business was located at 1718 First Avenue, North. In more recent years Southern Junior College of Business occupied the site. (SG.)

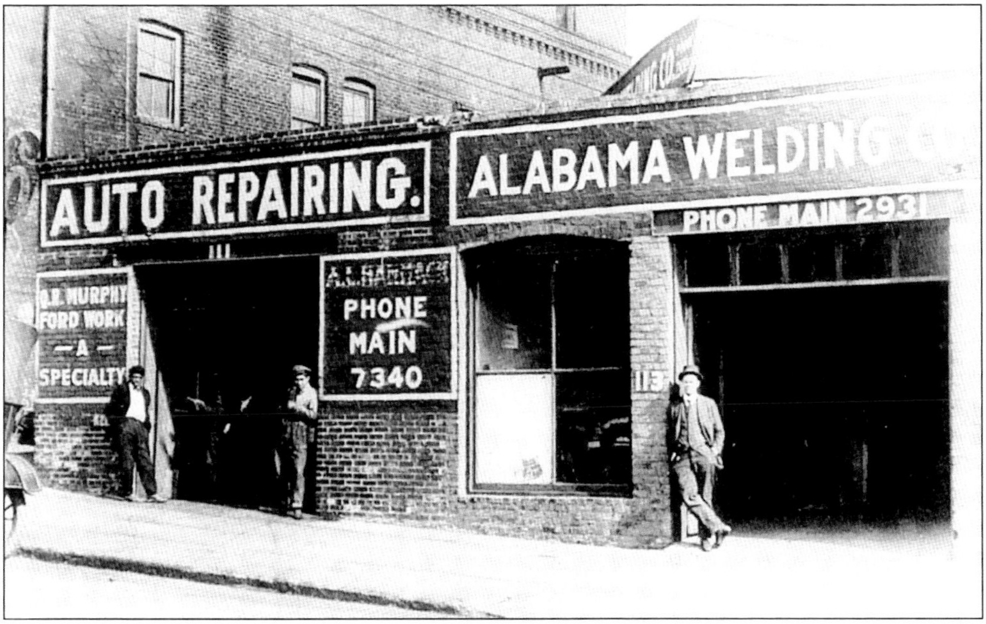

Around 1915 the business pictured to the left of the Alabama Welding Company was Murphy and Hammack Auto Repairing, and later Quinlan R. Murphy Auto Repairing. The building was located at 111 and 113 Twenty-first Street, South. (SG.)

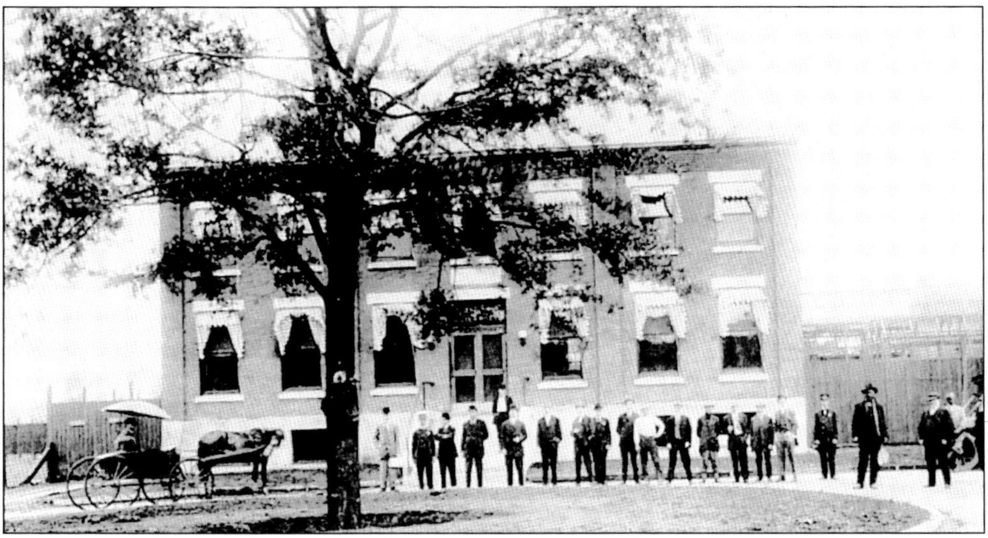

On the verso of this card, mailed in 1911, the sender writes, "Am sending you this card showing where I work. The office of the American Steel and Wire. This is a beautiful town. Think you would like it." The "beautiful town" is Corey, later called Fairfield. American Steel and Wire also had an office in Birmingham at the Brown-Marx Building. (SG.)

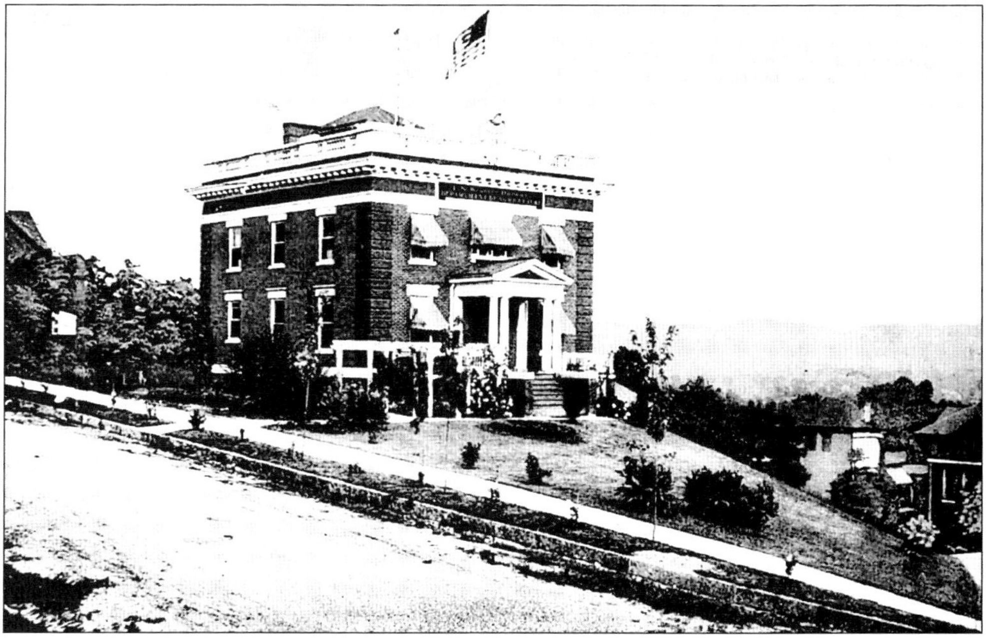

Early in the century various local weather forecasters worked from this building on the corner of Eleventh Avenue and Thirteenth Street, North, including W.F. Lehman (who lived nearby with his wife, Marie) and Edgar C. Horton (who lived just up the street with his wife, Carrie). (BPLA.)

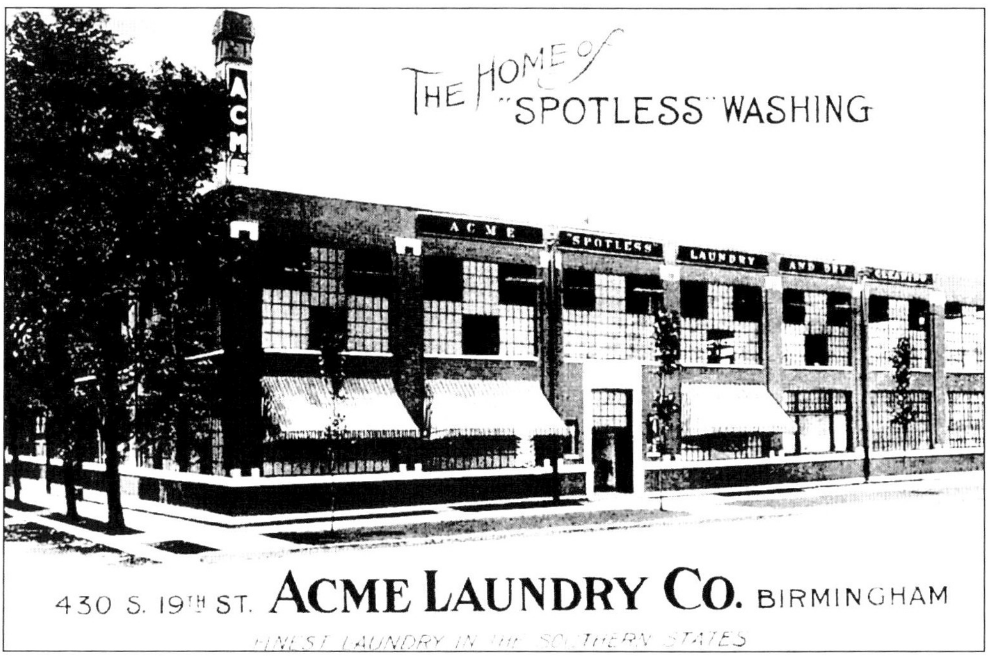

This postcard showing the Acme Laundry Company, located on Nineteenth Street, South, is typical of cards produced for companies as advertisement. (SG.)

Five

Places of Governance

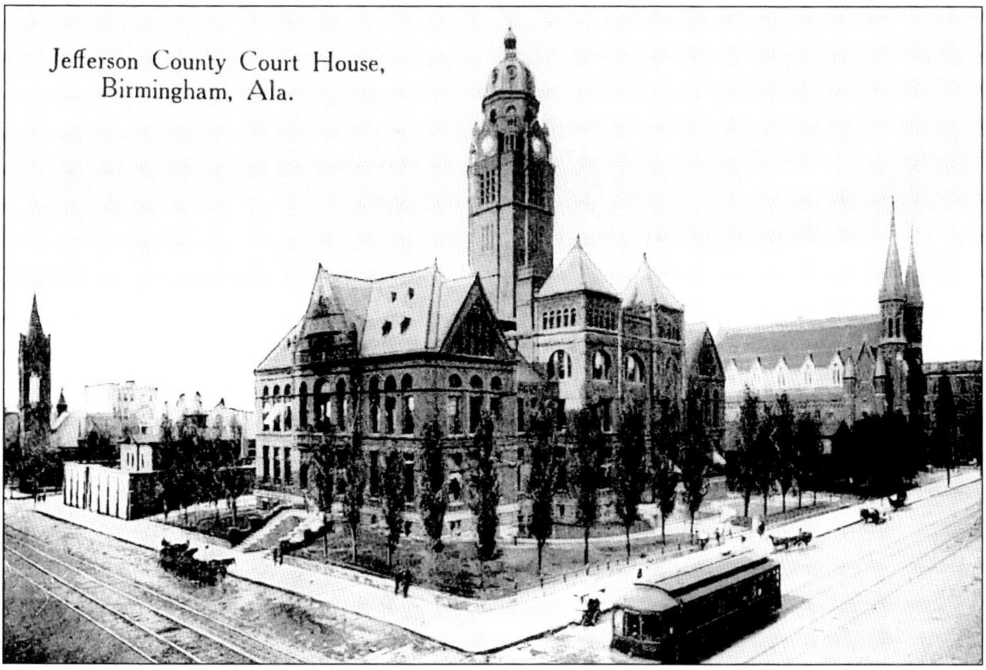

Jefferson County's first courthouse, after the county was established in 1819, was a log cabin in Carrollsville (now Powderly). The county seat moved to Elyton in 1820, and a new courthouse was constructed (near present-day Center Street and Tuscaloosa Avenue in Birmingham). A more substantial structure was built in 1841, but that courthouse burned in 1872—just in time for the scrappy new city of Birmingham to wrestle the county seat away from Elyton. The new courthouse was built at the corner of Third Avenue and Twenty-first Street, North. This structure was torn down in 1887, and the courthouse pictured above was constructed on the same site, opening in 1889. The central clock tower was 180 feet tall and doubled as a lookout point for fires. The structure served as the county courthouse until 1931, and was torn down in 1937. A parking lot now occupies the site. (BPLA.)

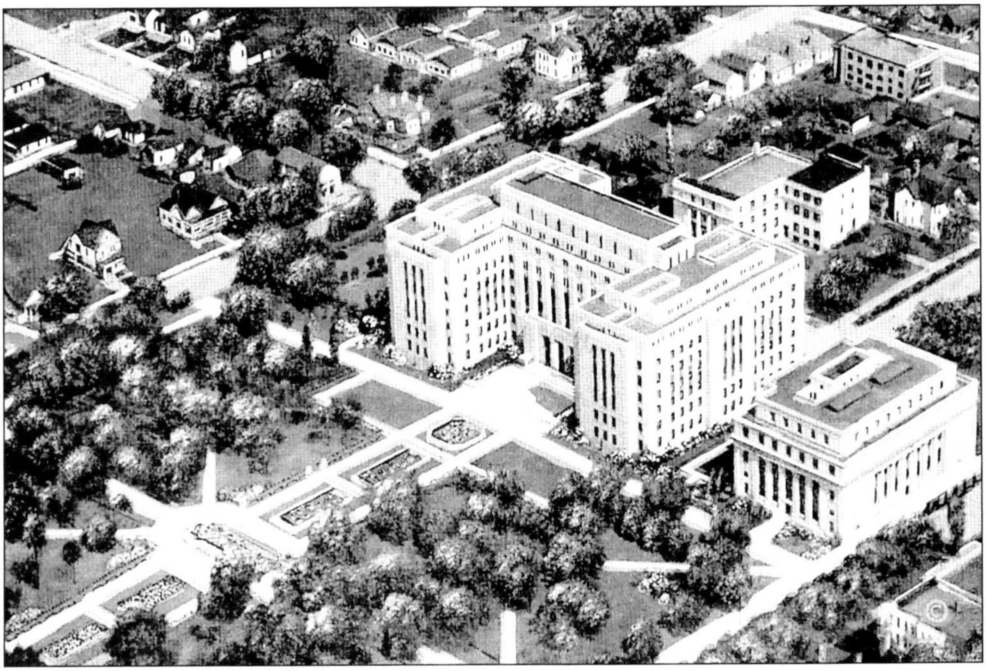

On this page and the top of the facing page are three views of the current Jefferson County Courthouse, which opened in 1929. Along with the Birmingham City Hall, the Birmingham Public Library, the Birmingham Board of Education, Boutwell Auditorium, and the Birmingham Museum of Art, the courthouse makes up the municipal complex, a series of public buildings that ring Linn Park. The verso of the card above reads, "Jefferson County's $3,000,000 Court House, one of the handsomest in the South is constructed of white Indiana limestone and marble. The jail occupies the top floor. A unique fact is that eighty per cent of those entering the Court House come in through the back door, reached through a small but very beautiful park." The courthouse was designed by Jack B. Smith of the Chicago architectural firm Holabird and Root. Note in these two images the large number of homes still in the area at the time of the courthouse opening. (BPLA.)

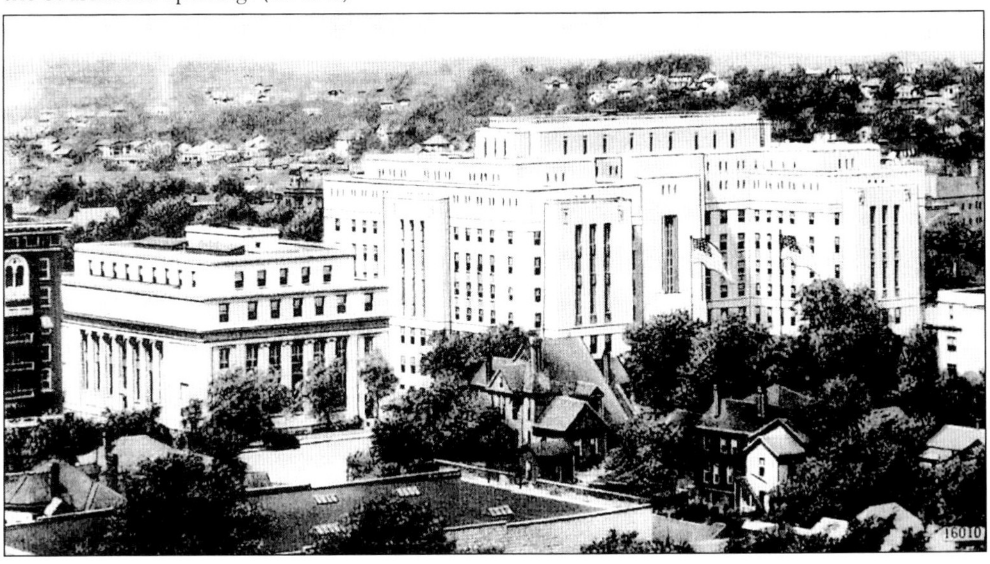

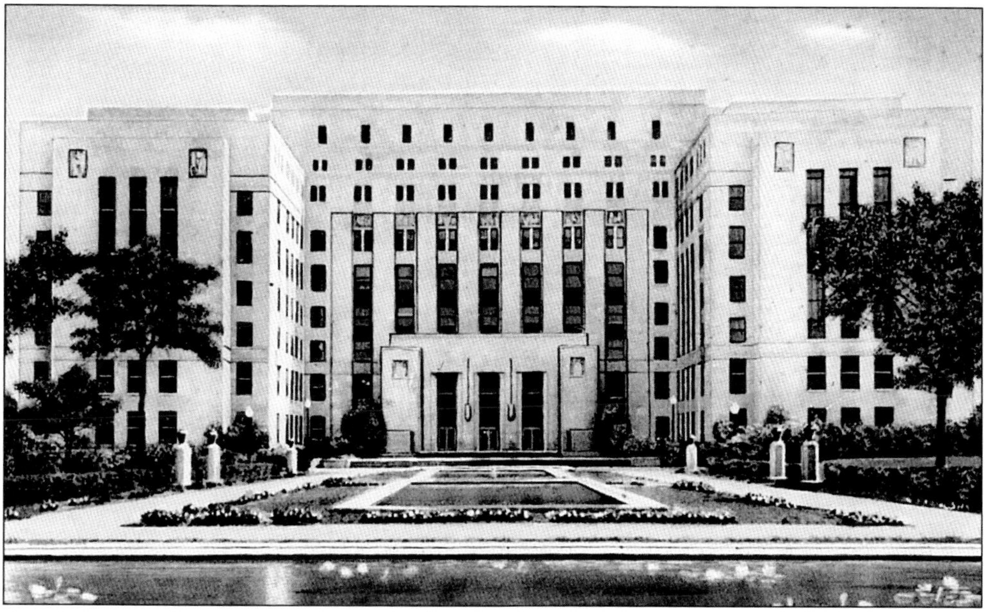

This is the courthouse as seen from Woodrow Wilson Park (now Linn Park). (BPLA.)

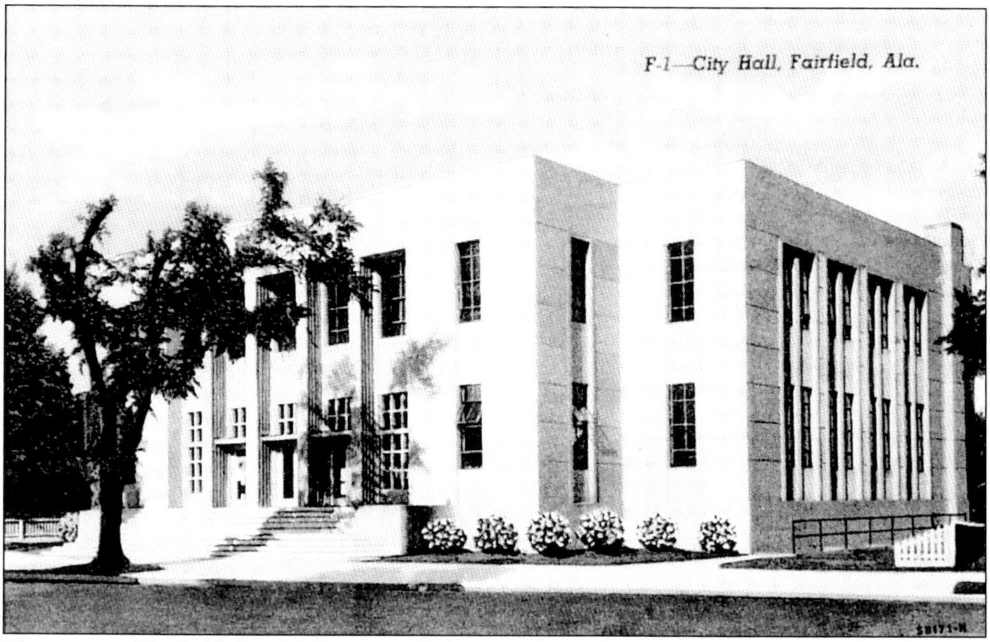

The present Fairfield City Hall, pictured above, is located on Gary Avenue. The building was constructed in 1945 with assistance from the Works Progress Administration. (WS.)

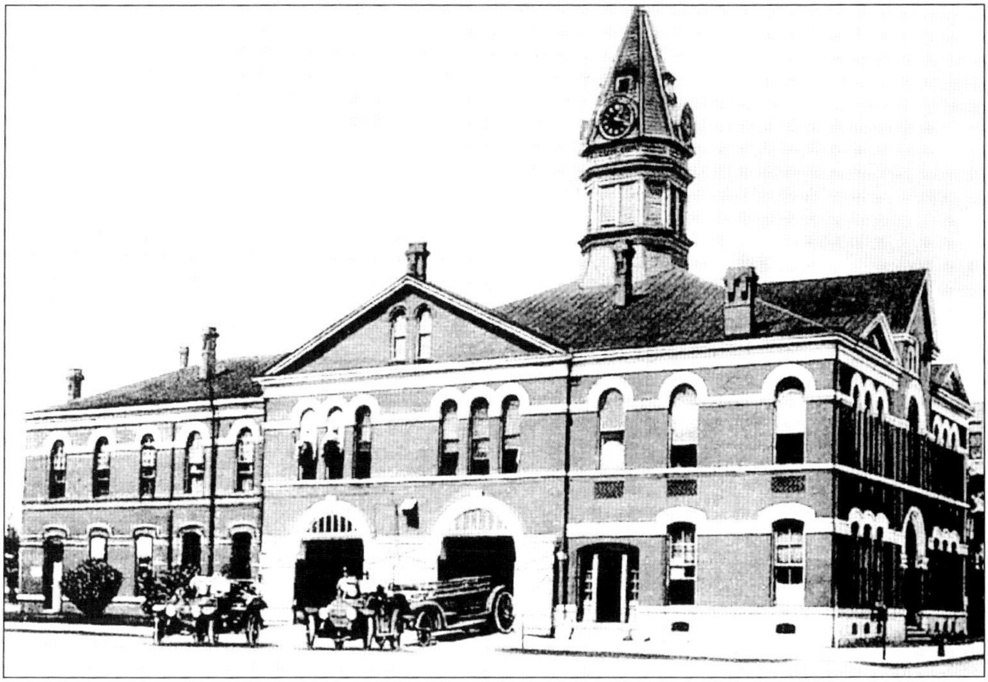

Bessemer's first city hall and fire station, pictured above, was designed by architect G.M. Torgenson and built in 1889 at a cost of $12,000. Located on the corner of Eighteenth Street and Third Avenue, this structure was replaced in 1938 with the new city hall, pictured below. Designed by Charles H. McCauley, this structure was remodeled in 1984. The clock from the tower of the old city hall was saved and placed on the tower of the new structure. (BHH.)

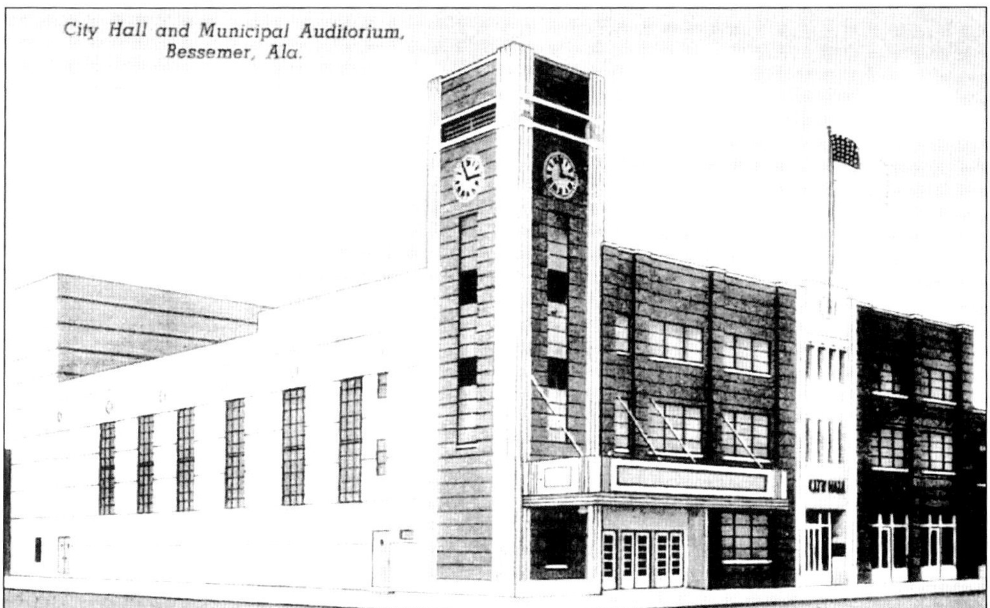

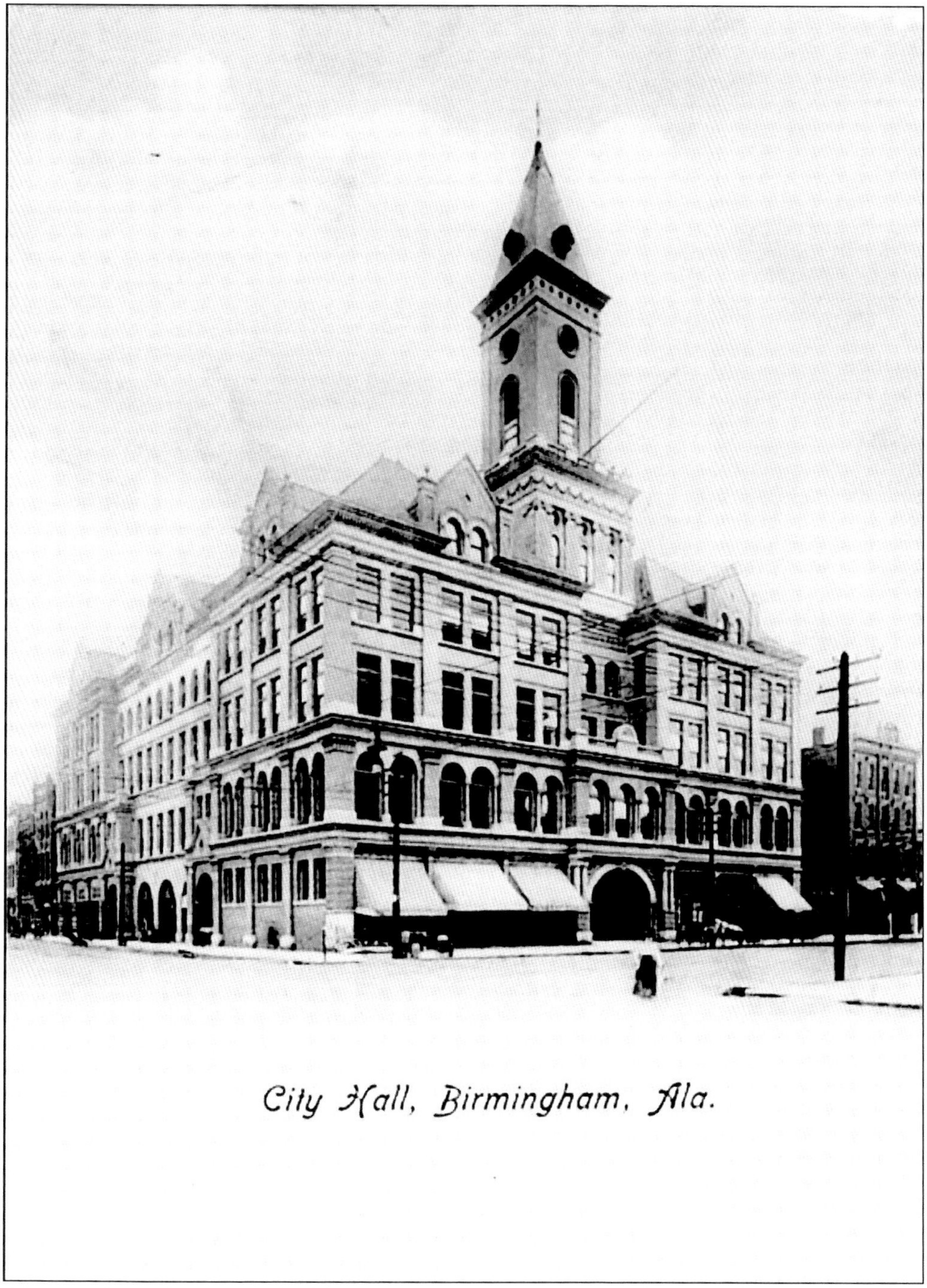

Above and on the top of the following page are two views of the second Birmingham City Hall, constructed in 1901 to replace a smaller structure that had served as city hall since 1881. Located on the corner of Nineteenth Street and Fourth Avenue, North, the building held offices of government, a city market, shops, a fire station, National Guard offices, the public library, and a small museum of art. The building was damaged by fire on at least two occasions, in 1925 and 1944. The first fire destroyed many city records and the public library. (BPLA.)

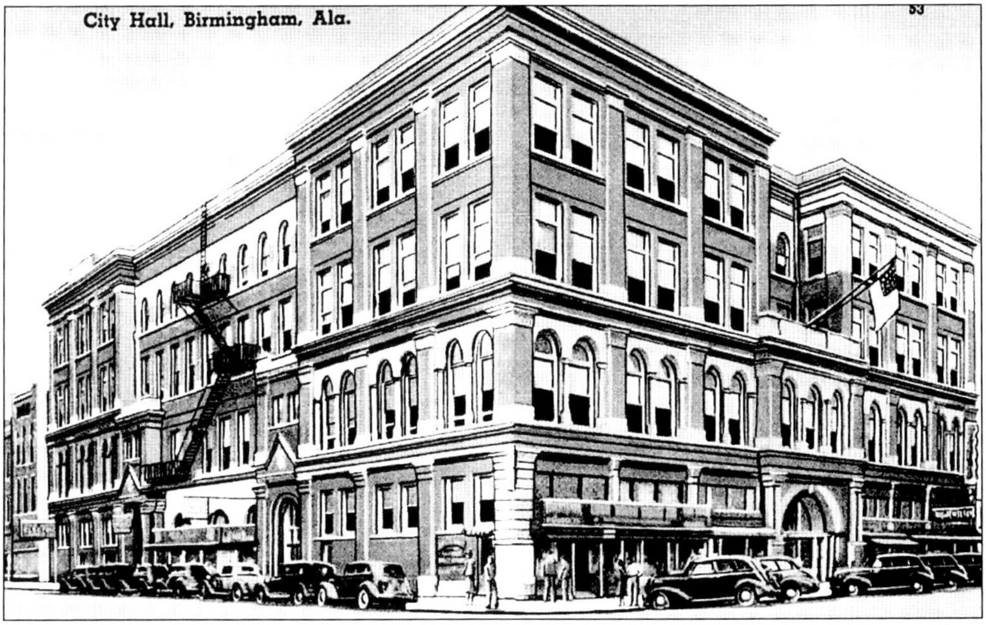

This card shows Birmingham City Hall after the 1925 fire. The damaged tower and upper floor were removed and the building remained in service until a new city hall opened in 1950.

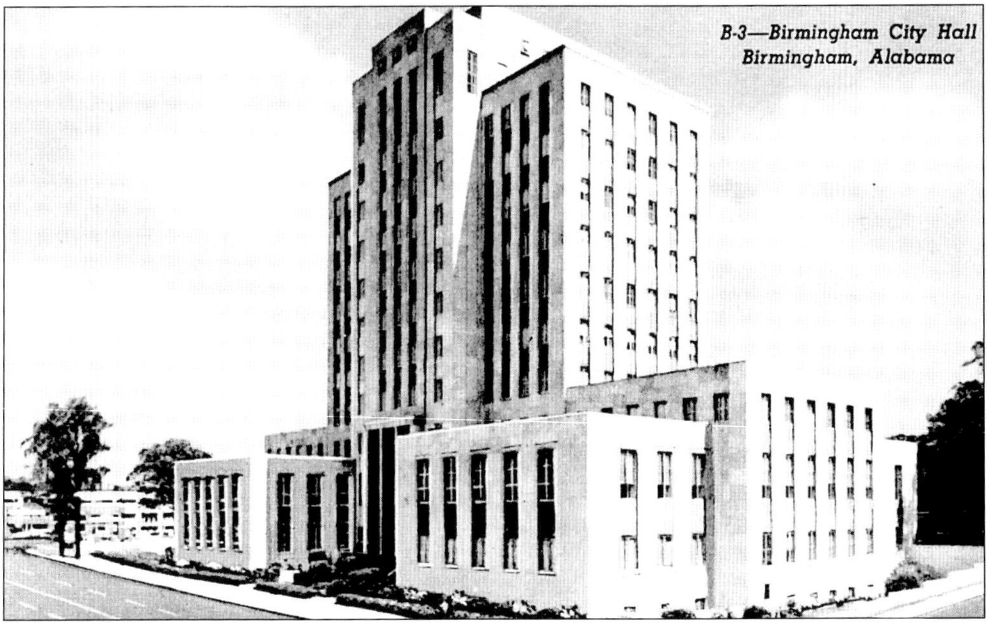

Birmingham's current city hall, seen above and on top of the facing page, opened in 1950. Architect Charles H. McCauley designed the structure, and the city held a grand dedication and "centerstone" laying ceremony in August. Entertainment was provided by the Zamora Temple Shrine Band, and attendees included city officials, Governor Jim Folsom, and the president of the United States Conference of Mayors. Local clergy, including Rev. John W. Goodgame Jr. "Representing Negro Citizens of Birmingham," offered prayers. The city government that moved into this building was headed by three famous names in Birmingham politics—Commissioners James W. "Jimmy" Morgan, W. Cooper Green, and T. Eugene "Bull" Connor. (BPLA.)

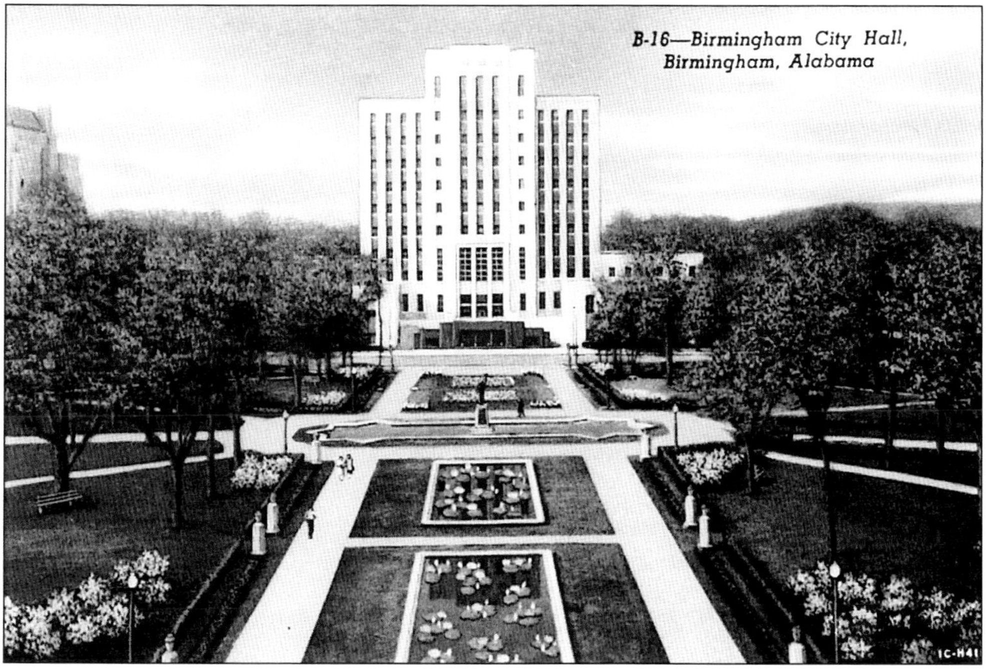

This is Birmingham City Hall as seen from Woodrow Wilson Park (now Linn Park). The view is looking the opposite direction from the view of the courthouse on the top of p. 83.

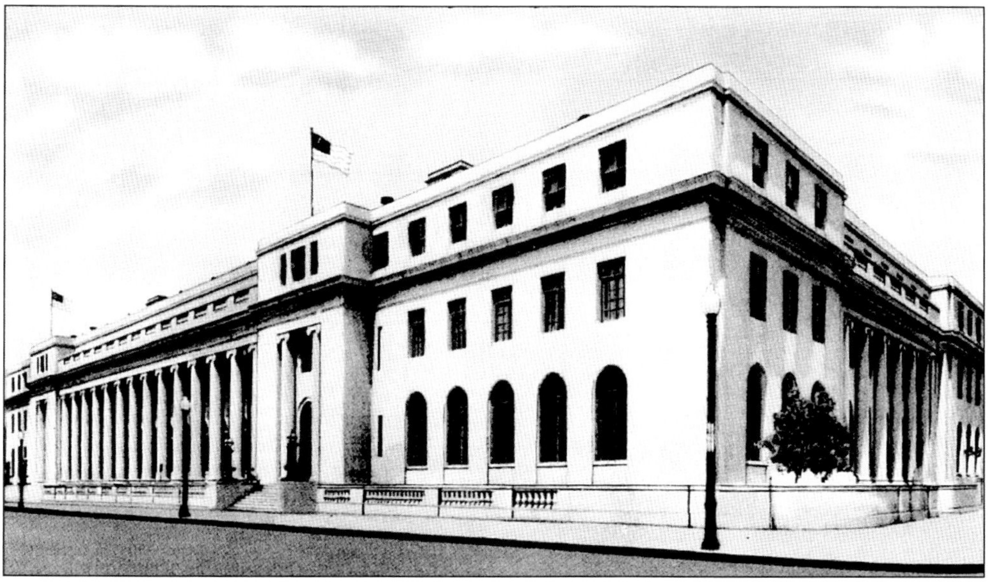

Originally constructed in 1921 to house the downtown post office, this building on Fifth Avenue, North between Eighteenth and Nineteenth Streets is now used primarily as a federal courthouse. The image above shows the building after a third floor was added in the 1940s. The building has been renamed to honor Judge Robert S. Vance, who was killed in a mail bomb attack at his home in 1989.

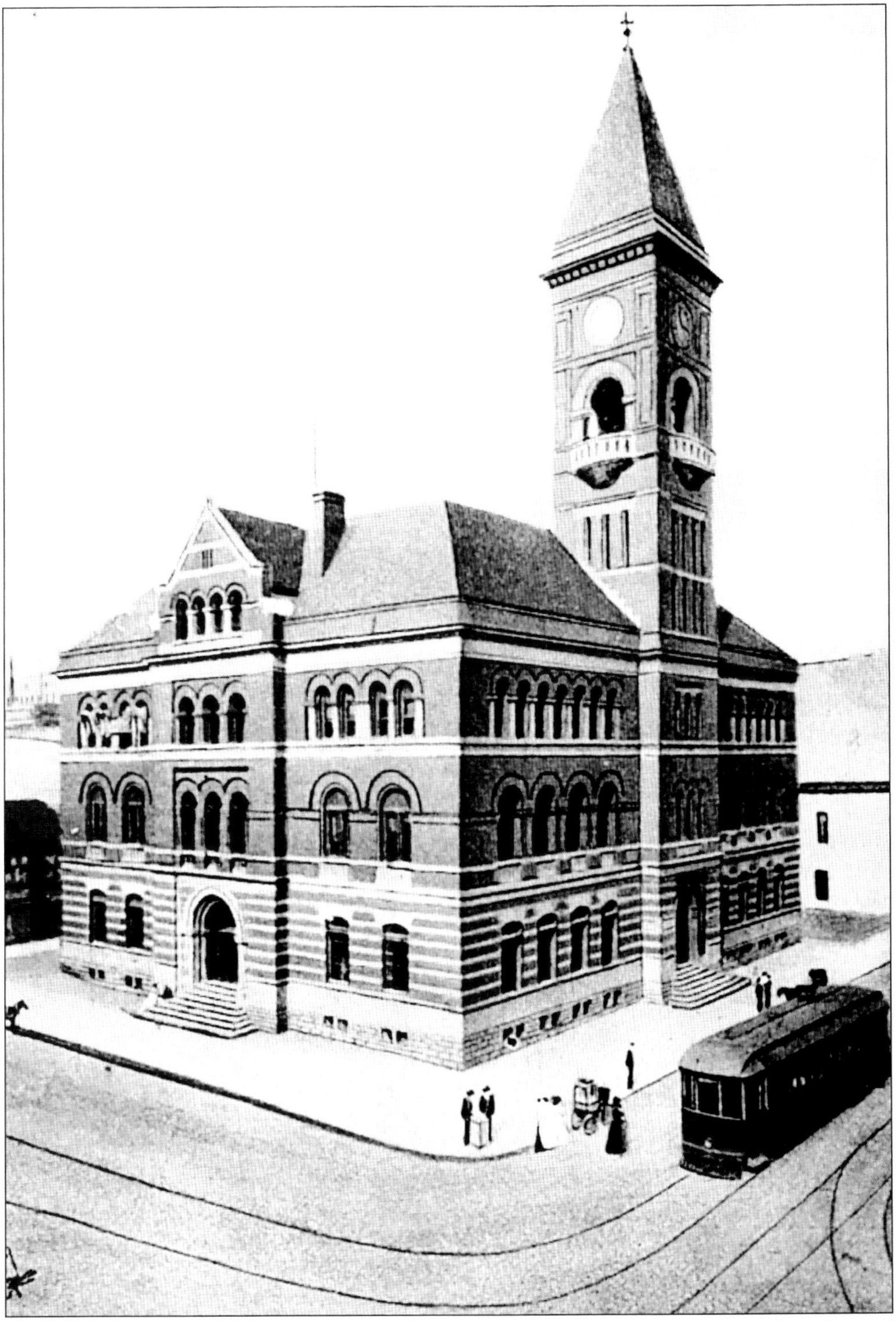

The post office and customhouse pictured above opened on September 1, 1893, and was located on the corner of Second Avenue and Eighteenth Street, North. (BPLA.)

Six

PLACES OF WORSHIP

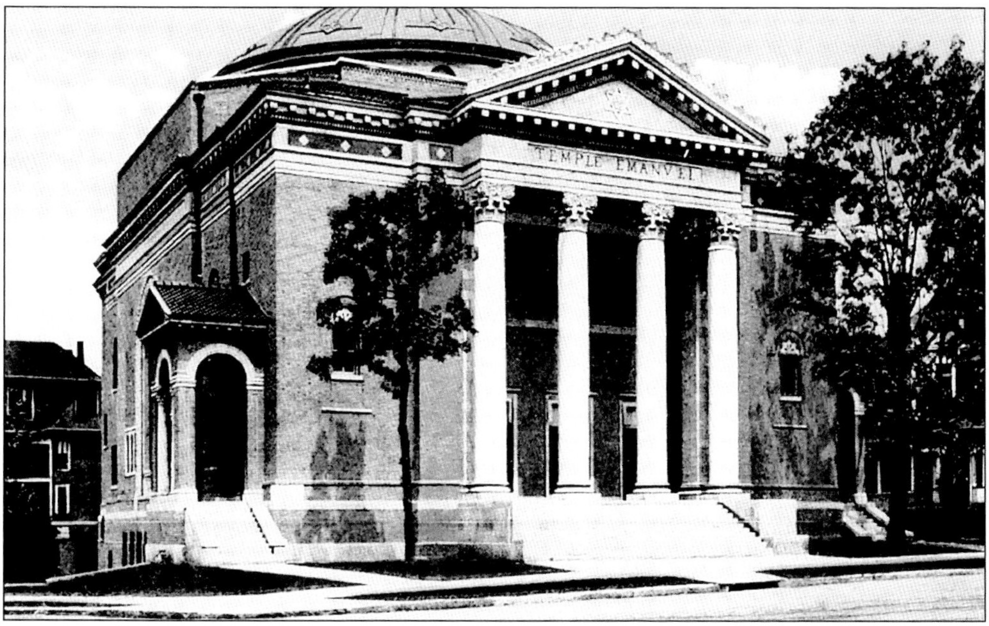

Temple Emanu-El is home to Birmingham's oldest Jewish congregation. The first temple was constructed in 1889 on the corner of Fifth Avenue and Seventeenth Street, North, across the street from the present Kelly Ingram Park. In 1913 the congregation moved to a new temple on Highland Avenue, pictured above. Designed by architect William C. Weston, the structure has very little steel reinforcement, but instead is held together by stress and supported by brick walls varying in thickness from 18 to 24 inches. The 72-foot brass dome is the largest in the Southeast. (BPLA.)

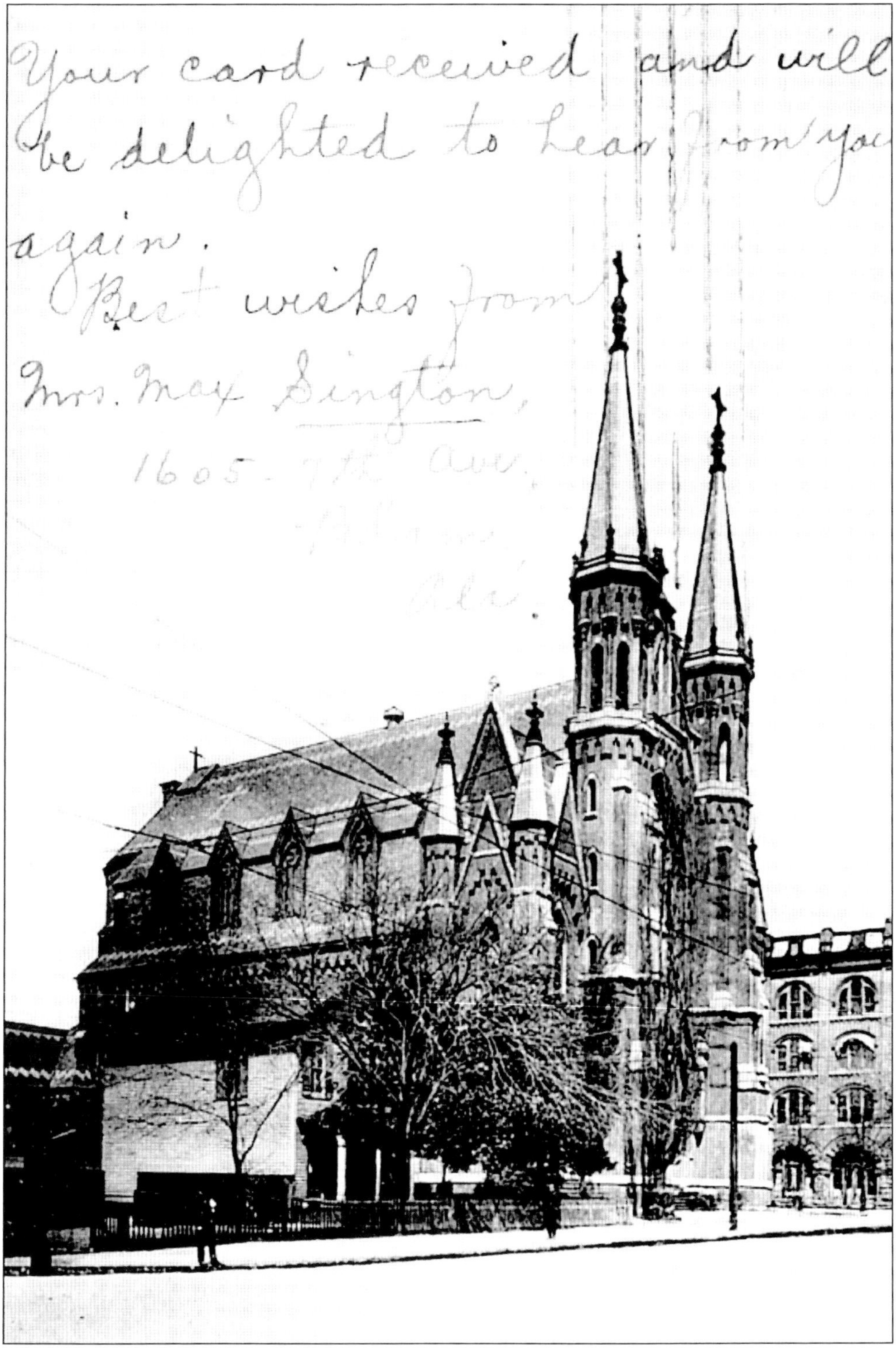
Your card received and will
be delighted to hear from you
again.
Best wishes from
Mrs. Max Sington,
1605 7th Ave.

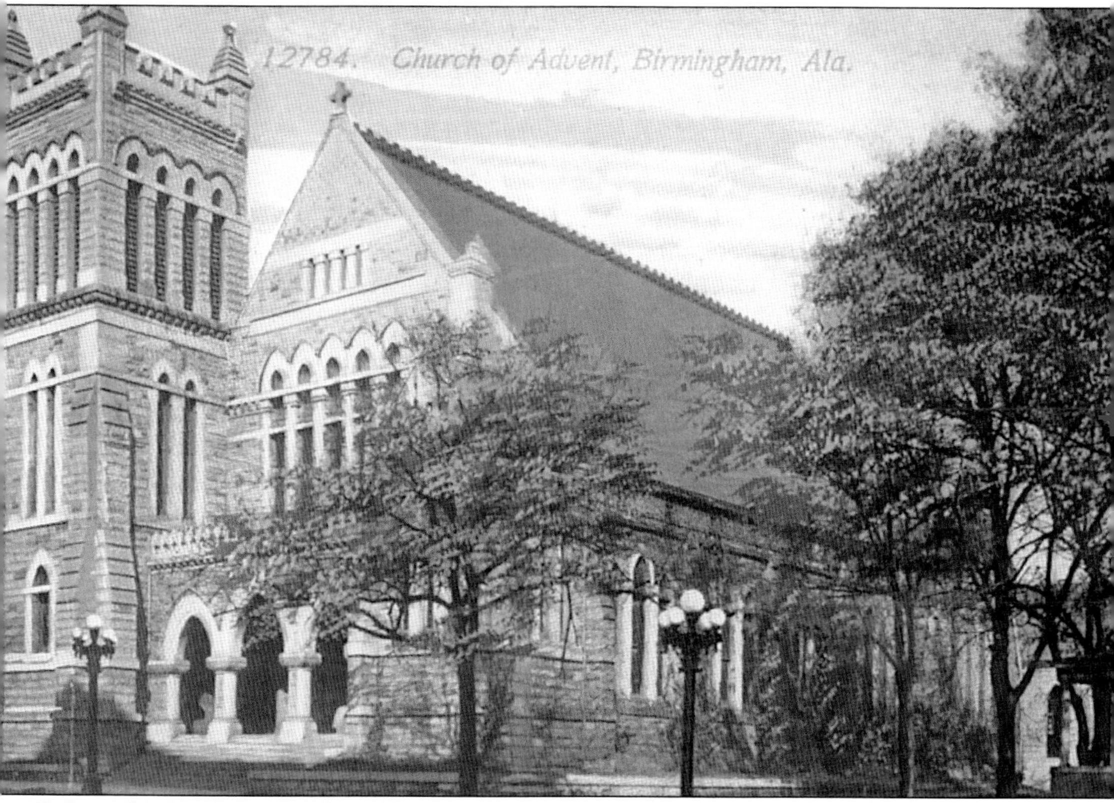

Early in the development of Birmingham, the Elyton Land Company announced that it would donate lots to congregations wishing to build churches in the new city. There is some question whether the first Temple Emanu-El and St. Paul's Catholic Church (pictured on the facing page) were constructed on donated or purchased lots, but at least four other structures—the Church of the Advent (pictured above), and First Methodist Church, First Presbyterian Church, and First Baptist Church (all pictured on the following pages)—were built on lots donated by the company.

On the facing page, St. Paul's Catholic Church, founded in 1872, was the first Roman Catholic Church in Jefferson County. A small wooden structure was built near the site, located on the corner of Twenty-second Street and Third Avenue, North, and replaced by the present building in 1893. Designed by the Druding Company, a Chicago architectural firm, the church now serves as the cathedral of the north Alabama Catholic diocese.

The postcard of St. Paul's, mailed in 1906, marks a milestone in postcard history. Prior to 1907 postal regulations allowed only for an address to be written on the verso of a postcard. If the sender wished to include a message, it had to be written on the image side of the card, as was done here. In 1907 this regulation was changed, leading to the introduction of the "divided back" card that we have today, with space on the right for the address and space on the left for a message. (BPLA.)

The Church of the Advent, pictured above, is the cathedral of the Episcopal Diocese of Alabama. Designed by architect Charles Wheelock, a member of the church, this 1893 structure replaced an earlier wooden building. Advent was the first Episcopal Church founded in Birmingham, and the second in Jefferson County. (BPLA.)

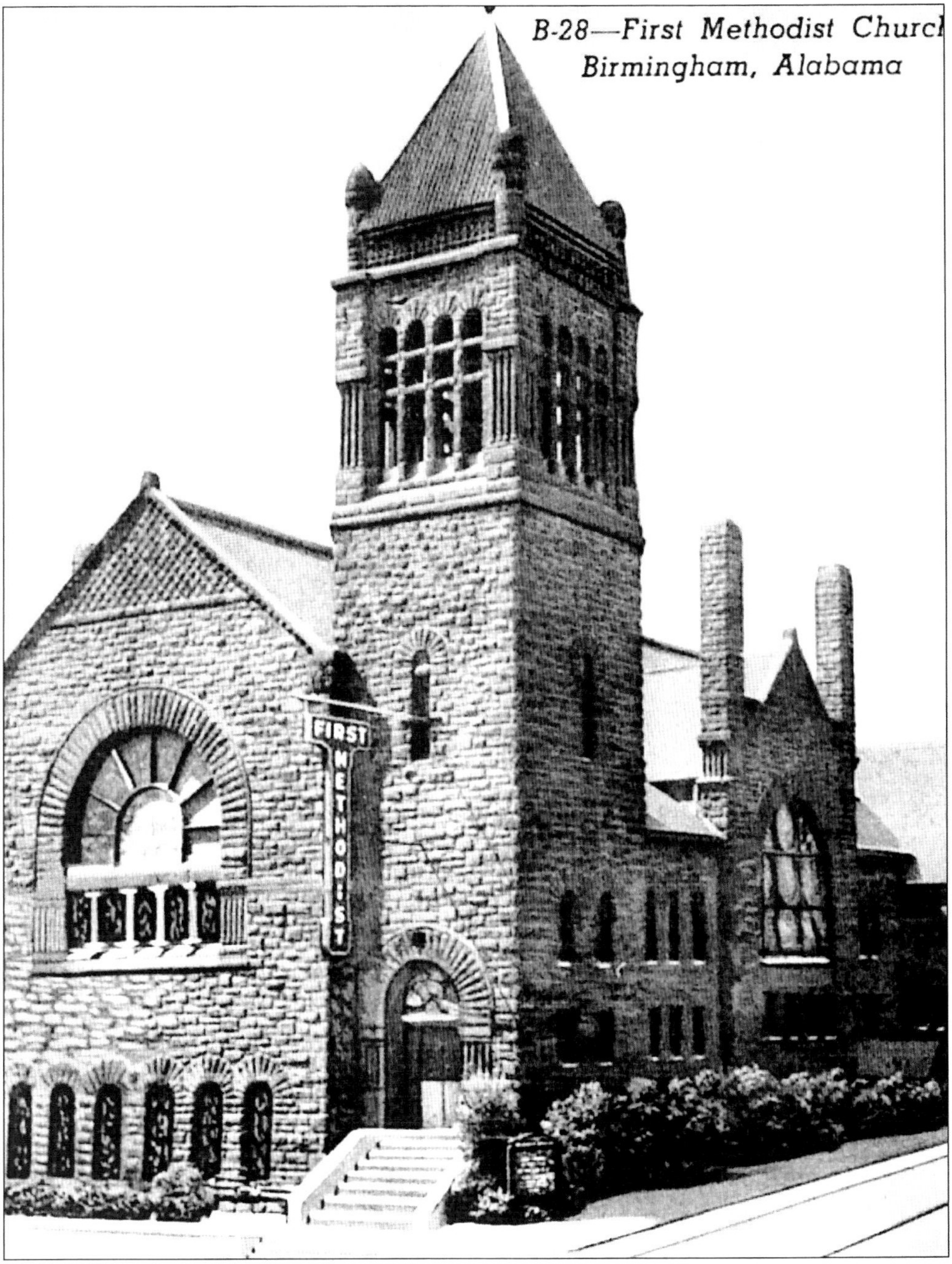

The present First United Methodist Church, pictured above, is the third home and third location for Birmingham's oldest Methodist congregation. Originally called the First Methodist Episcopal Church, South, the congregation occupied a building at the corner of Sixth Avenue and Twenty-first Street, North, later the site for the Essex House and now the site of Energen Plaza. By 1881 the church had moved to a new structure on the corner of Fourth Avenue and Nineteenth Street, North. In 1891 the church moved a final time to the building on the corner of Nineteenth Street and Sixth Avenue, North. This structure was designed by Weary and Kramer, Ohio architects. (BPLA.)

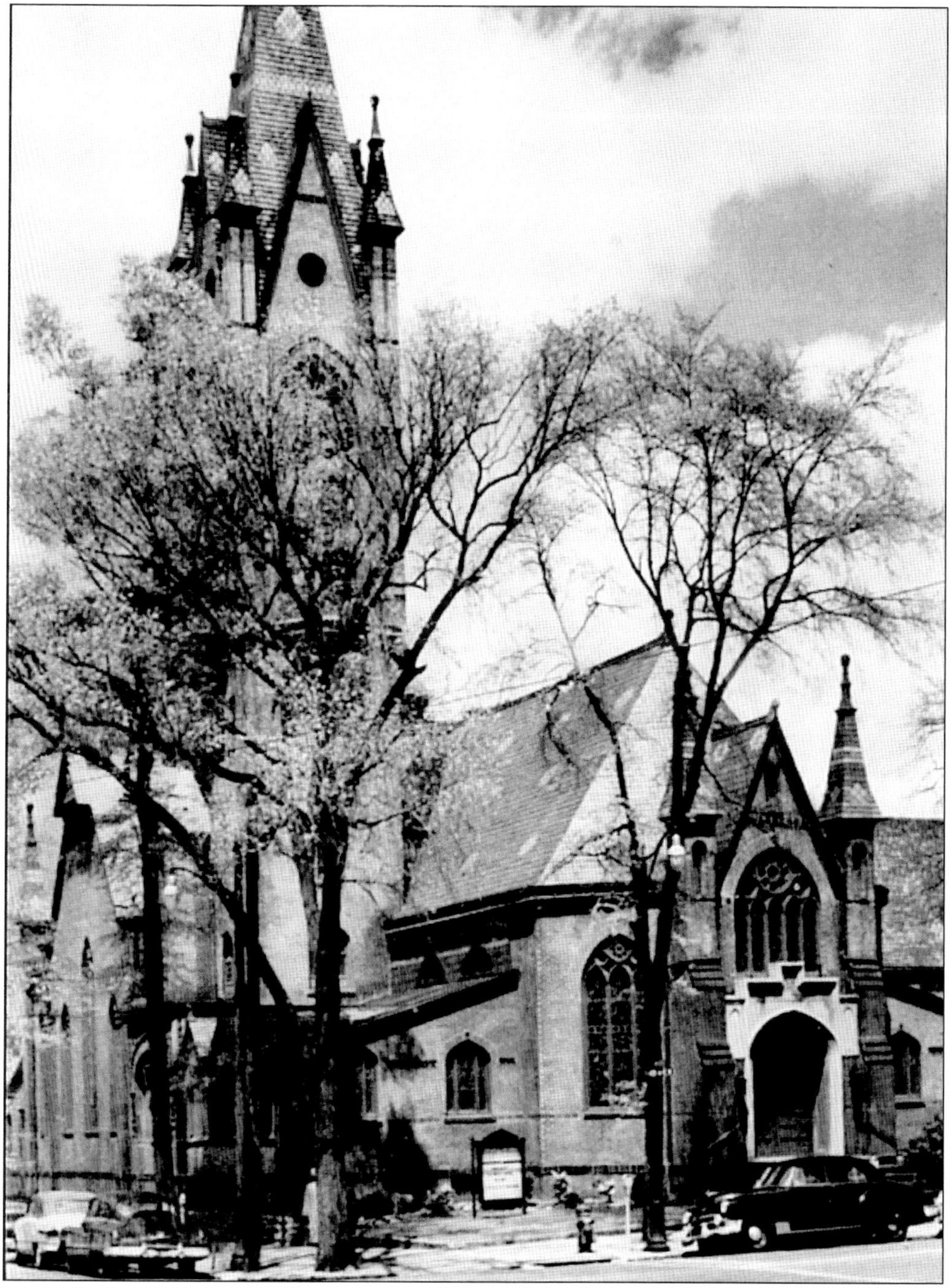

Established in 1872, First Presbyterian Church is another of Birmingham's "mother" or "pioneer" churches. The present structure, located on the corner of Fourth Avenue and Twenty-first Street, North, was completed in 1888, but the church began as the Old School Presbyterian Church in Elyton in 1858. When the Elyton Land Company announced the policy of giving free lots to churches, First Presbyterian was the first congregation to select a site and construct a building in 1872. The congregation quickly outgrew the church, and the present building was erected across the street. (BPLA.)

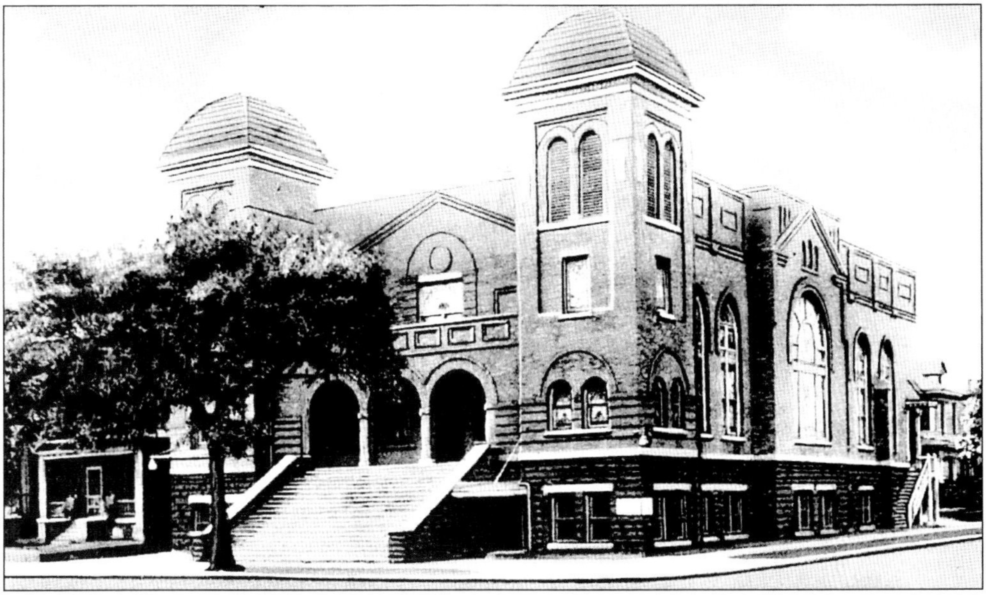

Founded in 1873, the First Colored Baptist Church of Birmingham became Sixteenth Street Baptist after moving to its present location in 1884. An earlier structure was replaced in 1911 with the building pictured above. Designed by African-American architect Wallace A. Rayfield, the church façade includes a stained-glass window donated by the people of Wales after the church was bombed by members of the Ku Klux Klan in 1963. Now a part of the Birmingham Civil Rights District, the church sits across the street from Kelly Ingram Park and the Birmingham Civil Rights Institute. (BPLA.)

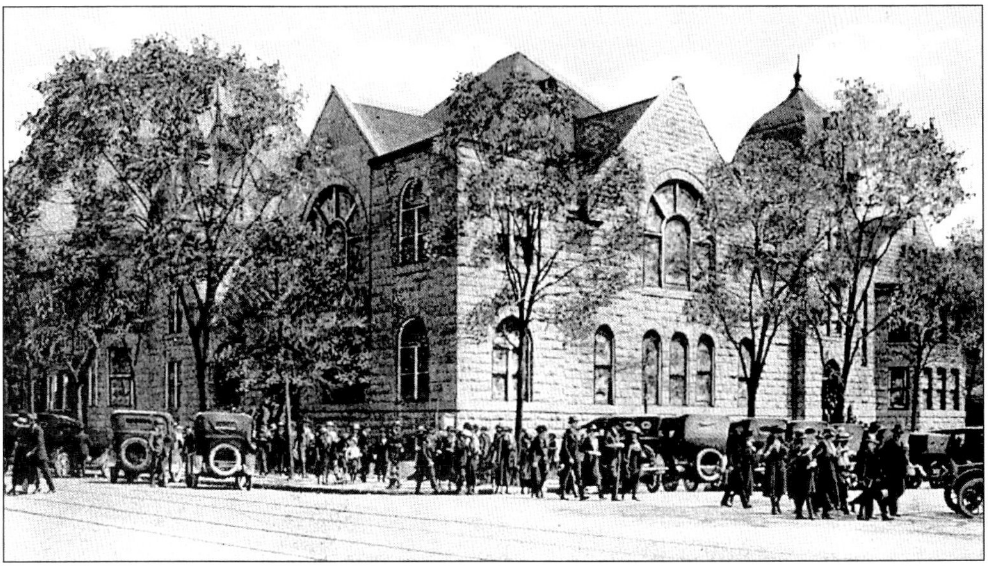

Like other early Birmingham churches, First Baptist Church grew and prospered along with the new city. Originally housed in a small wooden building, the church moved to a second wood frame structure (which was condemned in 1901) before settling into the Romanesque stone building pictured above. Designed by Chattanooga architect R.H. Hunt, this church was located on Sixth Avenue and Twenty-second Street, North. The present First Baptist Church is located on Lakeshore Drive. (BPLA.)

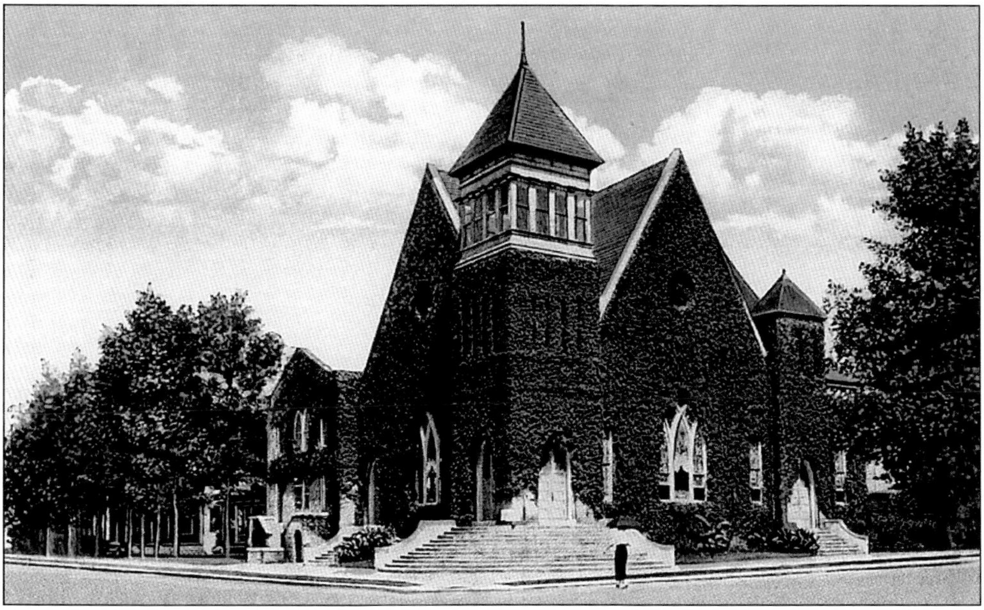

First Baptist Church of Bessemer was organized in 1881, and the nine original members met at the Red Mountain School. Later the congregation moved to a small wooden building on Nineteenth Street and Seventh Avenue. The church pictured here, located on the corner of Fifth Avenue and Eighteenth Street, was built on a pay-as-you-go plan. Construction began in 1904 but funds were soon depleted. In 1905 enough money was raised to roof the building, and in 1907 construction was completed. This building was razed about 1963 and the congregation moved to a new structure. (BPLA.)

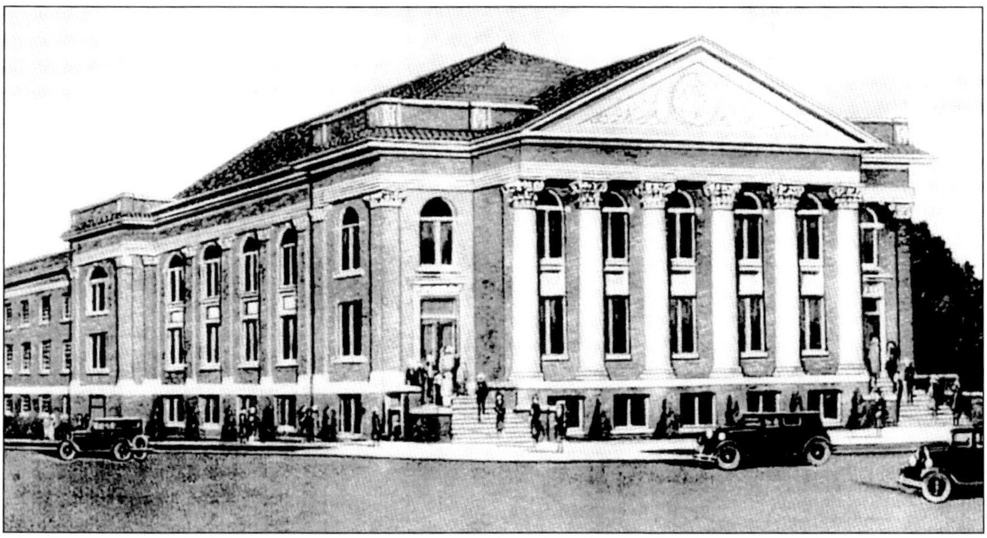

On September 15, 1929, the congregation of the South Highlands Baptist Church marched as a group down Dartmouth Avenue from their old church building to this new structure on Nineteenth Street, South. The stock market crashed six weeks later, and during the Great Depression the congregation struggled to make the payments on their new building. But in 1945 the mortgage was paid in full, with local mining engineer and philanthropist Erskine Ramsay donating the final $1,000. (BHH.)

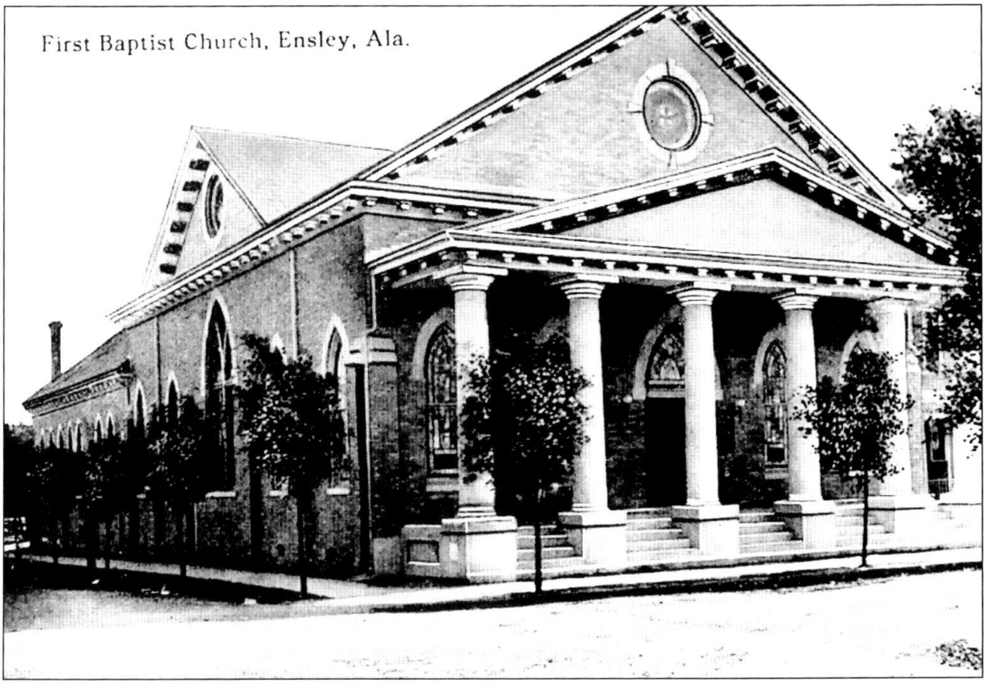

Ensley's First Baptist Church began in 1900 as a mission with a congregation of 55 people. By 1912 the church had grown large enough to construct the brick building of neo-classic design pictured above, on the corner of Eighteenth Street and Avenue G. Over the next two decades First Baptist would become one of the leading Southern Baptist churches, and would outgrow this building. The new, larger church pictured below was later constructed at Avenue E and Twenty-third Street. (BPLA.)

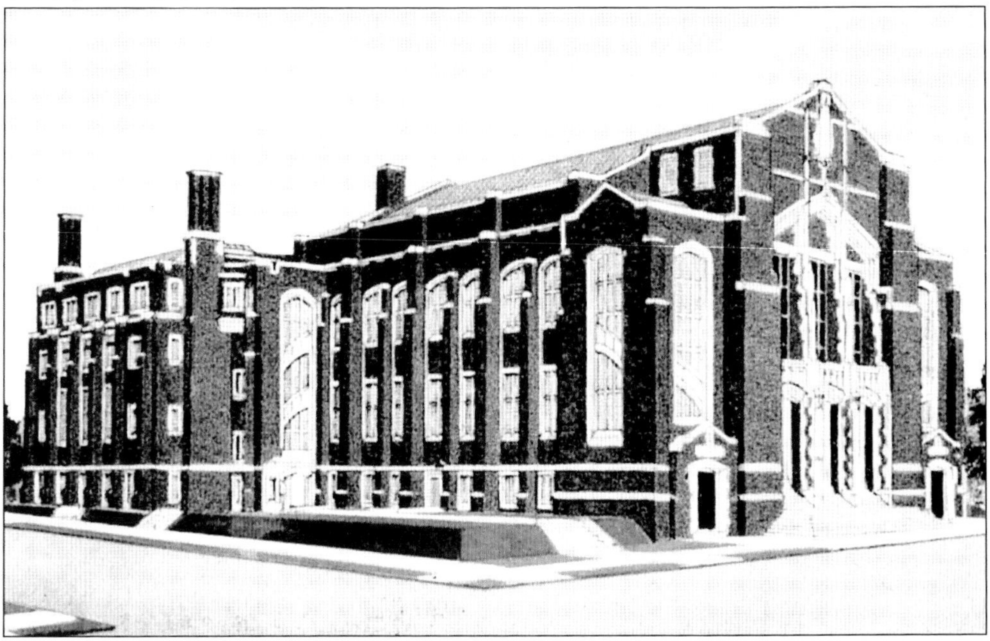

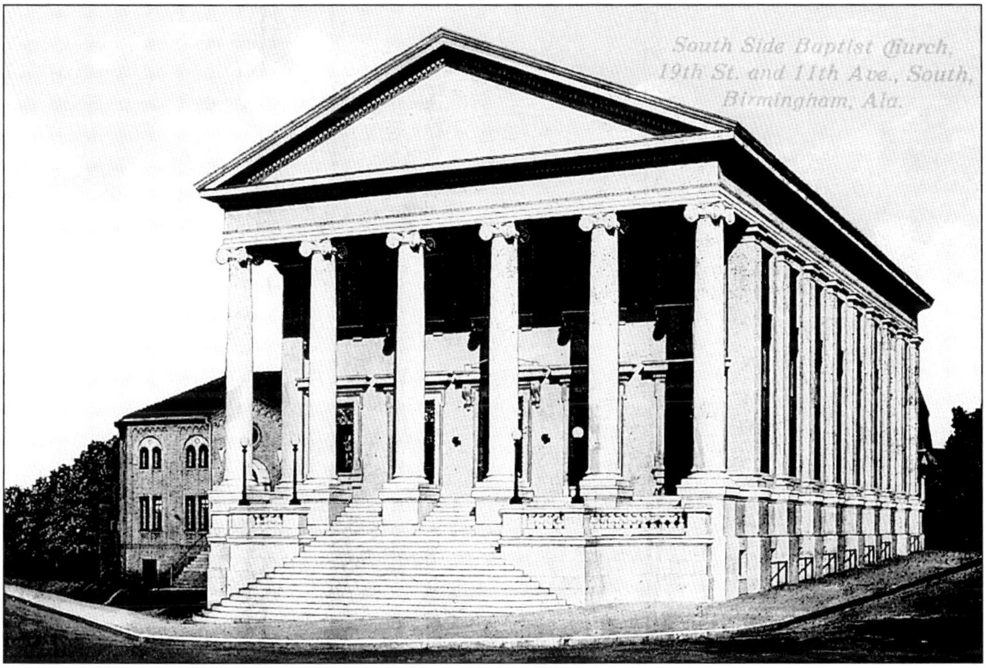

The Southside Baptist Church congregation was established in 1886. Forty-three of the church's original 70 members had defected from First Baptist downtown. In later years older members of the church would refer to their first wood-frame building as "the old barn." The congregation's fifth and present church, located just off Five Points South, is this 1911 structure designed by William Leslie Welton. (BPLA.)

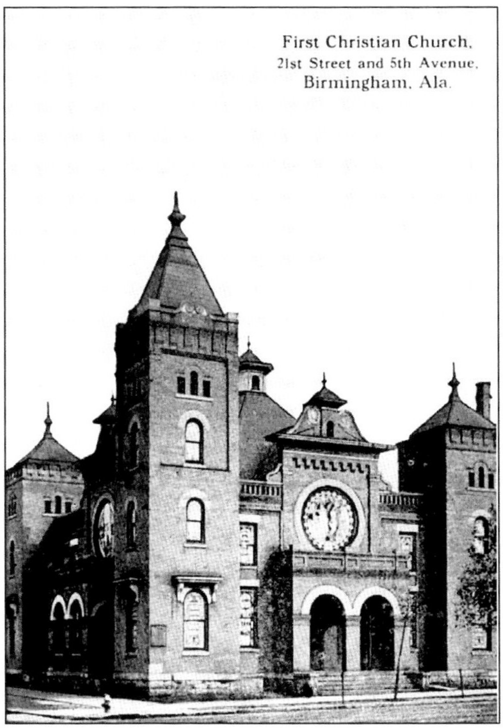

Members of the First Christian Church built this brick sanctuary in 1904 on the same site at Fifth Avenue and Twenty-first Street, North where they had worshiped in a frame building since 1899. The large stained-glass window over the entrance depicts angels surrounding the tomb of Christ. This window was moved with the church to a new Seventh Avenue location, where it was placed over the baptistery. The window was moved again when the church relocated to Valleydale Road. The Redmont Hotel now occupies the site pictured here. (BPLA.)

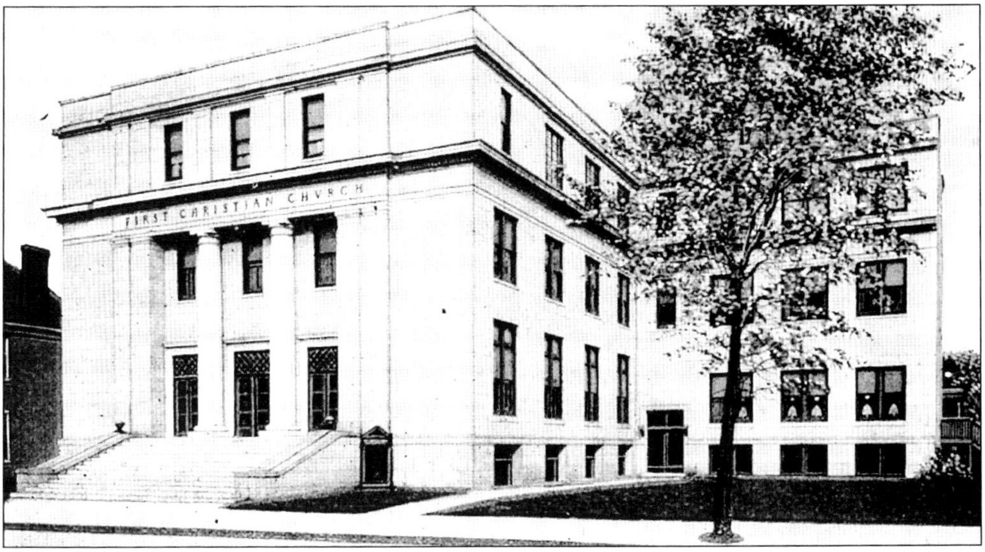

By 1924 the First Christian Church had outgrown the Fifth Avenue sanctuary pictured on the previous page. The structure shown above was constructed facing Twenty-first Street, North, and served as the church until 1955, when a Neo-Georgian sanctuary was erected at the corner of Seventh Avenue. The 1924 structure was remodeled and used as an education building. In 1980 the church held its last worship service here, and relocated to Valleydale Road in north Shelby County. The building pictured above is now part of the Jefferson County Courthouse complex. (BPLA.)

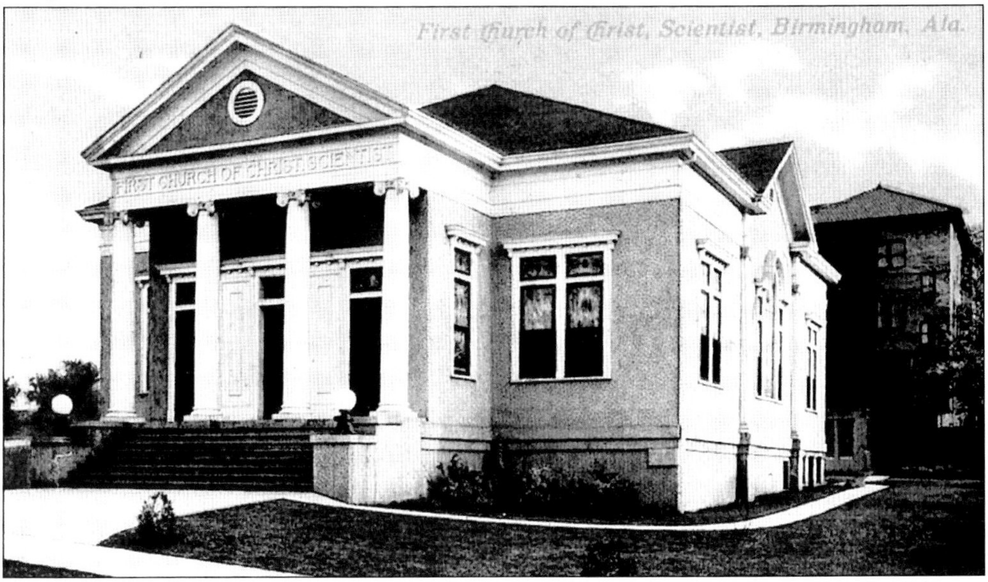

This stucco building was constructed in 1911 to serve the members of the First Church of Christ, Scientist, organized in Birmingham in 1899. Two large stained-glass windows graced the church, one representing the Bible and the other representing founder Mary Baker Eddy's concepts of "science and health." In 1950 the congregation moved to a larger structure on Highland Avenue. In the early 1950s Dr. Earl Conwell opened an orthopedic clinic in this building. The old church sat empty for a time in the 1960s, but the architectural firm of Giattina, Mitchell, and Crawford bought the building in 1974 and restored it for use as offices. (BPLA.)

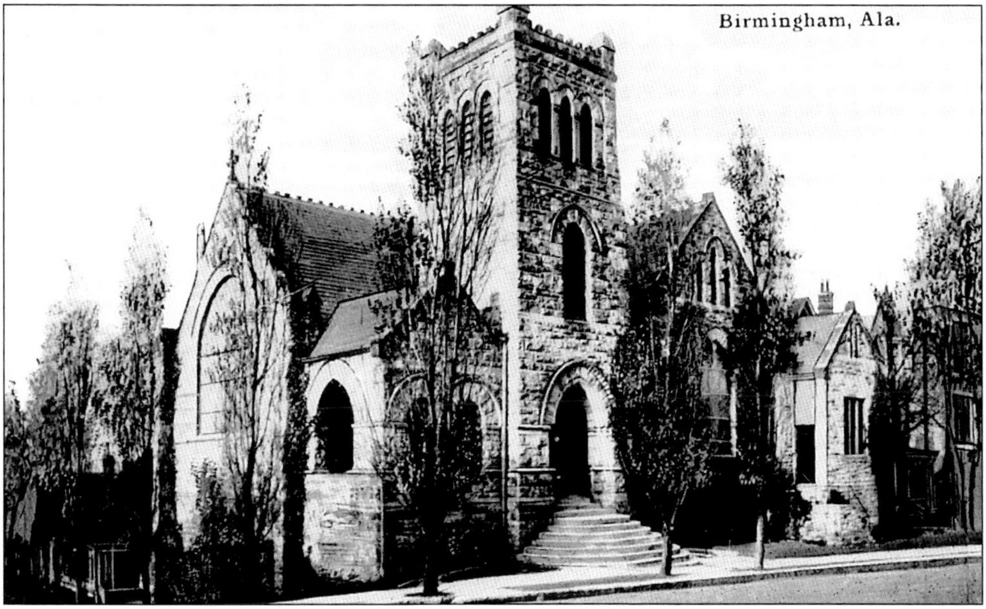

The first St. Mary's Episcopal Church was a wood-frame structure that stood approximately where the Pickwick Hotel (Medical Arts Building) is located today. After this church was destroyed by fire in 1890, the congregation purchased a lot on the corner of Nineteenth Street and Twelfth Avenue, South for a new stone structure. Pictured above, this church was designed by architect John Sutcliffe and completed in 1892. (BPLA.)

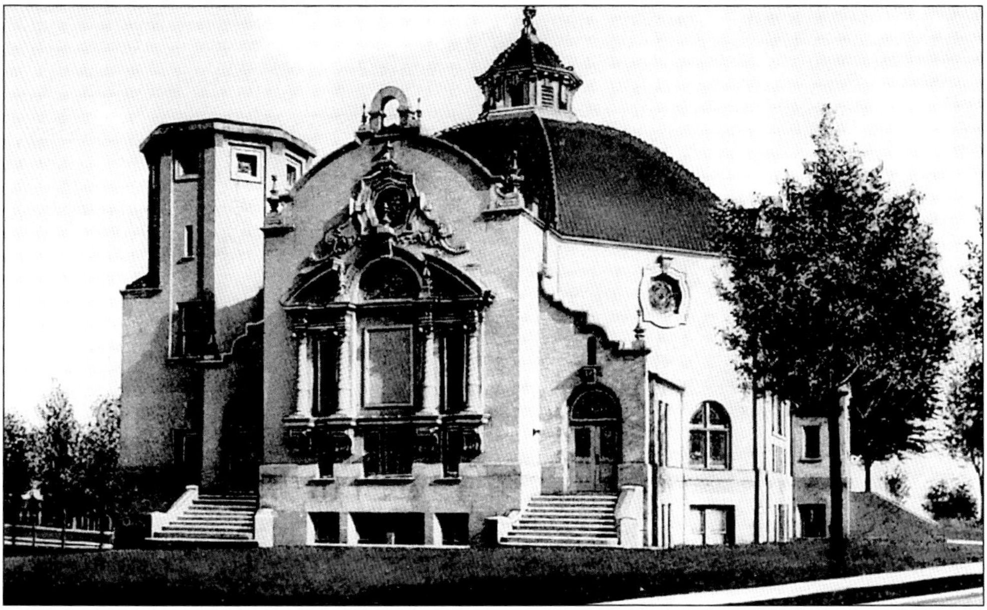

Although many argue that Highlands Methodist Church at Five Points South was designed by New York architect Stanford White, all evidence suggests that the designer was actually P. Thornton Marye of Atlanta. Marye also designed Birmingham's Terminal Station. Opening in 1909, many of the charter members of this church had come from First Methodist downtown to found a new church in Highland. The image above shows the building before the completion of the tower. (BPLA.)

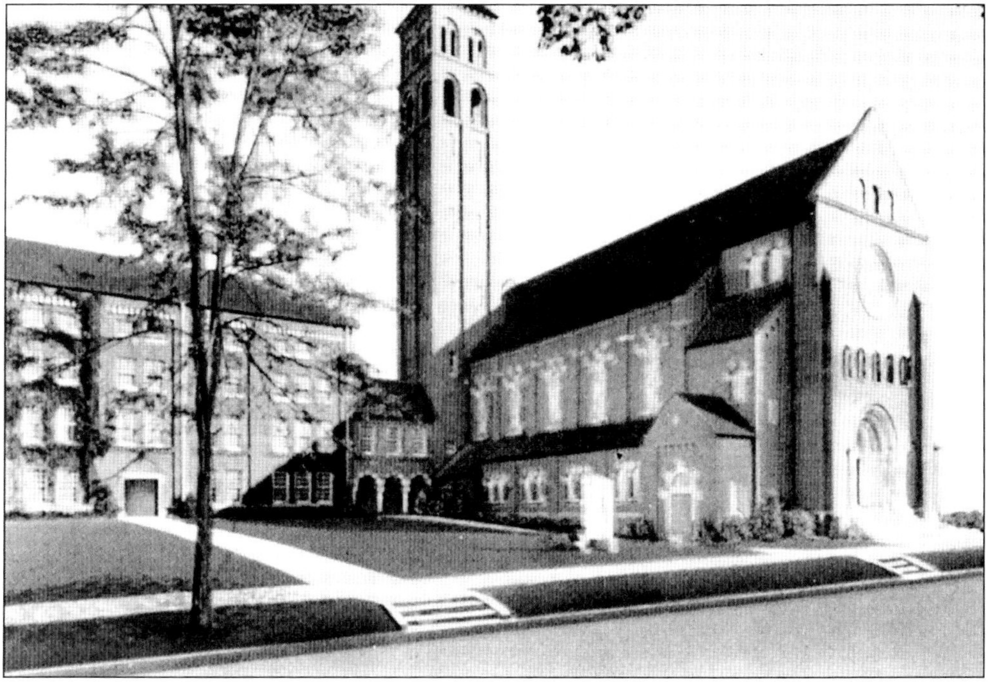

The East Lake Methodist Church was organized in 1887 as a mission. The first church building was constructed in 1889 on a lot sold to the congregation by the East Lake Land Company for $1. Less than two years later the first church had been outgrown, and a second building was completed in 1891. The building shown above, called the "brick sanctuary," opened in 1948. (BPLA.)

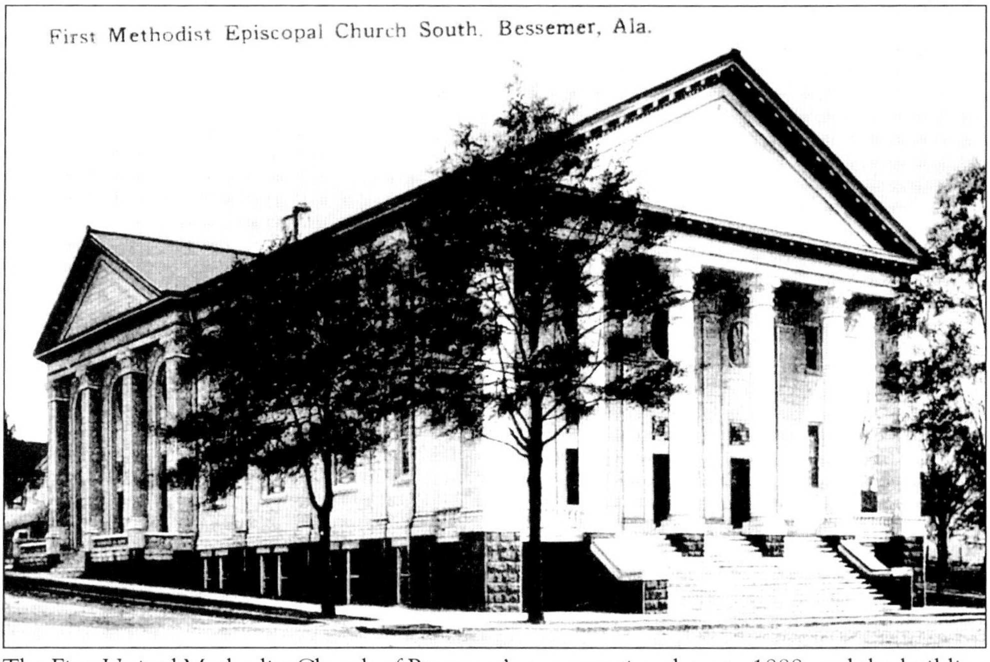

The First United Methodist Church of Bessemer's congregation dates to 1888, and the building pictured here was completed in 1911. The church is located on Arlington Avenue. (BHH.)

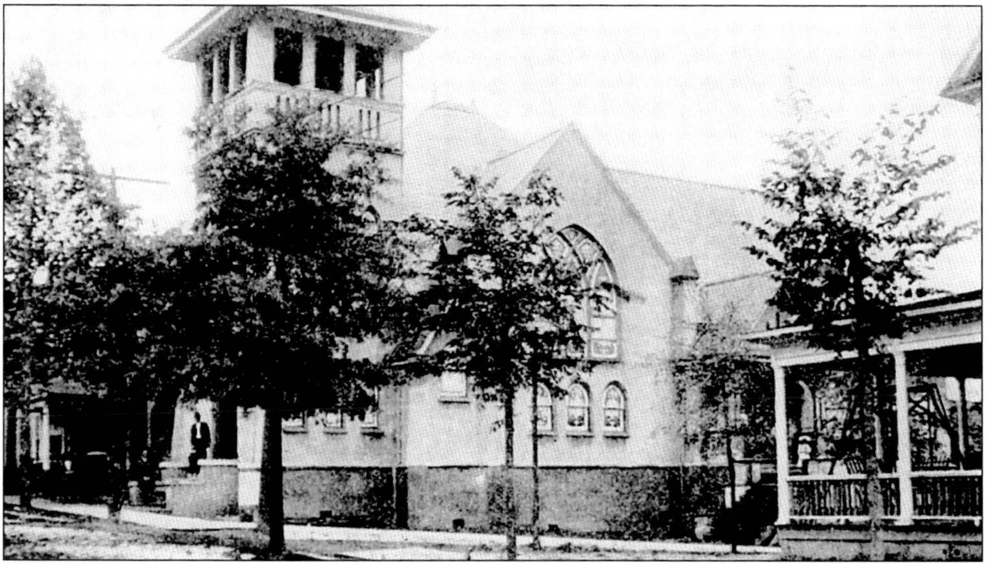

A Methodist congregation was first organized in Pratt City in 1884 and named the Pratt Mines Methodist Episcopal Church, South. The first meeting place was a short distance from Slope #1 of the Pratt Coal and Coke Company mines. In 1938 the church shown here was located at Third Avenue (now Avenue U) and Third Street. The building housed the First M.E. congregation until 1973, and is now home to the Original Miracle Deliverance Temple. (SG.)

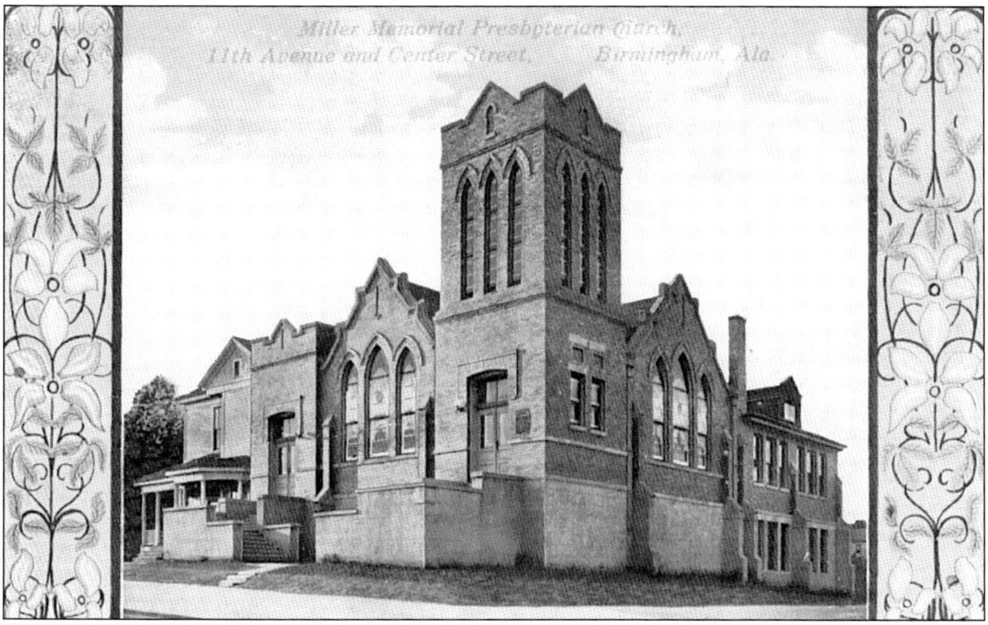

The red brick church pictured here was constructed in 1905 in part with funds provided by the Board of Mission for Freedmen of the Presbyterian Church, USA. The Miller Memorial Presbyterian Church took its name to honor J.H. Miller, the African-American attorney who drafted the church's articles of incorporation in 1896. Adjoining the church on the left was the parsonage, and at the right rear was a two-story wing used for the church school and a community kindergarten. The building was demolished about 1966, but was replaced in 1971 with another church structure on the same site. (BPLA.)

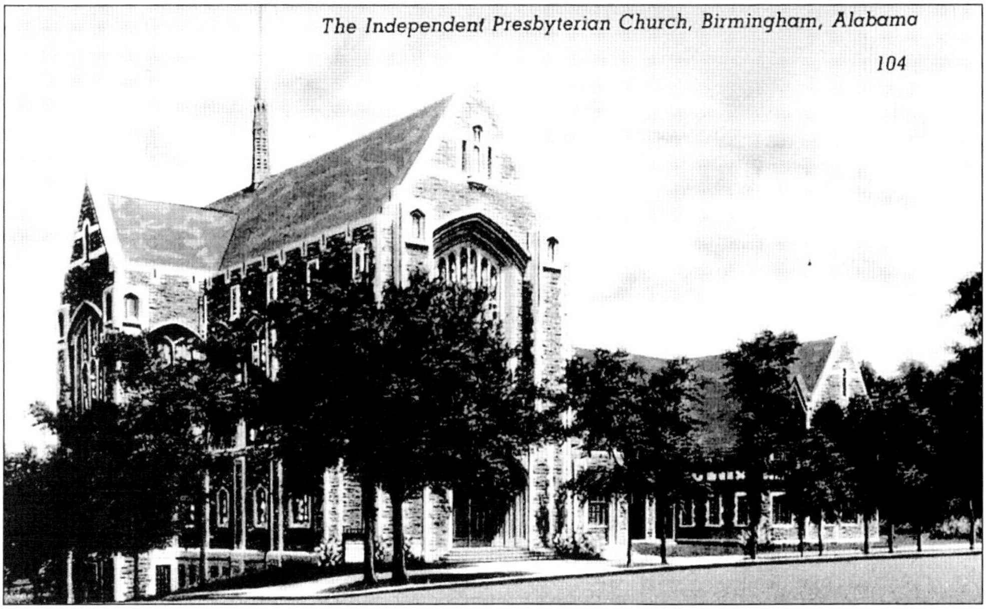

In 1915 Henry M. Edmonds, pastor of South Highlands Presbyterian Church, resigned his position in a doctrinal dispute with the North Alabama Presbytery. When Edmonds left South Highlands, more than half of the congregation chose to follow him and together they founded the Independent Presbyterian Church. After meeting for seven years at Temple Emanu-El (see p. 89), the congregation moved to the church pictured above when it was completed in 1926. Located on Highland Avenue, the English Gothic structure was designed by two architectural firms, Warren, Knight and Davis and Miller, Martin and Lewis. (BPLA.)

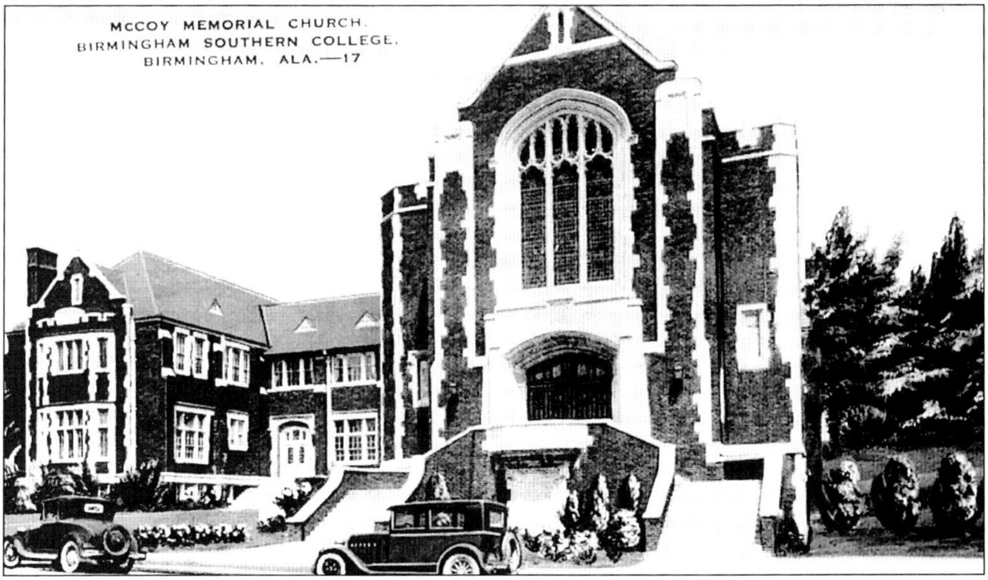

The congregation that would eventually become the McCoy United Methodist Church was organized in 1901 on the campus of the North Alabama Conference College (later Birmingham College, and finally Birmingham-Southern). The structure pictured on this postcard, located on Eighth Avenue, West and Arkadelphia Road across from the Birmingham-Southern campus, was completed in 1925. (BPLA.)

Seven

PLACES OF LEARNING

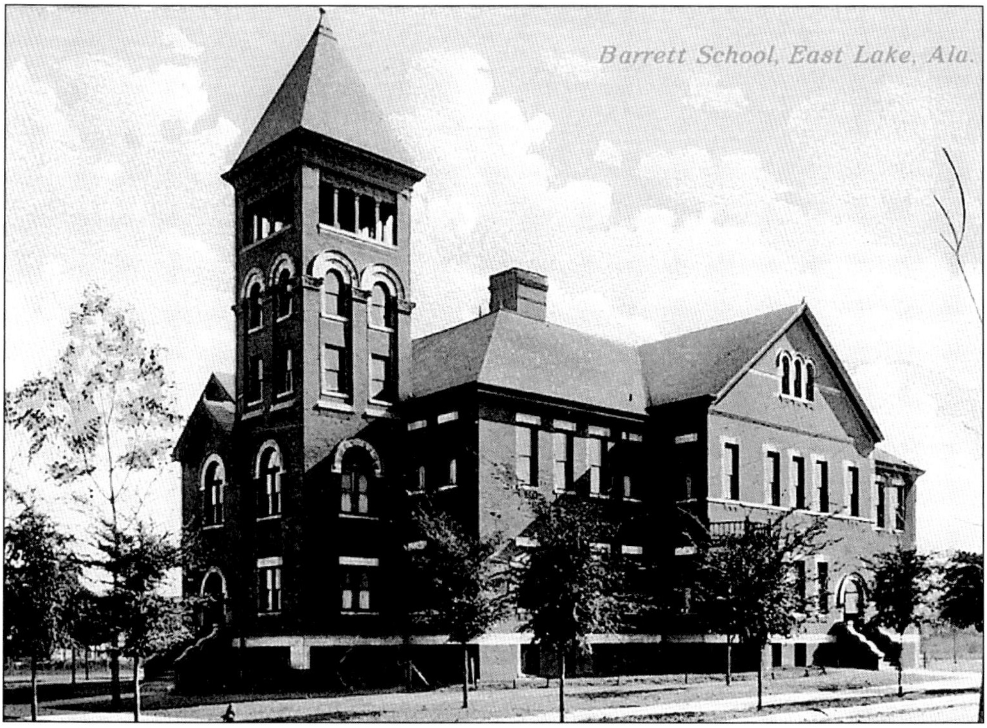

Barrett School was named for Dr. Nathaniel A. Barrett, a physician who served as mayor of East Lake before the town was annexed into Birmingham in 1910. Dr. Barrett was elected mayor of Birmingham in 1917 with the strong support of the "True Americans," a political faction that hoped to rid Birmingham of "immigrant influences." Built in 1901, Barrett School is located at Division Avenue and Seventy-sixth Street, South. (BPLA.)

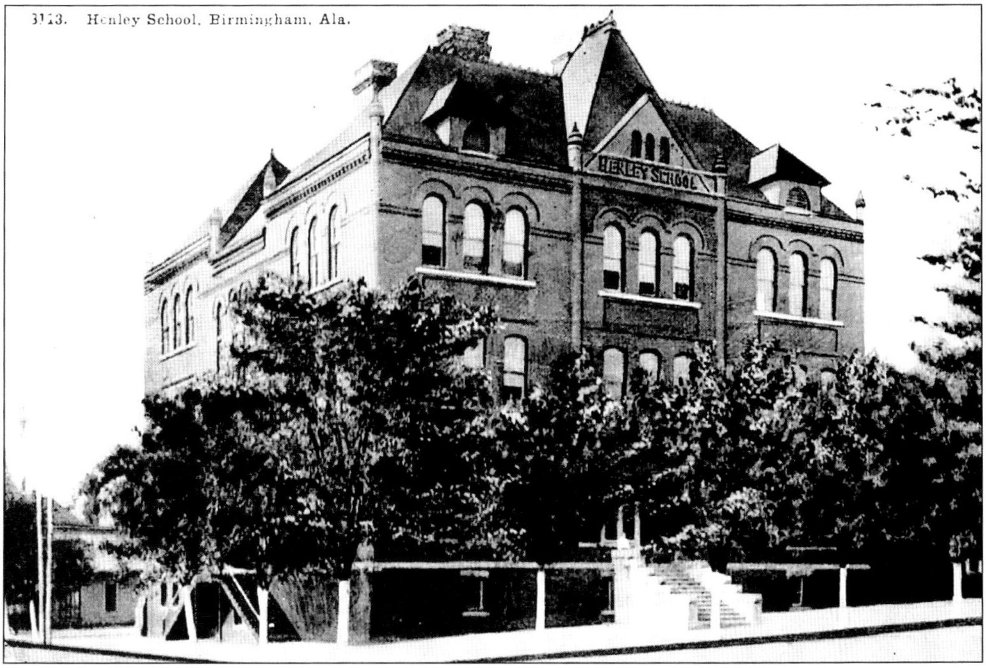

This postcard shows the second Henley School, named for Birmingham's first mayor Robert H. Henley, and located at Sixth Avenue and Seventeenth Street, North. The first Henley School was a wood-frame structure built in 1887 at the same site. (BPLA.)

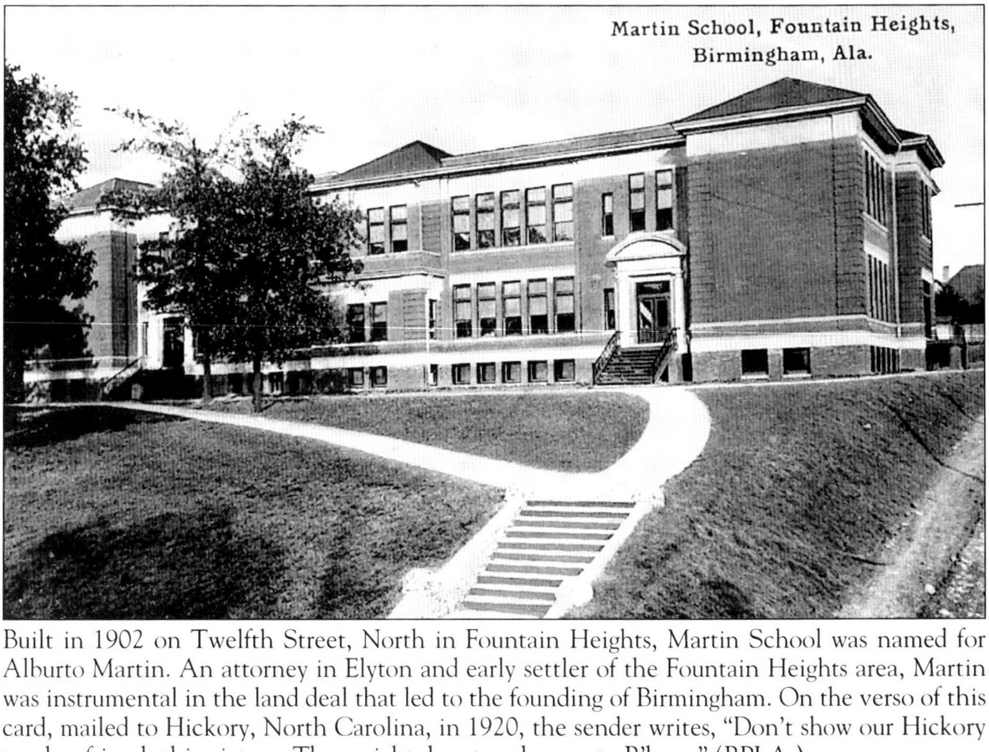

Built in 1902 on Twelfth Street, North in Fountain Heights, Martin School was named for Alburto Martin. An attorney in Elyton and early settler of the Fountain Heights area, Martin was instrumental in the land deal that led to the founding of Birmingham. On the verso of this card, mailed to Hickory, North Carolina, in 1920, the sender writes, "Don't show our Hickory teacher friends this picture. They might desert and come to B'ham." (BPLA.)

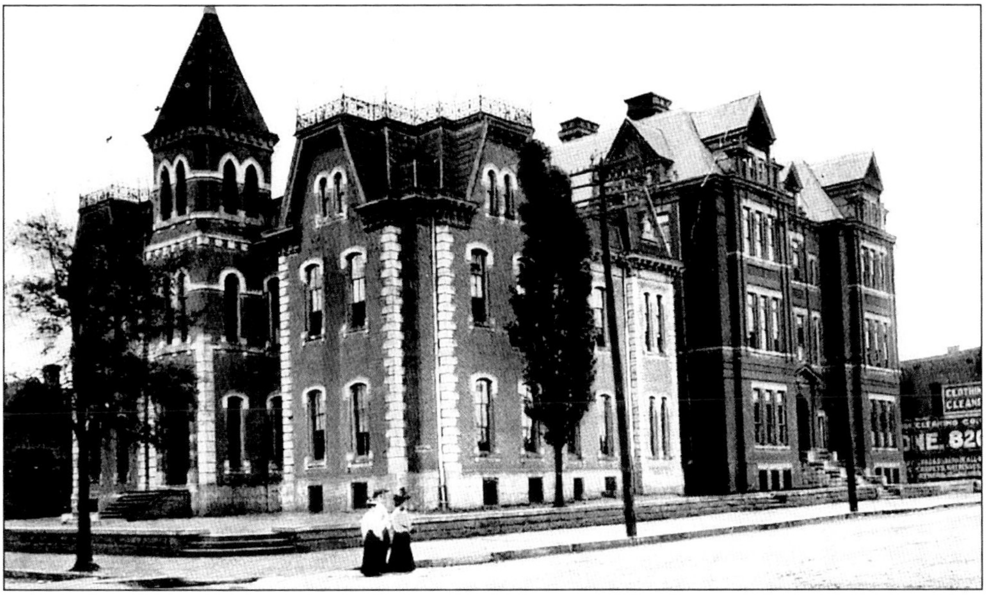

Located on the corner of Fifth Avenue and Twentieth Street, South and named to honor a South Carolina poet, Paul Hayne School was built in 1886 and served as an elementary school until 1918. Used briefly as a high school, the institution then became Paul Hayne Opportunity School, a vocational training center. The building was demolished in 1955. On the verso of this card, mailed in 1908, the sender writes, "I am so busy studying I haven't time to write anything but a postal. My birthday is Nov. 9. When is yours? I will be 'sixteen and never been kissed.' " (BPLA.)

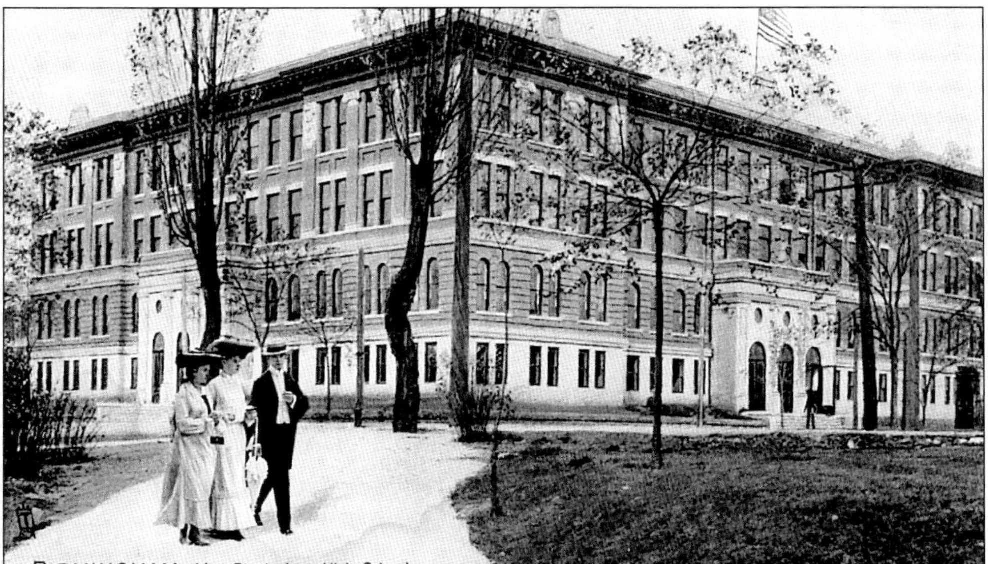

At various times different buildings in Birmingham have been referred to as "Birmingham High School" or as "Central High." The building pictured above, which the board of education described as "splendid," opened in 1906 at Sixth Avenue and Nineteenth Street, South. After this structure burned in the 1920s, it was replaced, at a different location, with Phillips High School (see p. 108). (BPLA.)

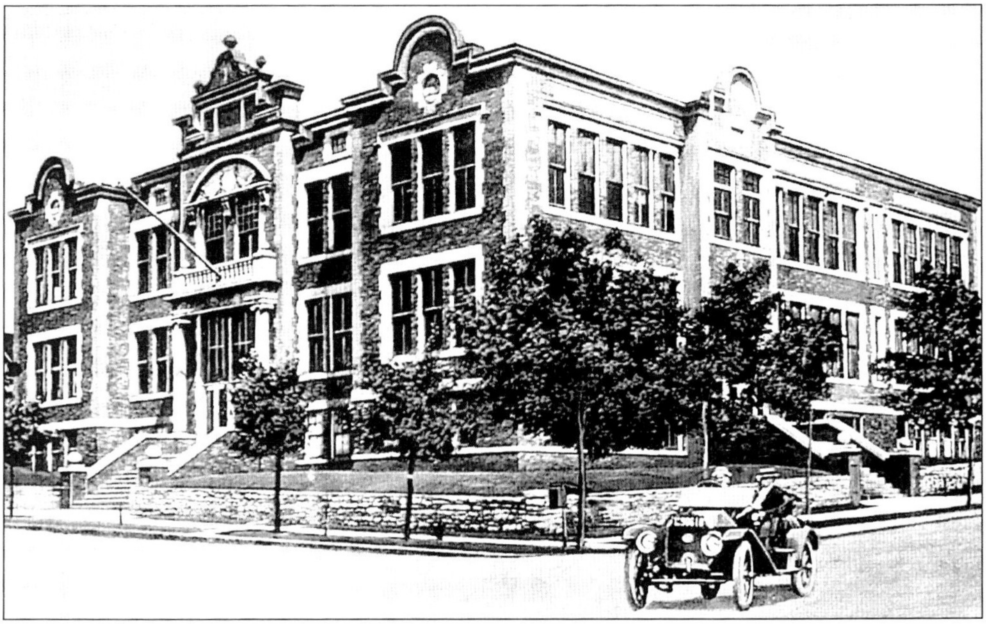

Located at 1901 Arlington Avenue, this was the first structure built as a high school in Bessemer. Opening in 1908, the building remained a high school until 1923, and then became Arlington School. Designed by architect W.E. Benns, the school features an auditorium with an arched proscenium of plaster decorated with a floral design. The building, now on the Alabama Register of Historic Places, is currently being restored. (BHH.)

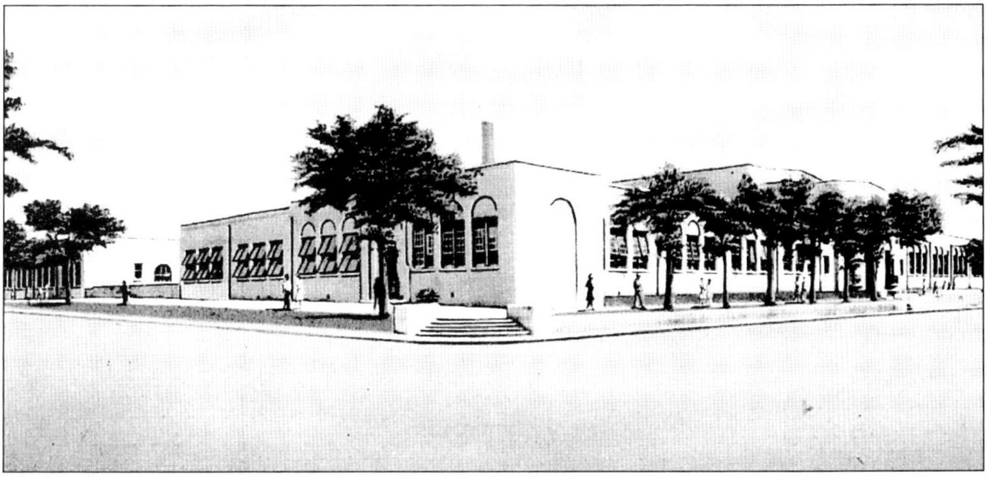

Many African-American families left rural Alabama and moved to Birmingham searching for economic opportunities and an education for their children. But prior to the 1960s and 1970s public education in Birmingham (like much of the United States) was racially segregated by law or by custom. By 1899 black parents in Birmingham were demanding a high school, and educator A.H. Parker opened the first high school for black students in a room at Cameron School. The first graduating class had 15 pupils. Called Industrial High School, the facility moved to an old theater building in 1910. The building pictured above opened in 1924 at Eighth Avenue and Eleventh Street, North. Later renamed Parker High in honor of the school's first principal, Industrial High taught both academic and vocational subjects, and included among its instructional facilities a "model housekeeping apartment." (BPLA.)

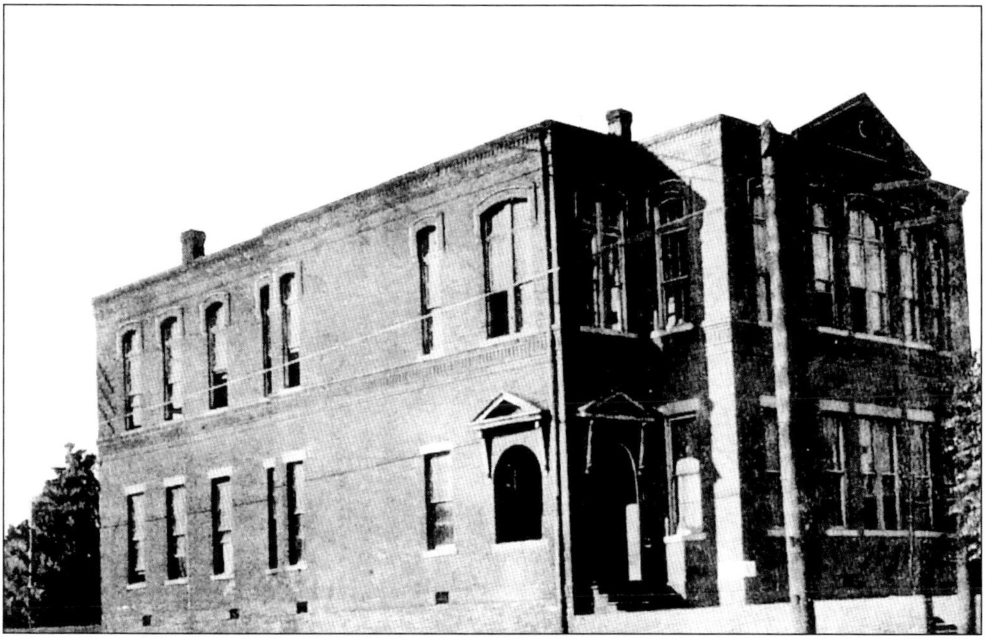

This card showing Pratt City High School was mailed in 1908. The sender writes, "I guess I will start and come Home this town is to big for me to get over it." (SG.)

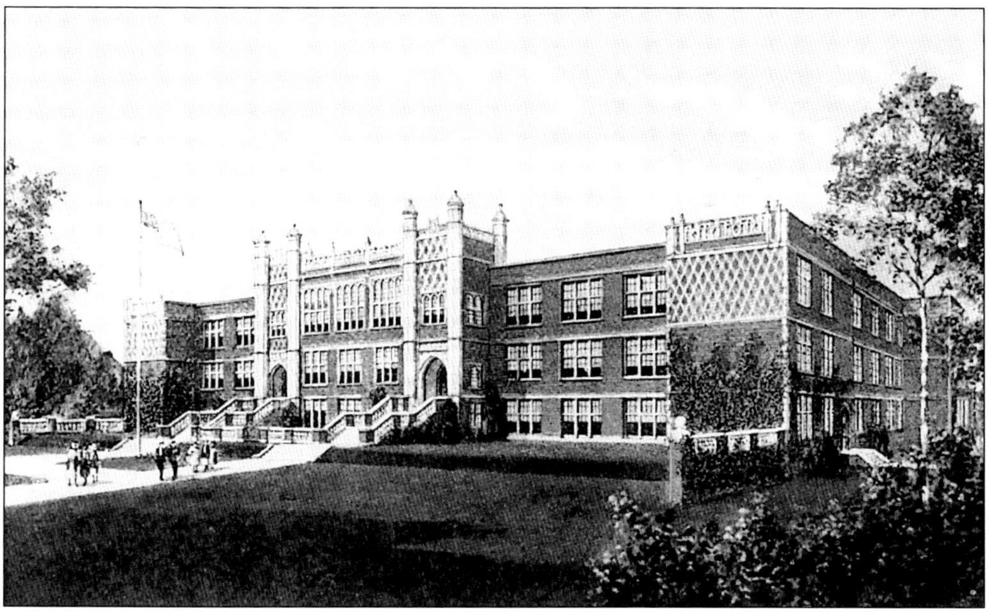

On the verso this cards reads, "Birmingham's newest High School Building, the Woodlawn High School. Opened Jan. 30th, 1922. 24 Instructors. 800 Pupils. Cost of present unit and equipment $300,000. Complete building to contain auditorium, gymnasium and 28 additional classrooms. A visit to this school and an inspection of its modern equipment will interest you." (BPLA.)

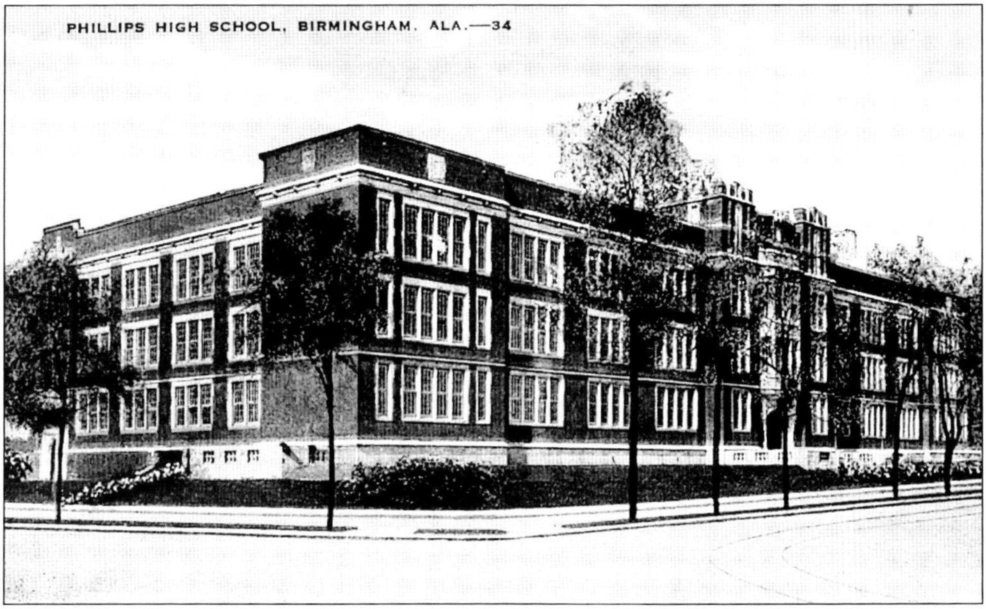

Named for John Herbert Phillips, Birmingham's first superintendent of schools, Phillips High School opened in 1923 at Seventh Avenue, between Twenty-third and Twenty-fourth Streets, North. A native of Ohio, Phillips came to Birmingham in 1883 to head the city's public schools. He issued Alabama's first public school course of study in 1884, and was a strong advocate for including the arts and languages in the school curriculum. Phillips served as superintendent until 1921, and is credited with establishing the city's first public library. (BPLA.)

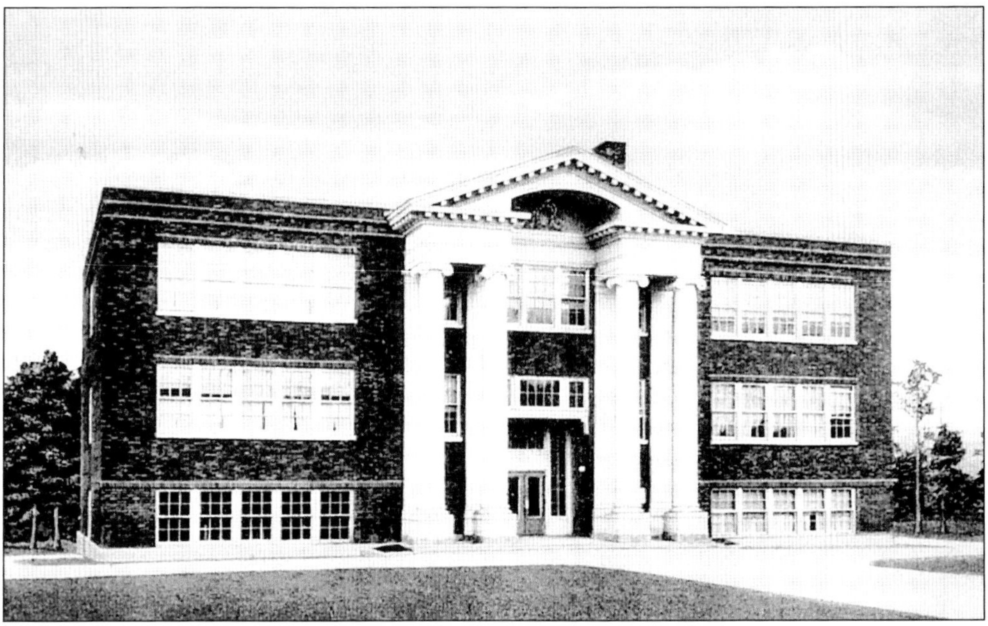

The Jefferson County High School was located at Boyles, near Tarrant. On the verso of this card the sender, apparently a child, writes, "Got here all right. We didn't sleep much on the train only in the morning. We are going to camp today." (SG.)

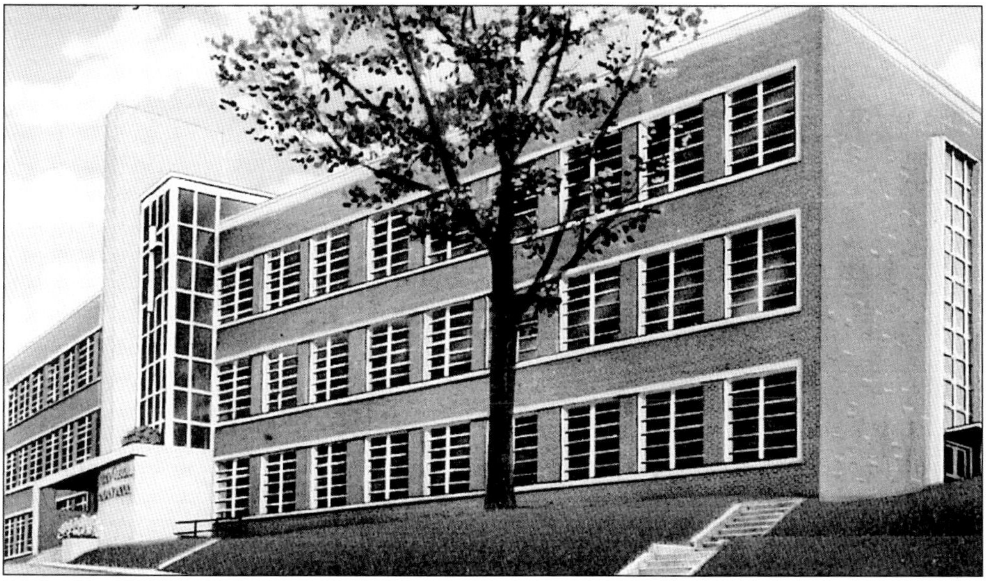

John Carroll High School, named for a benefactor instrumental in raising funds for the construction, opened as a Catholic high school in 1947. Located on Highland Avenue across from Caldwell Park, the building was designed by architect Charles H. McCauley. The modern design of the building is a departure from the early-20th-century schools shown on previous pages. A new John Carroll High School opened in 1992 on Lakeshore Parkway; the building pictured above has since been demolished. (BPLA.)

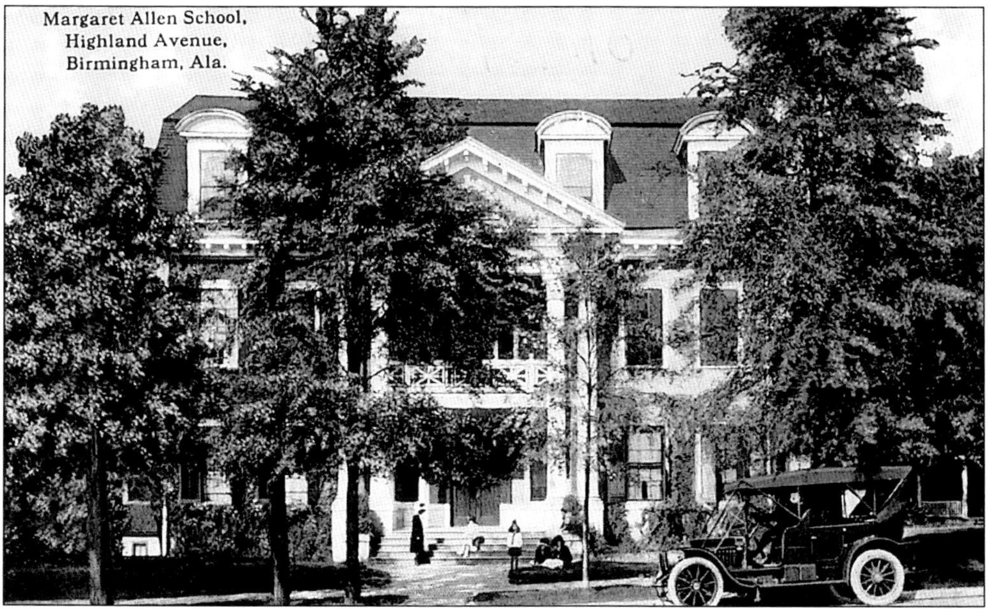

Located on Highland Avenue, the Allen School (later the Margaret Allen School) was a private institution stressing the classics, languages, art, music, and dance. Established in 1884, the school was originally operated by three sisters, Ruth, Willie, and Beffie Allen, who each taught various subjects. Other teachers at the Allen School included Birmingham artist Hannah Elliott. Although the majority of the school's pupils seem to have been girls, boys were not excluded. (BPLA.)

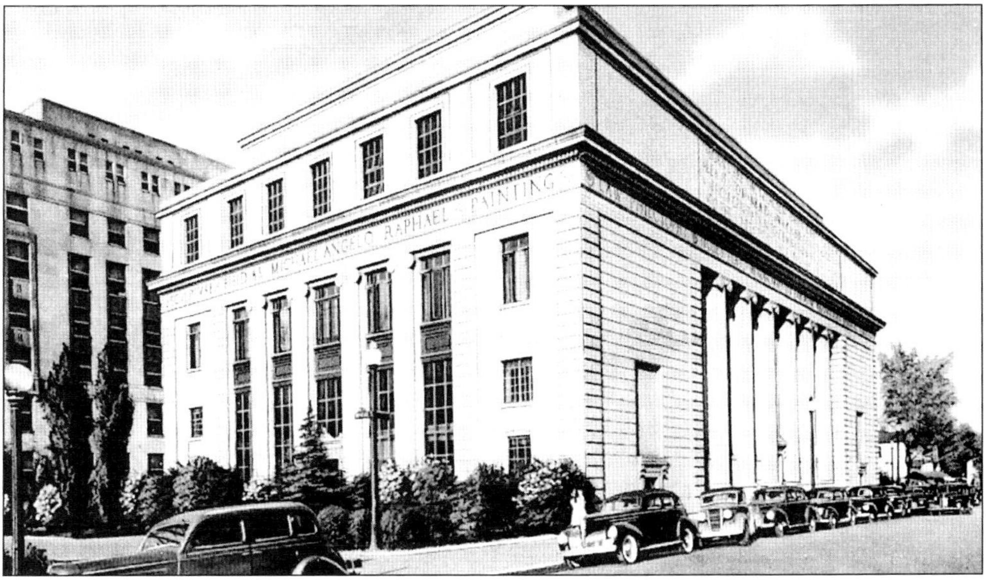

Following the 1925 fire at the Birmingham City Hall, which destroyed much of the public library located on the fourth floor, the need for a free-standing, "fire-proof" public library for Birmingham became more evident than ever. The city's first central library building, pictured above, opened in 1927. Designed by the architectural firm of Miller and Martin, the four-story neo-classical structure was constructed of Indiana limestone. Among the building's most impressive features are a series of murals depicting various literary traditions, painted by New York artist Ezra Winter. A new Central Library was completed in 1984. The old Central Library was renovated and now houses the Linn-Henley Research Library, which includes a collection of Southern history, a government documents department, one of the finest map collections in the nation, and an archives department. (BPLA.)

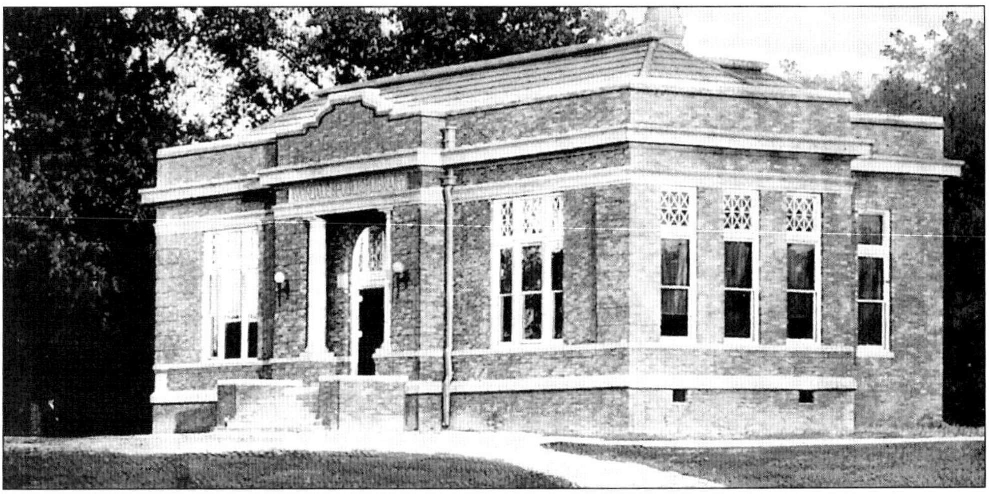

Millionaire industrialist Andrew Carnegie believed that wealth, once acquired, should be used for the common good. Between 1893 and 1918, Carnegie donated large sums of money to towns and cities across the United States to fund the construction of 1,689 public libraries. Fourteen Carnegie libraries were built in Alabama, including the Avondale Library pictured above, which opened in 1908. This facility later became a branch of the Birmingham Public Library system, and served the Avondale community until a new library was constructed in 1961. (BPLA.)

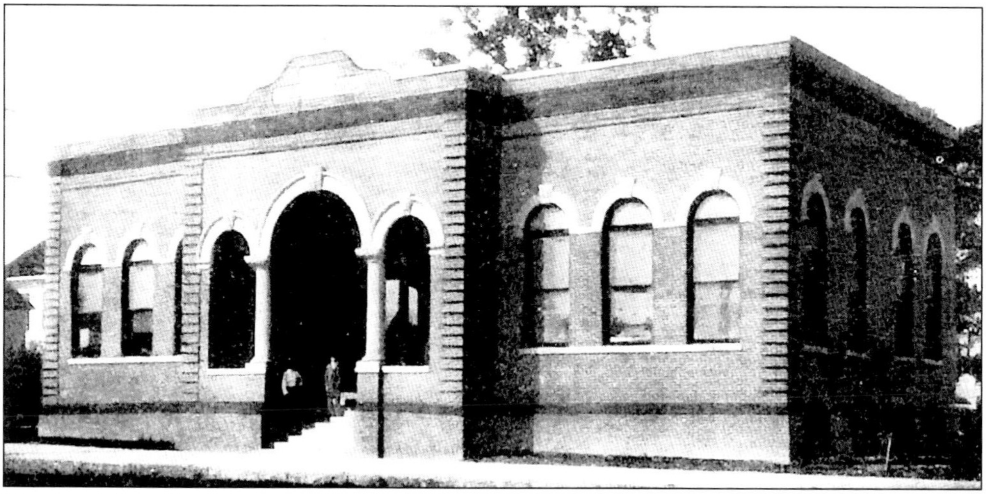

This card shows the Carnegie library in Bessemer as it looked when it opened in 1907. Recipients of a Carnegie grant were not required to include the name Carnegie in the name of their library, but some towns, including Bessemer, still chose to honor their benefactor in this way. Like some other Carnegie libraries in Alabama, the Bessemer structure no longer serves as a library but was saved and adapted for other uses. The Bessemer Chamber of Commerce has occupied the building since 1969. (JM.)

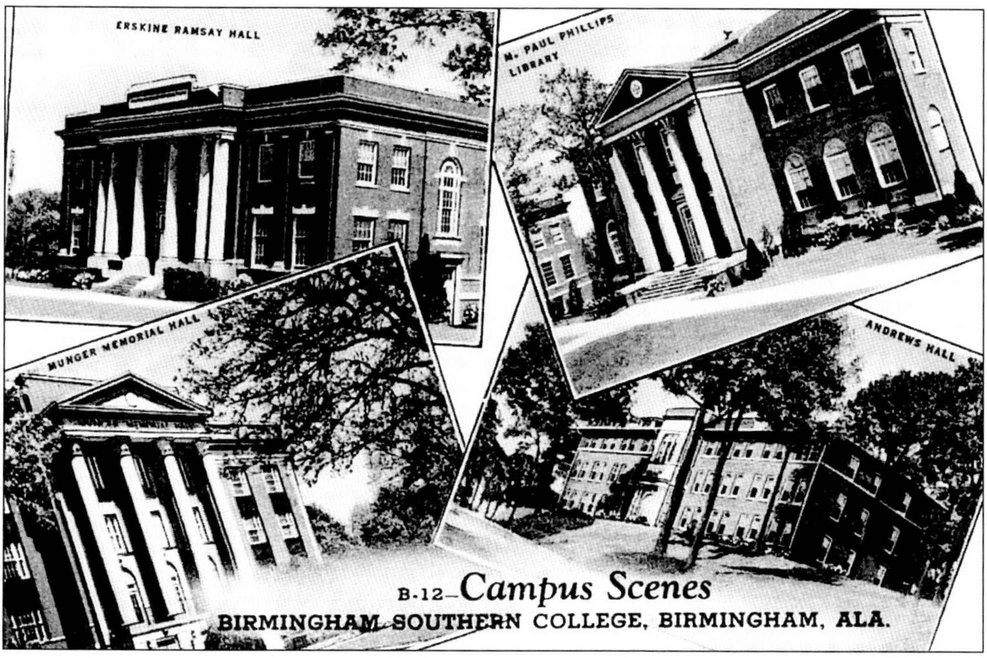

Prior to the Civil War, wealthy planters in Alabama's Black Belt recognized the need for a college to educate their sons close to home. In 1856 Southern University was founded at Greensboro, but the war that soon followed took away most of the school's students and depleted its endowment. In 1918 Southern University merged with Birmingham College, founded in 1898, to form Birmingham-Southern College. Mailed in 1953, this is one of the newer postcards included in this book. (SG.)

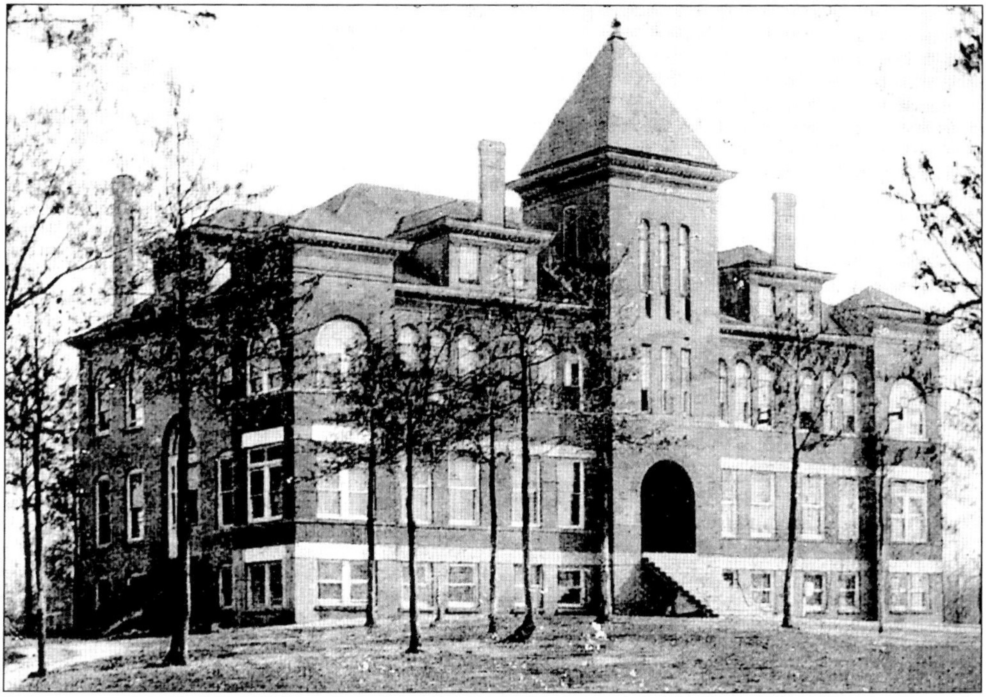

Rose Owen Hall, shown here, was already constructed when Birmingham College enrolled its first class. Owen was demolished to make way for Munger Memorial Hall, pictured below, which opened in 1928. (BPLA.)

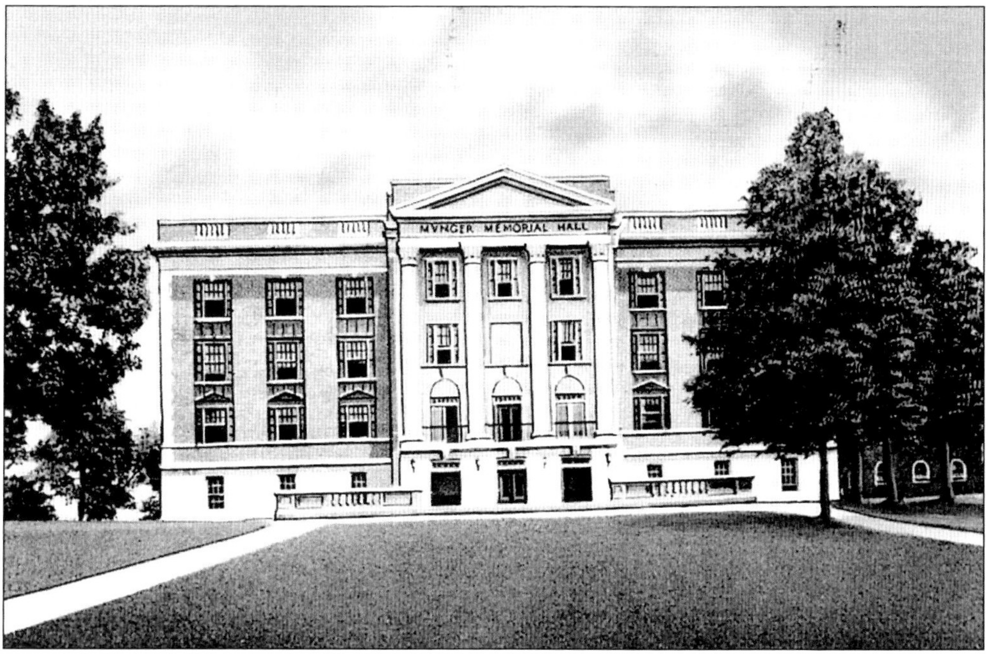

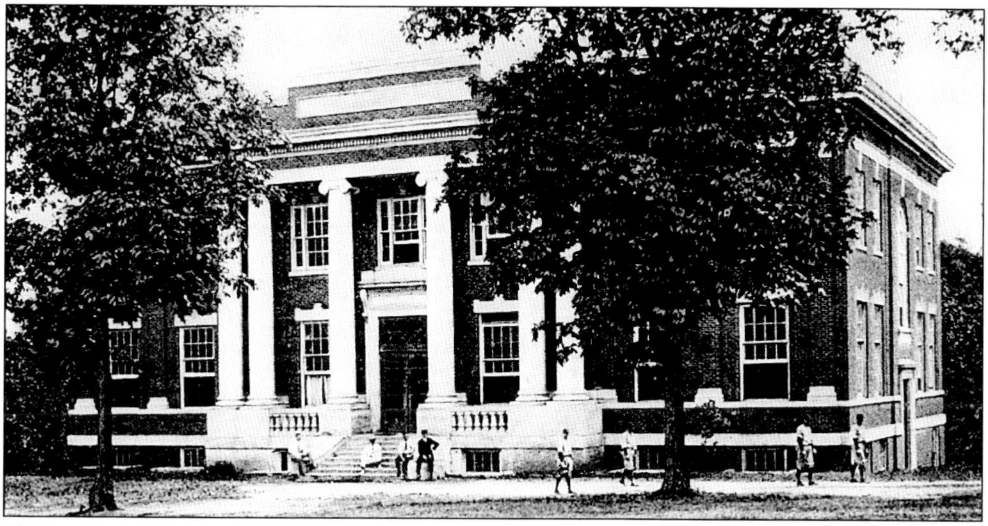

Shown here is the Birmingham-Southern College Science Hall as it appeared about 1920. (BPLA.)

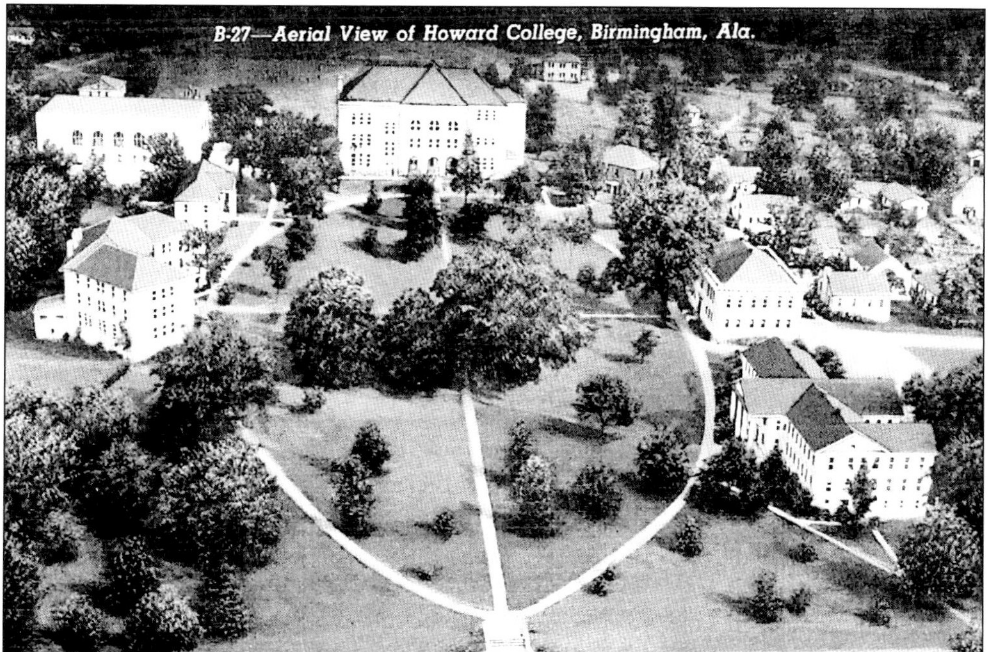

The verso of this card, dating about 1945, reads, "One of the state's oldest institutions, founded January 3, 1842, Howard College has been located the last fifty-seven years in Birmingham. This air view shows the college city of white nestled at the foot of the hills among the green foliage, with Berry Field where the Bulldogs romp in the background, and Main Hall, fifty-seven years old, at the top center, flanked by the gymnasium, boys' dormitory, science hall, library, sorority lodges an[d] other recitation halls. It is under the jurisdiction of the Alabama Baptist State Convention and numbers among its graduates some of the foremost citizens of the state and country." Howard, now Samford University, moved to a new campus on Lakeshore Drive in the mid-1950s. The East Lake buildings were torn down except for the women's dormitory, which became part of East End Hospital. (BPLA.)

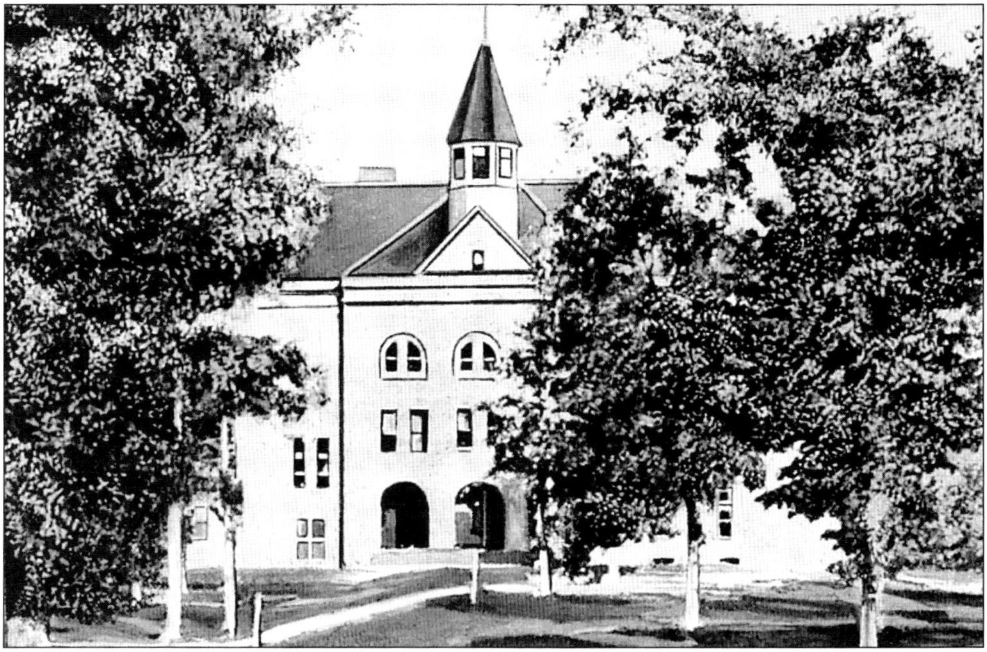

Like Southern University, Howard College was founded in the Alabama Black Belt before moving to Birmingham. Pictured above is the old Main Building, one of the earliest structures on the East Lake campus. (BPLA.)

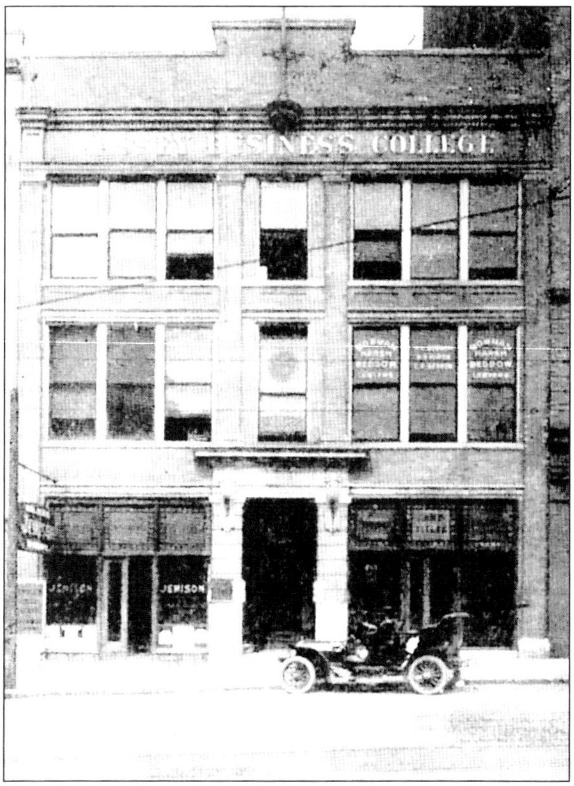

Richard W. Massey established Massey Business College in Birmingham in 1887. The institution became the first chain of business colleges in the South, eventually opening six schools in five states. Massey's colleges taught typing and shorthand, basic accounting (known as "business arithmetic"), business law, and other related subjects. Class schedules were flexible, and in many cases courses were structured to let students work at their own pace. Tuition could be paid in monthly installments. The building pictured here opened in 1905 on Third Avenue, North, and became the model building design for Massey's other schools. Massey would select a site in a downtown area and construct his own building. The ground floor would be rented as office or retail space, and the school would occupy the upper floors. (SG.)

Eight

Places of Healing

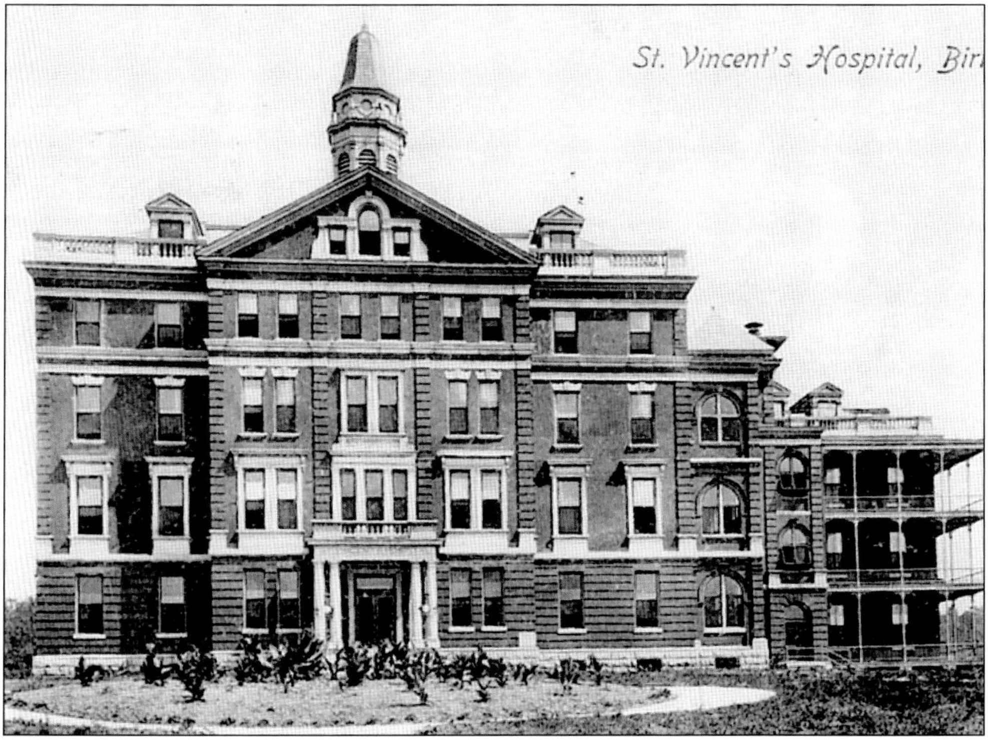

Father Patrick O'Reilly, pastor of St. Paul's Catholic Church, persuaded nuns from the Daughters of Charity to come to Birmingham in 1898 to establish and staff a badly needed hospital. St. Vincent's Hospital, shown here about 1910, opened its doors as a 100-bed hospital to serve the growing industrial city. By 1911 an east wing, designed by architect Harry F. Wheelock, was added. The wide, open porches off each floor provided patients with fresh air and a commanding view of the neighborhood. Early in 1900 the first school of nursing in northern Alabama opened at St. Vincent's. The school was founded by the first registered nurse in the state, Sister Chrysostom Moynahan. St. Vincent's still serves the Birmingham community, but none of the original structure has survived. A monument to Father O'Reilly, sculpted by Giuseppe Moretti, the artist who created the Vulcan statue, once stood on the lawn at the entrance to the old hospital. This statue now stands in the circle at the entrance to the present-day hospital. (BPLA.)

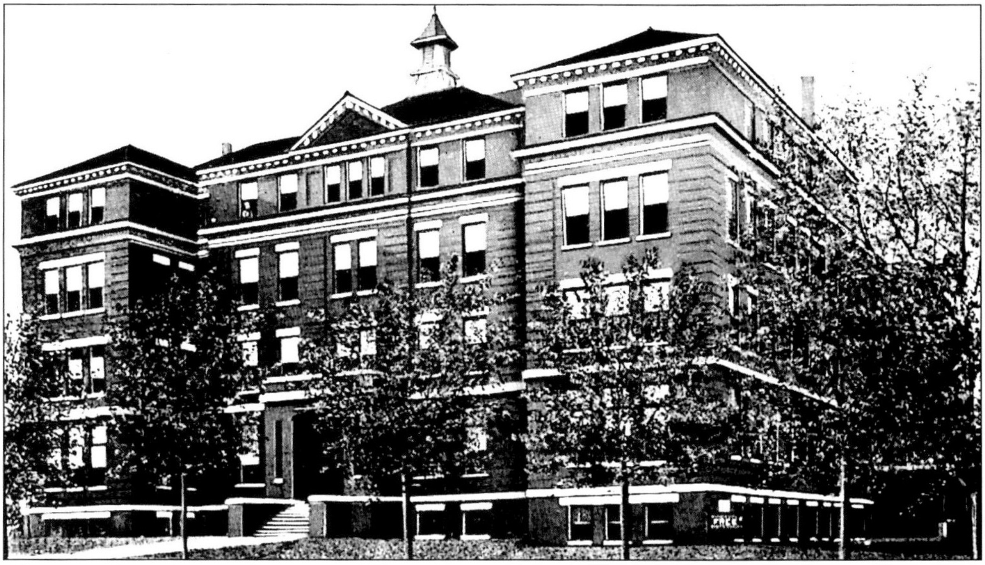

When Hillman Hospital, pictured here about 1920, first opened in 1903, the Board of Lady Managers (which had raised funds for the construction) named the facility after a benefactor, Birmingham industrialist T.T. Hillman. In 1907 the hospital contracted with Jefferson County to serve as a "free charity, non-sectarian hospital." One year later Hillman became a teaching hospital, and in an era of racial segregation offered treatment to patients of all races (on a segregated basis). Hillman no longer functions as a medical facility, but it serves as a nucleus of the University of Alabama at Birmingham Medical Center. At the time of this writing, UAB has announced plans to demolish the historic structure to build a new entranceway for the medical center. (BPLA.)

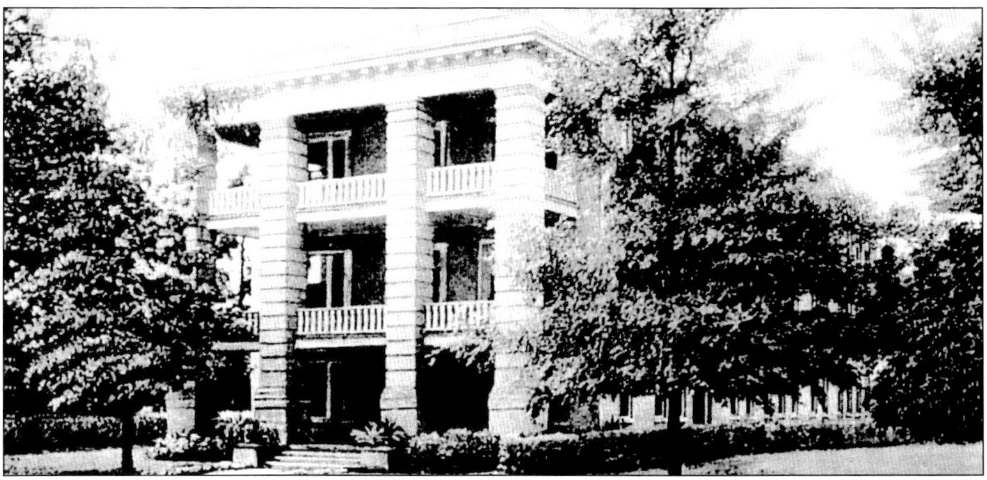

Elizabeth Duncan Memorial Hospital, located on Third Avenue between Seventeenth and Eighteenth Streets, was established around 1900 by two physician brothers. Dr. E.M. Robinson and Dr. Thomas F. Robinson, both of whom had migrated to Bessemer from Blount County, named the hospital in honor of their mother. Around 1910 the brothers gave the facility to the United Charities, and the name was later changed to Bessemer General. After leaving Bessemer, E.M. Robinson established an infirmary and nursing school on Birmingham's Southside. Thomas F. Robinson stayed in Bessemer and served on the city council. Bessemer General was razed in the 1960s. A parking lot now occupies the site. (BHH.)

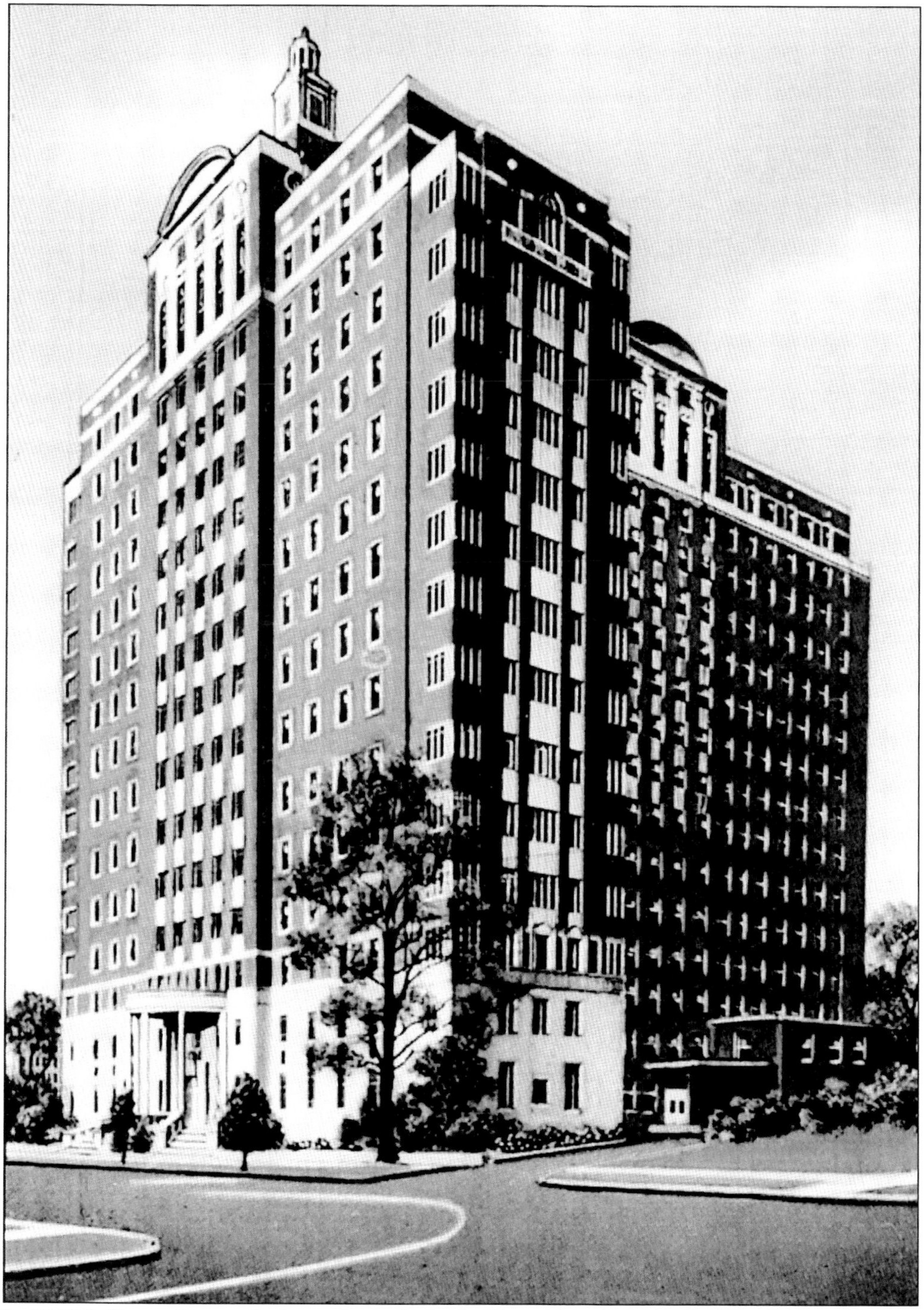

In 1945 Jefferson Hospital, shown here, became the teaching hospital for the newly relocated University of Alabama medical school. By act of the state legislature the medical school had been moved from Tuscaloosa to Birmingham, where the university already operated an extension campus. Today Jefferson Hospital has become University Hospital, part of one of the finest medical research and teaching complexes in the United States. (BPLA.)

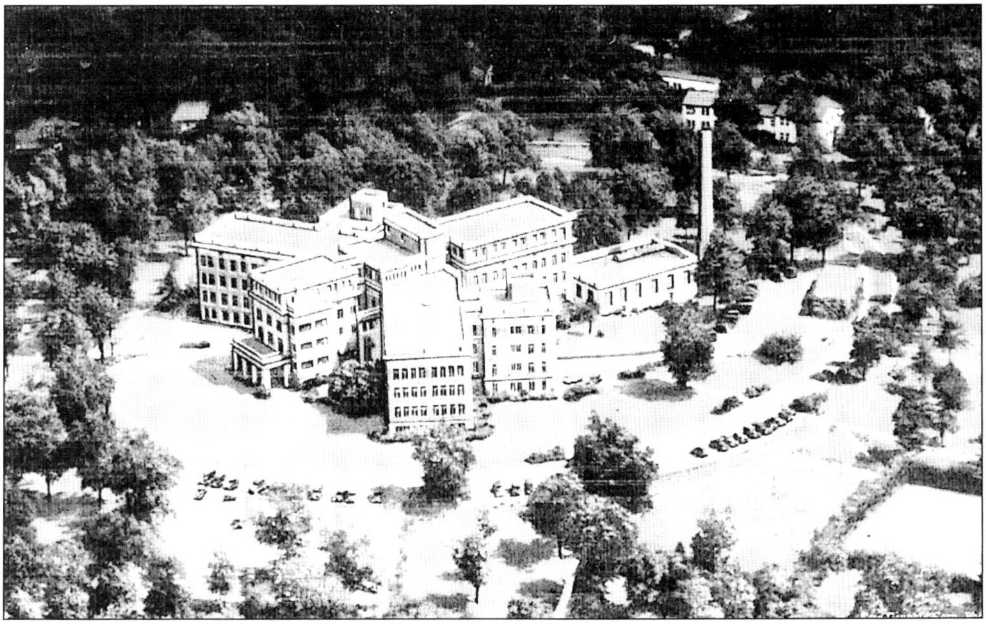

Dr. Lloyd Noland created a nationally recognized health care system to care for the employees and their families of Tennessee Coal, Iron and Railroad Company (TCI). Built in 1919 overlooking the Fairfield Works, the facility, originally called the TCI Employees Hospital, was renamed Lloyd Noland Hospital in 1950. Pictured above is the 345-bed health care center as it appeared at that time. One year later the United States Steel Corporation, the parent company of TCI, gave the hospital to the community. (BPLA.)

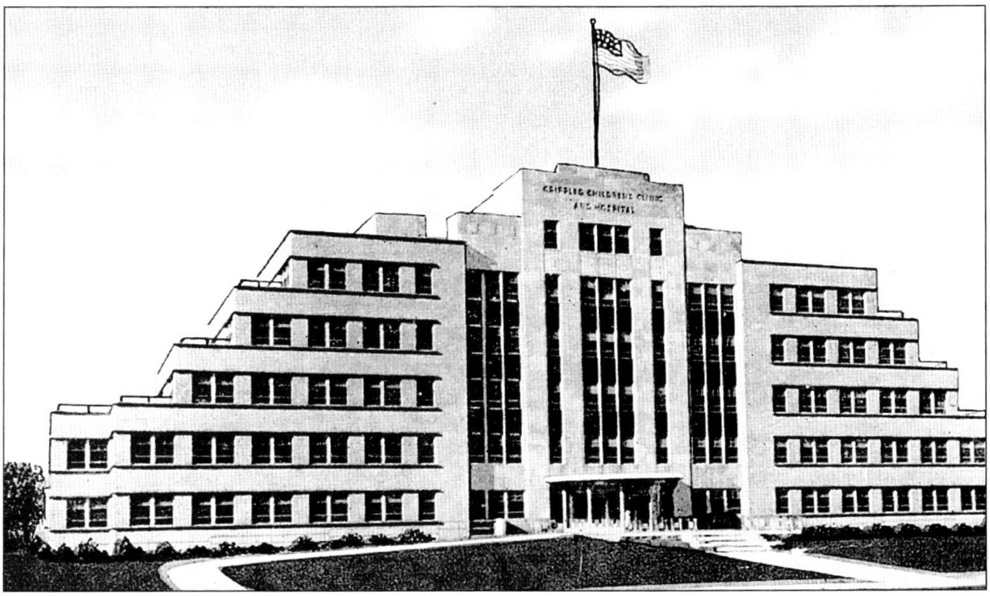

Crippled Children's Hospital, a 100-bed orthopedic facility that offered free medical services to all crippled Alabama children, is shown here soon after its completion in 1951. The facility became known as the "football hospital" because one-third of its funding came from the proceeds of an annual Thanksgiving Day high school game. UAB acquired this structure in 1970 for use as the University Ambulatory Center. (BPLA.)

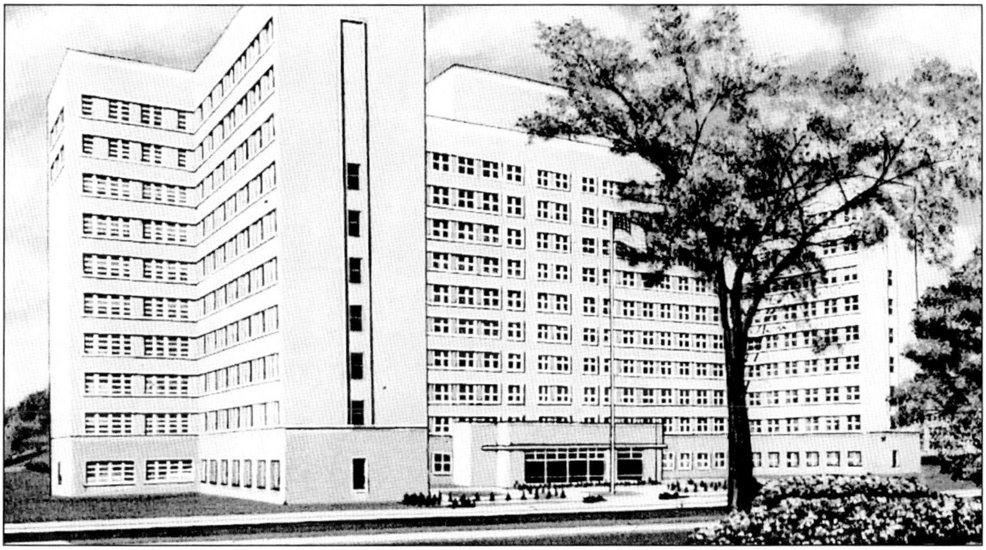

The Veterans Administration Hospital, located on Nineteenth Street, South, opened in the 1950s with 479 beds. Closely affiliated as a teaching hospital with the UAB Medical Center, VA Hospital is one of the few "dean hospitals" in the VA system. As such, all department heads are selected in consultation with the UAB Medical Center administration. (BPLA.)

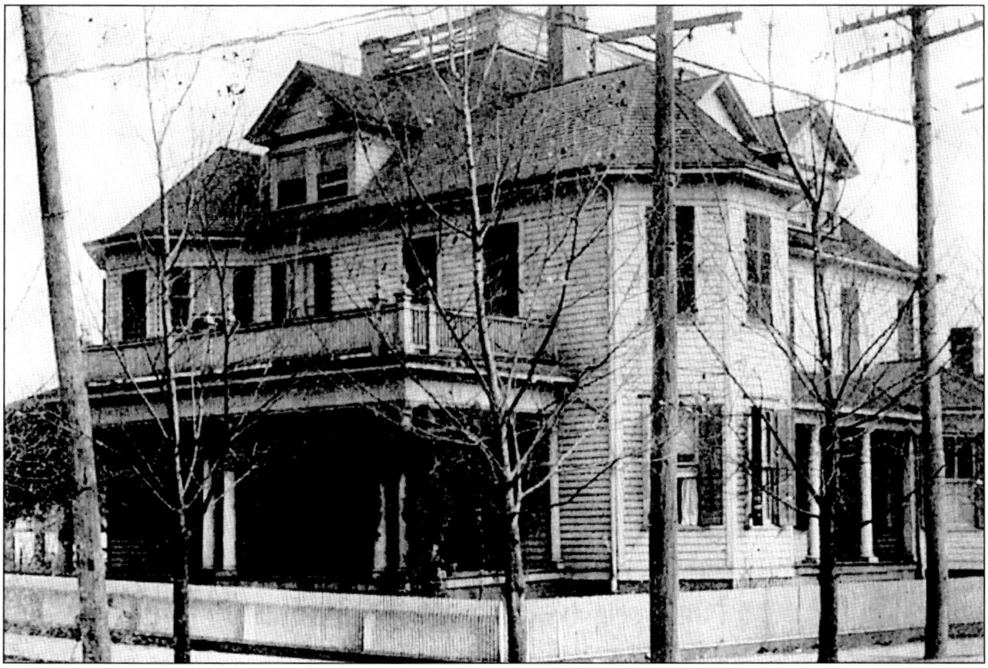

During the late 19th and early 20th centuries, quality health care was sometimes difficult to find in the still new city of Birmingham. In addition to early hospitals like St. Vincent's and Hillman, a number of infirmaries were opened around the turn of the century. Dr. Russell Cunningham, concerned for the health and welfare of TCI employees, especially the convicts leased by the state to work in area mines, opened the infirmary pictured above in 1899. Cunningham continued to work here, at Eighteenth Street and Avenue F in Ensley, until 1914. He later became the medical officer for Jefferson County. (BPLA.)

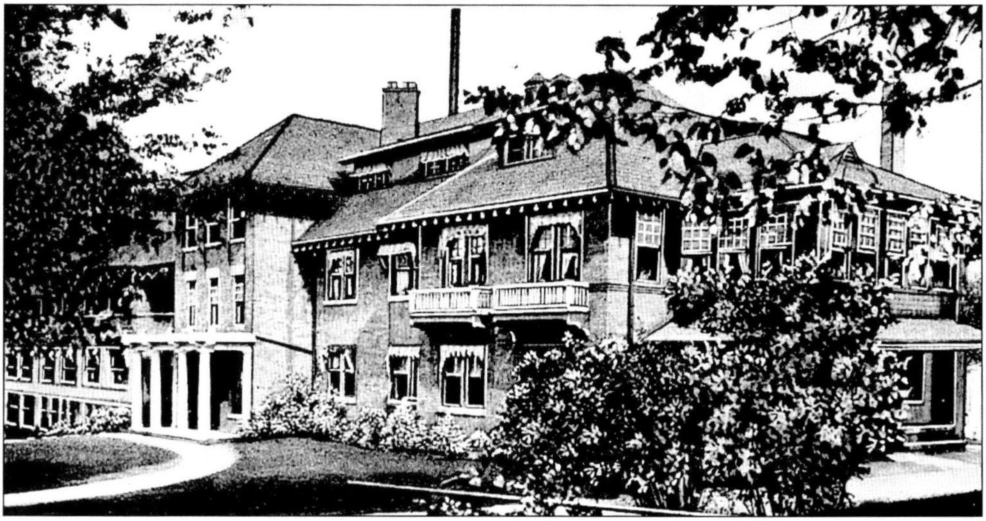

Located at 1127 Twelfth Street South, the South Highlands Infirmary opened in 1910. Dr. Edmond Mortimer Prince raised $92,000 locally and borrowed, at high interest, another $30,000 from sources in New York. Furniture for the hospital was purchased "on time" from a local supplier. The infirmary also operated a school of nursing. Today the HealthSouth Medical Center occupies this site. (BPLA.)

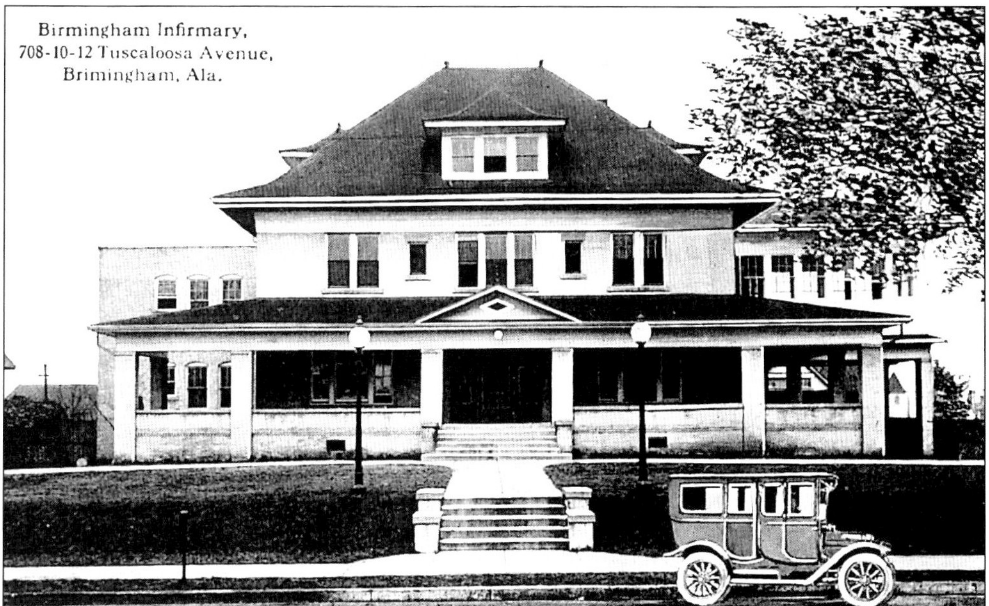

This card shows Birmingham Infirmary on Tuscaloosa Avenue as it appeared about 1920. Rooms had been added to the side and rear of the building. Dr. W.C. Gewin opened the facility in 1906 to serve the West End community. A physician and surgeon, Gewin was a pioneer in the use of radium. Gewin sold the infirmary to the Birmingham Baptist Hospital in the early 1920s. The facility's nursing school became the first to be accredited in the state. Student nurses referred to the original building, pictured above, as the "old plantation house" because of the grand dining room and crystal chandeliers. This site is now occupied by Baptist Medical Center, Princeton. (BPLA.)

Nine

PLACES OF TRANSPORT

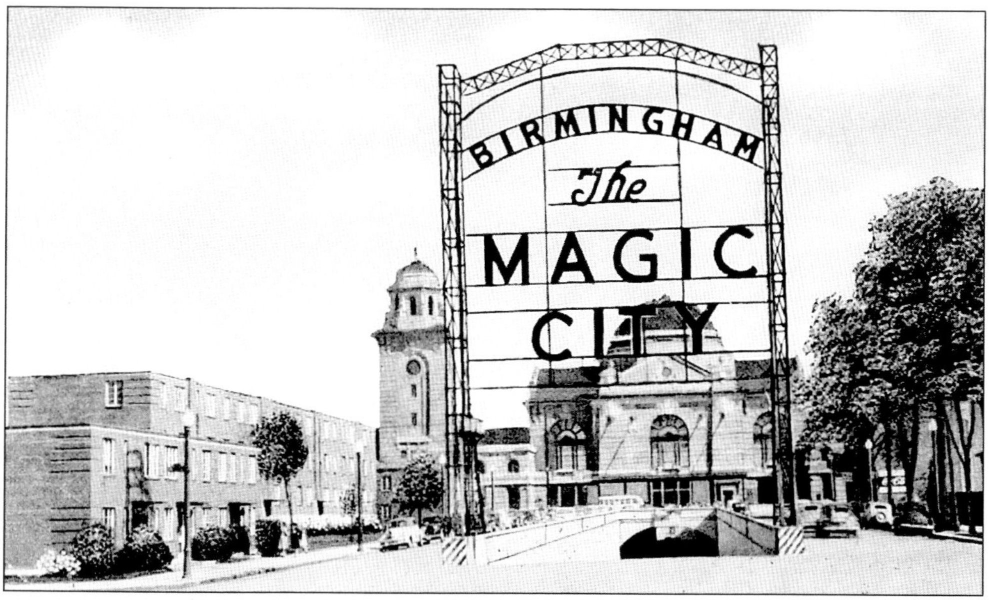

Located at Fifth Avenue and Twenty-sixth Street, North, Birmingham's Terminal Station opened in 1909. The central dome of the beaux arts-style structure was 64 feet in diameter and 100 feet in height. The twin towers were 130 feet tall. As rail travel declined in the 1950s and 1960s, Southern Railway no longer needed the station, and other proposals for its use were not taken up. The grand building was demolished in 1969, and the site is still vacant. "Remember Terminal Station" has become a battle cry of local preservationists. This card appears to have been copied from a famous photograph of the station by Birmingham photographer O.V. Hunt. The Magic City sign, which should read backwards from this direction, has been reversed in this image. The actual sign faced the station to welcome visitors who had arrived by train. (BPLA.)

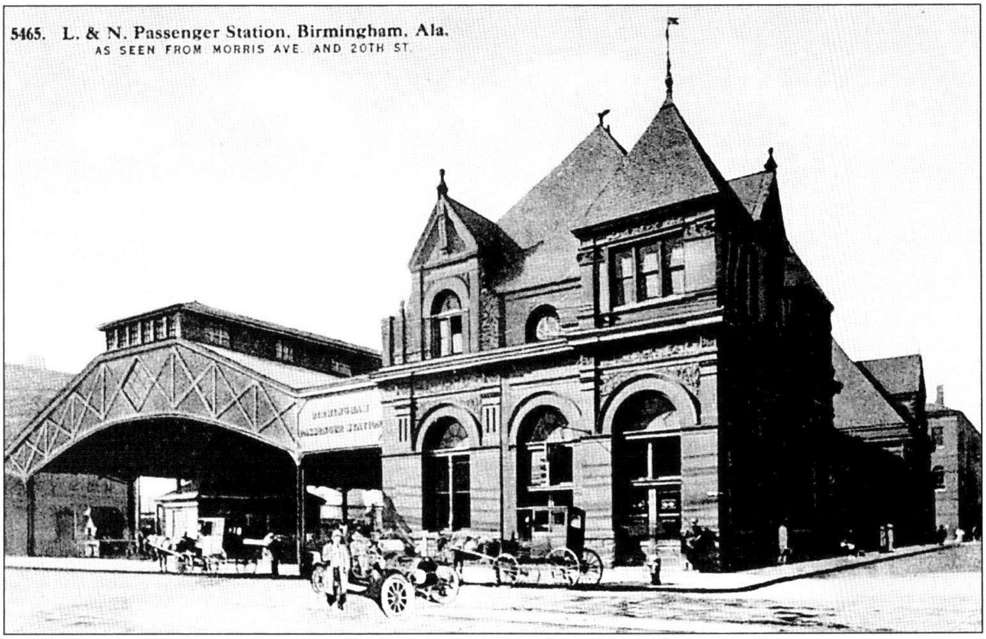

Birmingham, mid-way through its second decade, had grown sufficiently to need a better train station than the old wood-frame Relay House. Designed by Louisville and Nashville Railroad Company architect J.W. Walters, the Union Depot opened on Morris Avenue and Twentieth Street in 1886. Union Station was demolished in 1960. The Bank for Savings Building now occupies the site. (SG.)

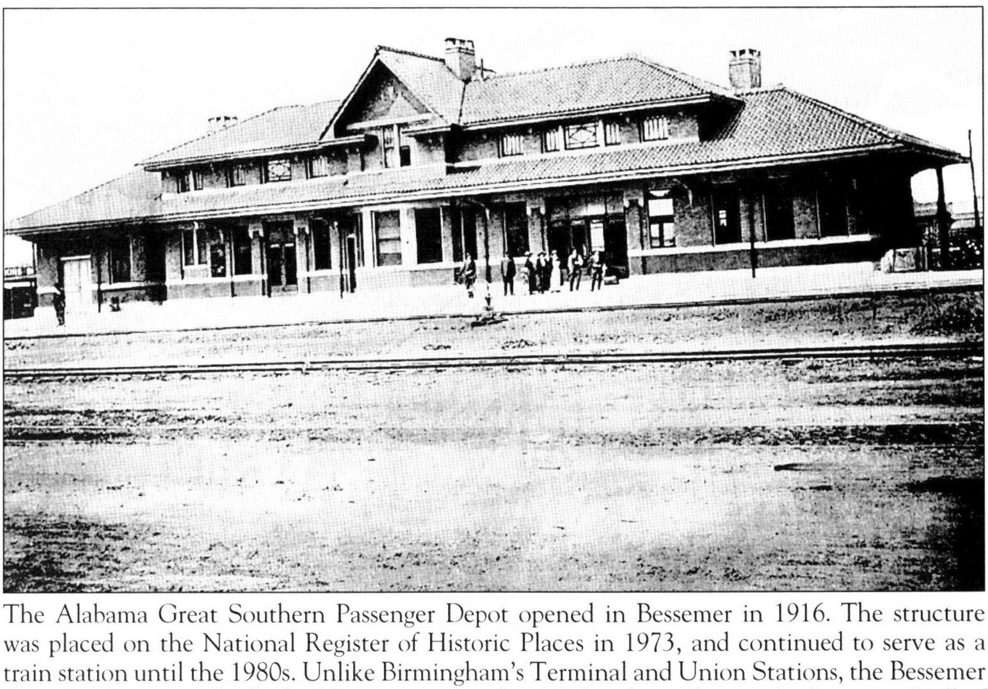

The Alabama Great Southern Passenger Depot opened in Bessemer in 1916. The structure was placed on the National Register of Historic Places in 1973, and continued to serve as a train station until the 1980s. Unlike Birmingham's Terminal and Union Stations, the Bessemer depot has been saved. The building was restored in 1986 and now houses the Bessemer Hall of History Museum. (BPLA.)

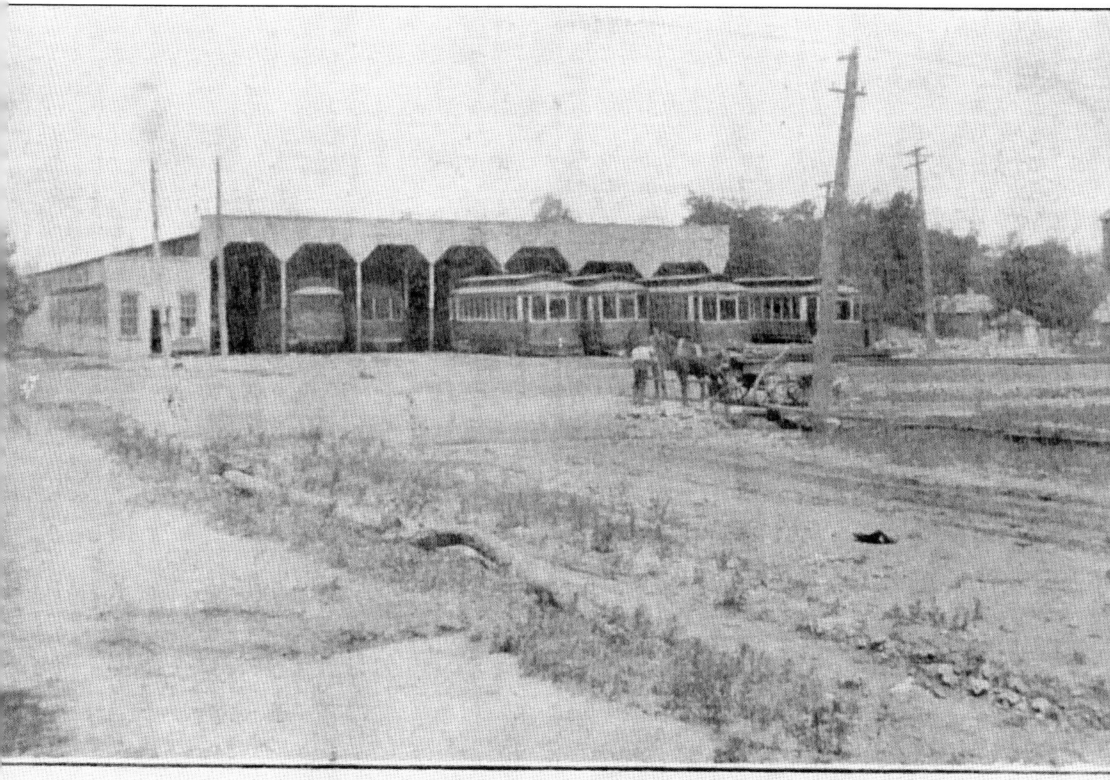

CAR BARN, EAST LAKE, ALA.

As the city of Birmingham grew during its first few decades, so did the small towns and mining camps in the outlying areas. Between 1880 and 1890 the population of Jefferson County, outside of Birmingham, tripled. This growing but scattered population needed good public transportation.

During the late 19th century the streetcar transformed city life in the United States. For the first time it became practical for people to live miles from their place of work and from shopping. Birmingham's first streetcar, a horse-drawn vehicle, ran in January 1884. Four months later the city's first steam-powered car, known as a "dummy," went into service.

Streetcar lines eventually ran throughout the city and into the surrounding areas. The convenience of the streetcar led to the development of bedroom suburbs like Highland and East Lake, and the development of resorts and amusements like Lakeview, Cascade Plunge, and East Lake Park (all pictured earlier in this book).

The postcard above shows one of the car barns in East Lake. Dummy car service began to East Lake in October 1887, and the operating company contracted to have a car barn and shop constructed on the northeast corner of First Avenue and Seventy-eighth Street, North. Through some mix-up the barn was built across the street on someone else's property, and to avoid legal entanglements the company had a group of workers move the barn in the middle of the night. The structure burned a year later and a new barn was built.

Automobiles and buses eventually brought about the demise of the street railway. Streetcar service to East Lake ceased in 1952, and all service in Birmingham ended the following year. (SG.)

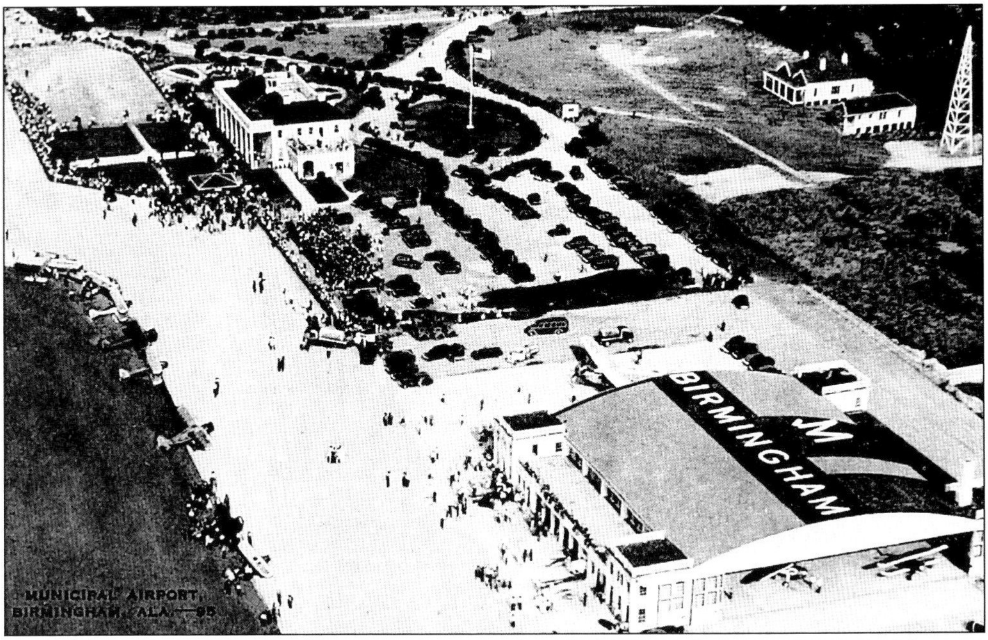

Birmingham's experience with aviation began early. World War I flying ace James A. Meissner founded the Birmingham Flying Club in 1919, and the group later reorganized as a unit of the Alabama Air National Guard. The area's first airfield, Roberts Field, was built in 1922 on land donated by Republic Steel. Because the field had no runway lights, pilots landing at night found their bearings by the glow from Republic's furnaces. The Birmingham Municipal Airport, shown on the cards above and below and at the top of facing page, opened in 1931 on the site of the current airport. The terminal building, strongly reminiscent of George Washington's home, Mt. Vernon, contained a waiting room for passengers, ticket counters, and a restaurant. Visitors could also dine on a second-floor balcony that provided a good vantage point for watching takeoffs and landings. Before lights were installed on the runway a worker would go out each evening and light smudge pots to guide the pilots. (BPLA.)

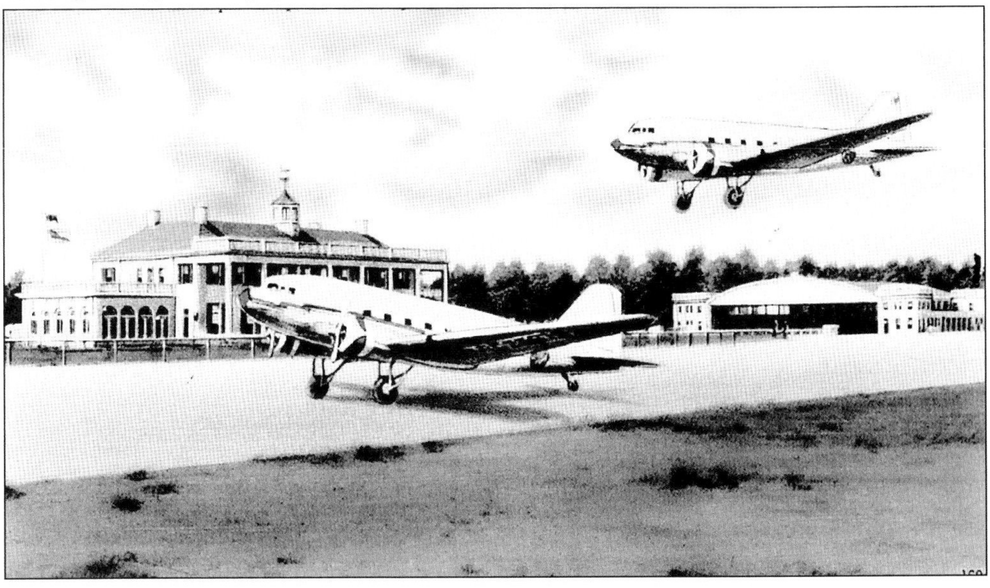

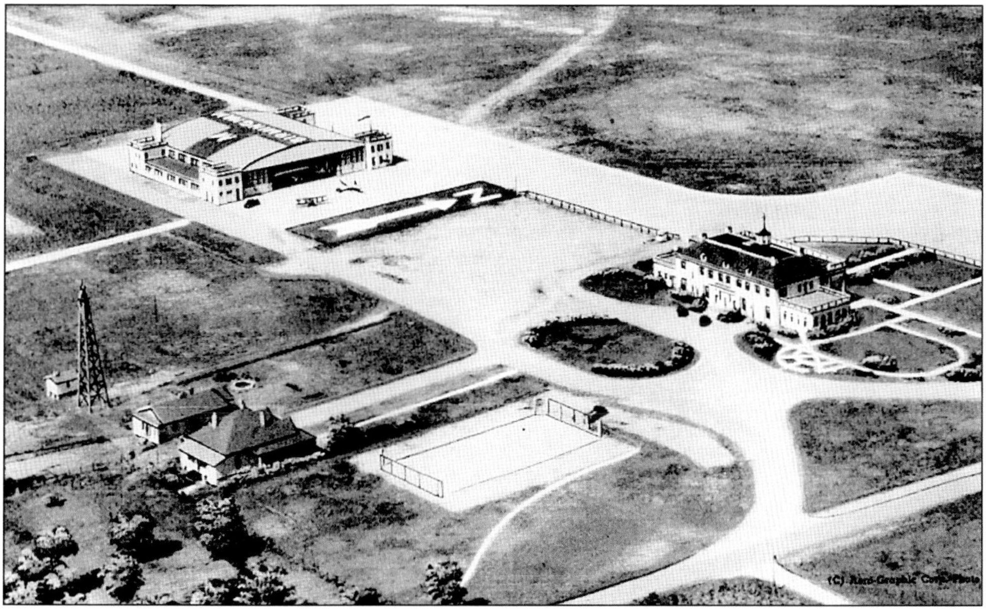

The verso of this card, which shows the airport in about the 1940s, reads, "Dedicated on June 1, 1931, Birmingham's Million Dollar Airport covers 315 acres and has accommodations for 300 to 500 planes. It is located about five miles northeast of the heart of the city and this unusual view shows the Municipal Hanger and the beautiful Administration Building." (BPLA.)

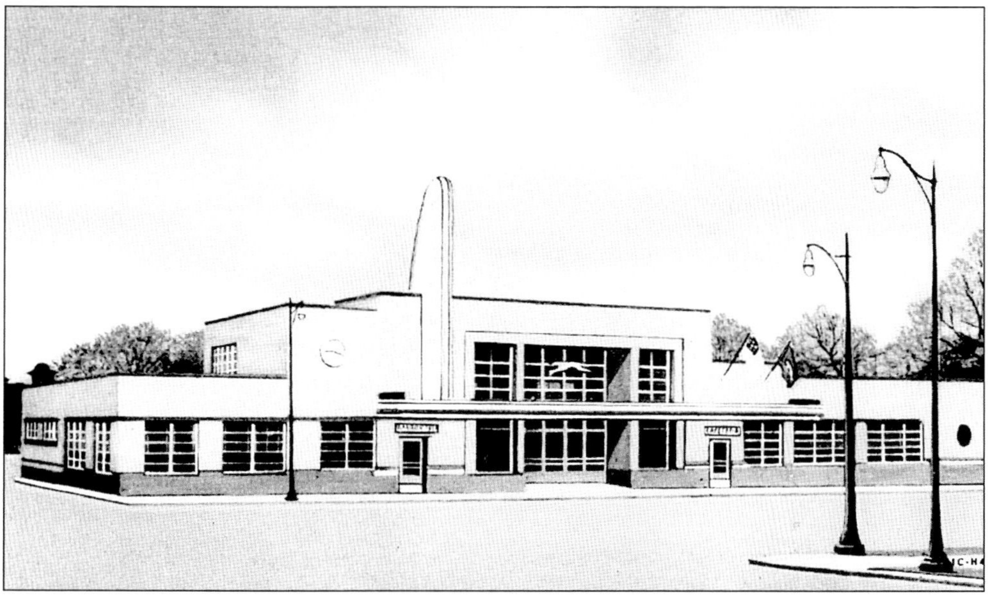

Birmingham's Greyhound Bus Depot, pictured above, opened in 1951 on the corner of Seventh Avenue and Nineteenth Street, North, just behind city hall. Promoters touted the station's "spacious waiting lobby . . . bright modern cafeteria . . . and scientifically-planned loading," that made it "impossible to get on the wrong Greyhound bus!" The depot location was selected because it was close to downtown stores and hotels, businesses that would, for the most part, leave downtown over the next two decades. The Greyhound Station still stands and is still used as a bus depot. (BPLA.)

BIBLIOGRAPHY

Postcards

The postcards reproduced in this book come from six collections. The source of each card is indicated in parenthesis after the corresponding caption. The collections are as follows: Bessemer Hall of History (BHH); Birmingham Public Library, Department of Archives and Manuscripts (BPLA); Leeds Chamber of Commerce (LCC); Steven Gilmer (SG); Mrs. and Mrs. Jim Ed Mulkin (JM); and William J. Skelton (WS).

Books, Pamphlets, and Articles

Alabama: A Guide to the Deep South. New York: Hastings House, 1941.

Alabama Blast Furnaces. Woodward, AL: Woodward Iron Company, 1940.

Annual Report of the Birmingham City Schools for the Year Ending June 30, 1907. Birmingham: Roberts and Sons, 1907.

Apartment Inventory and Housing Implementation Program. Birmingham: Birmingham Regional Planning Commission, 1973.

Atkins, Leah Rawls. *The Valley and the Hills: An Illustrated History of Birmingham and Jefferson County*. Tarzana, CA: Preferred Marketing in cooperation with the Birmingham Public Library, 1996.

Baggett, James L., "Legion Field, Birmingham's 'Old Glory.' " *The Reader*, Vol. 6, No. 3 (August, September, October 1996).

Belasco, Warren James. *Americans on the Road: From Autocamp to Motel, 1910–1945*. Cambridge, MA: The MIT Press, 1979.

The Best People in the World Live in Wylam. Birmingham: Birmingfind, 1981.

Birmingham City Directory. Birmingham: R.L. Polk and Company, various years.

"Birmingham's High Schools." *Alabama School Journal*, February 1925.

Breedlove, Michael A., "Progressivism and Nativism: The Race for the Presidency of the City Commission of Birmingham, Alabama in 1917." *The Journal of the Birmingham Historical Society*, Vol. 6, No. 4 (July 1980).

Brown, Virginia Pounds and Mabel Thuston Turner, "The Birmingham Public Library: From Its Beginning until 1927. Chapters III and IV." *The Journal of the Birmingham Historical Society*, Vol. VI, No. 1 (January 1979).

Brown, Virginia Pounds. *Grand Old Days of Birmingham Golf*. Birmingham: Beechwood Books, 1984.

Corley, Robert G. and Samuel N. Stayer. *View from the Hilltop: The First 125 Years of Birmingham-Southern College*. Birmingham: Birmingham-Southern College, 1981.

Dillon, Elsie H. *A Brief History of the Birmingham Public Schools, 1883–1972*. Birmingham: The author, 1972.

Ensley Baptist Church, 1912–1929: 65th Anniversary and Homecoming. Birmingham: The church, 1929; copy available in the Special Collections Department, Samford University.

First Baptist Church [Bessemer], *1887–1993.* N.P., n.d.; copy available in the Special Collections Department, Samford University.

First United Methodist Church, 1872–1972: The Story of a Century of Service to God and Man. Birmingham: First United Methodist Church, 1972.

Fisher, Virginia E. *Building on a Vision: A Fifty-Year Retrospective of UAB's Academic Health Center.* Birmingham: The University of Alabama at Birmingham, 1995.

Flynt, J. Wayne. *Mine, Mill and Microchip: A Chronicle of Alabama Enterprise.* Northridge, California: Windsor Publications, 1987.

Guthrie, Emily. *The Spirit of One Hundred Years: A History of East Lake United Methodist Church.* N.P., 1986.

Haslip, Eleanor S. and N.K. Thomas. *History of Miller Memorial Presbyterian Church.* N.P., n.d.; copy available in the Birmingham Public Library, Department of Archives and Manuscripts.

Hearn, Mildred (ed). *Recollections, Reminiscences . . . And More Legacies from the Crossroads: A History of the Development of Northeast Jefferson County in Alabama.* Birmingham: Roebuck Springs Garden Club, 1993.

Hudson, Alvin W. and Harold E. Cox. *Street Railways of Birmingham.* Forty Fort, PA: Harold E. Cox, 1976.

Jones, Theodore. *Carnegie Libraries Across America: A Public Legacy.* New York: John Wiley and Sons, 1997.

LaMonte, Ruth Bradbury, "The Origins of an Urban School System: Birmingham, 1873–1900." *The Journal of the Birmingham Historical Society,* Vol. V, No. 2 (July 1977).

Leeds Bicentennial Commission History Committee. *Leeds . . . Her Story.* Leeds, AL: The Commission, 1979.

Lewis, Pierce and Marjorie Longenecker White. *Birmingham View: Through the Years in Photographs.* Birmingham: Birmingham Historical Society, 1996.

Looking Back (Seventy-Five Years), 1901–1976. Birmingham: McCoy United Methodist Church, 1976.

McMillan, Malcolm C. *Yesterday's Birmingham.* Miami, FL: E.A. Seeman Publishing, 1975.

McCorquodale, Ann and Alice Meriwether Bowsher (ed), "Town Within a City: The Five Points South Neighborhood, 1880–1930." *The Journal of the Birmingham Historical Society,* Vol. 7, Nos. 3 and 4 (November 1982).

McCutcheon, Violet, *et al. A Walk Back Through Pratt City.* Birmingham: The Committee, 1987.

National Building Museum. *A Guide to the Building Records of S.H. Kress and Co. 5-10-25 Cent Stores at the National Building Museum.* Washington, D.C.: National Building Museum, 1993.

Owen, Thomas M. *History of Alabama and Dictionary of Alabama Biography,* Vol. 4. Chicago: S.J. Clarke, 1921.

Ragan, Larry. *True Tales of Birmingham.* Birmingham: Birmingham Historical Society, 1992.

Report of the Survey of Jefferson County Schools, School Years 1920–1930. Birmingham: Jefferson County, 1932.

Reuse, Ruth Beaumont. *Molton, Allen and Williams: The First One Hundred Years.* Birmingham: Birmingham Publishing Company, 1988.

Rumore, Sam, "Historic Jefferson County Courthouses." *Birmingham Bar Bulletin,* 1982.

Satterfield, Carolyn Green. *Historic Sites of Jefferson County, Alabama.* Birmingham: Jefferson County Historical Commission, 1985.

Schnorrenberg, John M. (ed). *Papers on Some Buildings of Birmingham.* Birmingham: Department of Art, University of Alabama at Birmingham, 1994.

Smith, Jack H. *Postcard Companion: The Collector's Reference.* Radnor, PA: Wallace Homestead Book Company, 1989.

South Highlands Infirmary. Birmingham: The Infirmary, 1935.
Staff, Frank. *The Picture Postcard and Its Origins*. New York: Frederick A. Praeger, 1966.
Stoves, Doris H. *History of South Highland Church* [Bessemer], *1917–1992*. N.P., 1992; copy available in the Special Collections Department, Samford University.
Sulzby, James F. *Historic Alabama Hotels and Resorts*. Tuscaloosa: The University of Alabama Press, 1960.
Sulzby, James F. *Toward a History of Samford University*, Volumes I and II. Birmingham: Samford University Press, 1986.
Thomas, Bernice L. *America's 5 & 10 Cent Stores: The Kress Legacy*. New York: John Wiley and Sons, 1997.
Waldrep, B. Dwain, "Henry Edmonds and His Controversy with the Southern Presbyterian Church." *The Journal of the Birmingham Historical Society*, Vol. 9, No. 1 (December 1985).
Walker, Alyce Billings. *It's Nice to Live in Birmingham*. Birmingham: *The Birmingham News*, 1963.
White, Marjorie Longenecker. *The Birmingham District: An Industrial History and Guide*. Birmingham: Birmingham Historical Society, 1981.
———. *Downtown Birmingham: Architectural and Historical Walking Tour Guide*. Birmingham: Birmingham Historical Society, 1980.
Whiting, Marvin Y. (ed). *Fairfield: Past, Present, Future, 1910–1985*. Fairfield, AL: The Seventy-fifth Anniversary Celebration Committee, 1985.
Windham Kathryn Tucker. *The Ghost in the Sloss Furnace*. Birmingham: Birmingham Historical Society and First National Bank of Birmingham, 1978.
Witt, Timothy. *Bases Loaded with History, The Story of Rickwood Field: America's Oldest Baseball Park*. Birmingham: The R. Boozer Press, 1995.
Wofford, Tom. *The St. Vincent's Story: A Century of Caring*. Birmingham: St. Vincent's Hospital Foundation, 1997.

Archives and Manuscripts

Akenhead, Linda and Barbara Mitchell. Survey of six religious structures in Birmingham, Department of Archives and Manuscripts, BPLA.
Biographical files on Birmingham architects, Department of Archives and Manuscripts, BPLA.
Birmingfind papers and related documents, BPLA.
Birmingham Board of Education photographs, BPLA.
Ferguson, Hill. Papers, BPLA.
First Church of Christ, Scientist, archival file.
General Collection photographs, BPLA.
Gild, Winnifred. Scrapbook, BPLA.
Gillespy, J.A. Journal, original in possession of Virginia Pounds Brown.
Hunt, O.V. Photographs, BPLA.
Jefferson County Board of Equalization appraisal files, BPLA.
Jefferson County Historical Commission site survey, BPLA.
Leeds Chamber of Commerce files.
Prince, Robinson and allied families. Photographs and miscellaneous material, BPLA.
United Episcopal Church South Archives files.
Ward, George B. Scrapbooks, BPLA.

Interviews

Gilmer, Steven. Interview with James L. Baggett, June 4, 1998.